ASSASSINATIONS
THAT CHANGED
THE WORLD

D1468478

ASSASSINATIONS THAT CHANGED THE WORLD

NIGEL CAWTHORNE

First published in 2020 by Ad Lib Publishers Ltd
15 Church Road
London, SW13 9HE

www.adlibpublishers.com

Text © 2020 Nigel Cawthorne

ISBN 978-1-913543-86-0
eBook ISBN 978-1-913543-85-3

All rights reserved. No part of this publication may be
reproduced in any form or by any means – electronic,
mechanical, photocopying, recording, or otherwise – or stored
in any retrieval system of any nature without prior written
permission from the copyright holders.
Nigel Cawthorne has asserted his moral right to be
identified as the author of this work in accordance with
the Copyright, Designs and Patents Act of 1988.

A CIP catalogue record for this book is available from the
British Library.

Every reasonable effort has been made to trace copyright-
holders of material reproduced in this book, but if any have
been inadvertently overlooked the publishers would be glad to
hear from them.

Printed in the UK

10 9 8 7 6 5 4 3 2 1

CONTENTS

INTRODUCTION

Assassination is murder by another name, usually for political or religious reasons. However, in some cases, it can be justified. Who would condemn the attempts made by the Allies and the Germans themselves to assassinate Hitler? Millions might have been saved if they had succeeded. More recently Donald Trump gave the order to assassinate Qassem Soleimani because he was the architect of terrorism that destabilised the Middle East and threatened the lives of US troops. Barack Obama had authorised the assassination of Osama bin Laden and Abu Omar al-Baghdadi for similar reasons.

These killings clearly have consequences both in the Middle East and worldwide. They were conducted clinically from thousands of miles away using drones. Such targeted killings are bound to continue as long as it can be argued that their motive is self-defence.

In earlier times, assassins were not so fastidious and there is a long history of murder for political gain. Indeed, assassination has always been part of the political repertoire since Cain killed Abel and went on to take power in the land of Nod. Alexander the Great established the greatest empire in the ancient world after his father, Philip II of Macedon, who had imperial ambitions of his own, was murdered, along with the children of Philip's second wife who might have challenged Alexander for the throne of Macedonia. The murder of Julius Caesar was supposed to protect the Roman Republic. Instead it led to Caesar's adopted son Octavius becoming the first emperor of Rome as Caesar Augustus. The Empire's subsequent expansion had a profound effect on European history.

Before the birth of the drone, the assassin's knife, sword or gun were wielded at close quarters. Extrajudicial murder was a messy business and often the assassin did not benefit personally. Nineteen-year-old Gavrilo Princip, who assassinated Archduke Franz Ferdinand precipitating World War I, died in jail before the end of the war due to tuberculosis exacerbated by the poor prison conditions. The assassins of leading *SS* officer Reinhard Heydrich killed themselves after being cornered in the crypt of a church. Their supporters were murdered, along with most of the populations of the towns of Lidice and Ležáky, arbitrarily held to blame by the Nazis.

The original assassins were an Islamic sect that flourished in the Middle East between the eleventh and thirteenth centuries. The Order of the Assassins was founded by Hassan-i Sabbah who died in 1124, in Daylam, Iran. He was the leader of the Nizari Ismailites, a breakaway group from the Ismaili branch of Shia Islam. In its early years, it considered murdering its enemies a religious duty.

The Arabic name assassin or *hashishi* means 'hashish smoker', referring to the Assassins' alleged practice of taking hashish to induce ecstatic visions of paradise before setting out to face martyrdom. The historical existence of this practice is doubtful. The stories that were told by Marco Polo and other travellers about the gardens of paradise where the drugged devotees were given a foretaste of eternal bliss are not confirmed by any known Ismailite source. Nor did the sect inhabit gardens stocked with fine food and beautiful women. Their dusty mountain forts were often besieged and the presence of women was prohibited during military campaigns.

In 1090, with some Persian allies, Hassan-i Sabbah seized the hill fortress of Alamut in Daylam in Iran. Opposing the growing empire of the Seljuq Turks, he established a loose but cohesive state, which he defended by sending Assassins into enemy camps and cities to murder the generals and statesmen who opposed him. Unable to confront the superior Seljuq armies on the battlefield, the Nizaris sent devotees to infiltrate the households of enemy leaders and kill them. Murders were often carried out in public in broad daylight for maximum effect.

Their terror tactics resulted in a truce between the Seljuq and the Nizaris. The Assassins were given pensions and were allowed to collect their own taxes. During the Third Crusade, they even made attempts on the life of the Muslim leader Saladin, who was a Sunni Kurd who opposed the Ismaili Shia sect.

Over the three centuries of their existence, the Assassins killed two caliphs, along with many viziers, sultans and crusaders who greatly feared them – though the crusaders were not averse to using murder as a tactic themselves. The Assassins selected their victims strategically. They eliminated those who posed the greatest threat to Ismailis, particularly those who had committed massacres.

Assassin power came to an end when the Mongols invaded Persia. One by one their castles fell. However, the subsequent

Mamluk governors used them as paid killers. Nizaris were also used as mercenaries by the kings of Hungary, before they were expelled by the Inquisition. As the influence of the Nizaris continued to wane, their beliefs were considered a minor heresy. But cult followers are still found in Iran, Persia, India, Pakistan and Central Asia.

The Muslim world still seems to be the epicentre of assassination – both as its perpetrators and its victims. America also has a formidable record. Four presidents and several candidates have fallen foul of the assassin's bullet.

Assassinations often have terrible consequences. They can also change the world. Here are forty-eight of them which might be thought significant.

Nigel Cawthorne
Bloomsbury
March 2020

1

QASEM SOLEIMANI 2020

Major General Qasem Soleimani was the head of the Quds Force, the unit of Iran's Revolutionary Guard responsible for unconventional warfare and military intelligence. It specialised in extraterritorial activities, supporting Hezbollah in the Lebanon, Hamas and Palestinian Islamic Jihad in the Gaza Strip and the West Bank, Yemeni Houthis fighting the Saudis, and Shia militias in Iraq, Syria and Afghanistan. Considered by the CIA as 'the single most powerful operative in the Middle East', Soleimani was designated a terrorist by the United States and sanctioned by the European Union and United Nations.

On 2 January 2020, Soleimani flew from Tehran to Damascus. From there he was driven to Beirut where he met Hezbollah's secretary general Hassan Nasrallah. They discussed the latest developments in Iraq, especially the US air strikes that had hit Iraqi Shi'ite paramilitary group Kataeb Hezbollah and the attack on the American embassy in Baghdad a few days earlier. Their aim was to co-ordinate the work of Iran-backed armed factions in the region, preparing them to comprise a united front in any confrontation with the US.

That evening Soleimani returned to Damascus. There he boarded a regular Cham Wings passenger flight to Baghdad scheduled to depart at 8.20pm, but the departure was delayed until 10.28pm. The revised arrival time was sent to Abu Mahdi al-Muhandis, deputy head of the Hashd al-Shaabi Iraqi paramilitary in Syria, a longstanding ally of the Iranian general and a close friend. Muhandis headed to the airport with a small reception party and two vehicles, ready to whisk Soleimani back to the comparative safety of Muhandis' home in the Green Zone of the Iraqi capital.

Like Soleimani, Muhandis had been on the US most-wanted list for years and was seen as the most dangerous man in Iraq. They both avoided using electronic devices like smartphones and followed strict security measures to keep them below the American radar. The number of people who had access to the details of their movements was strictly limited. They always travelled without announcing their destination or advance dates, using regular airlines. They did not pass through formal channels to have their passports stamped at airports, and they moved around on the ground in undistinguished cars accompanied by the fewest number of people. This made it difficult to track them, though both Damascus and Baghdad airports were full of American intelligence assets. Nevertheless, it is clear that Soleimani's movements were being closely monitored.

Muhandis called Mohammed Redha, a close aide responsible for the Hashd al-Shaabi's arrangements in the airport, and gave him orders to drive him to the airport to collect a special guest. Security at the airport was managed by the British company G4S under the supervision of the Iraqi intelligence and national security services. Security measures required ordinary passengers heading in and out of the airport to pass through several checkpoints deployed along ten kilometres of road from Abbas ibn Firnas Square on the outskirts of Baghdad to the airport itself. However, travellers and officials who had a special escort were allowed to pass along a VIP route that required only informing a single checkpoint of the travellers' identity and the vehicles' physical and registration details. This information was shared with airport security, national security and intelligence, and G4S.

It was known that Redha only drove for Muhandis, while Muhandis would only travel to the airport to meet Soleimani. They arrived in time to collect Soleimani and his two companions, one of whom was his son-in-law, who landed at 12.32am. The meeting was kept deliberately low-key. National security officials handled the distinguished guests' travel documents and collected their luggage, which was loaded onto a Hyundai Starks minibus and a Toyota Avalon.

Already a US Air Force MQ-9 Reaper drone and other military aircraft were loitering in the sky above. At 12.47am, as the two vehicles were heading down the VIP route towards western Baghdad, the Reaper launched three missiles. One hit the Hyundai Starks which was travelling around 100 to 120 metres from the other vehicle. The second missed the Toyota, which attempted to speed away. A third finished the job.

The Iraqi authorities needed several hours to identify the victims, some of whom had been completely vapourised. However, Soleimani's remains were easy to spot, thanks to a large and distinctive ring carrying a dark red stone he wore on his left hand.

US President Donald Trump had ordered the assassination in June 2019 if Iran's increased aggression resulted in the death of an American, though he retained the final signoff on any specific operation to kill Soleimani. He did so when thirty-three-year-old defence contractor Nawres Hamid, an immigrant from Iraq who had become a naturalised American citizen, was killed in a rocket attack on an Iraqi military base by Iranian proxies on 27 December. The attack also wounded four US military personnel.

Targeting Soleimani specifically had been under consideration since 2017 and his movements had been tracked by US intelligence. As early as 2007, President George W. Bush had designated the Quds Force a foreign terrorist organisation. Four years later, the administration of Barack Obama announced new sanctions on Soleimani and three other senior Quds Force officials in connection with an alleged plot to assassinate the Saudi ambassador to the United States.

Then in April 2019 Trump designated the entire Islamic Revolutionary Guard Corps a foreign terrorist organisation. White House officials at the time refused to say whether that meant the United States would target Revolutionary Guard leaders as it does the leadership of other terrorist groups, such as the Islamic State militant group and al-Qaeda. Iran retaliated by designating the US military a terrorist organisation.

Justifying the attack, the US Defense Department issued a statement saying: 'General Soleimani was actively developing plans to attack American diplomats and service members in Iraq and throughout the region. General Soleimani and his Quds Force were responsible for the deaths of hundreds of American and coalition service members and the wounding of thousands more.'

Born in 1957, as a teenager, Soleimani had come under the thrall of radical preacher Hojjat Kamyab, a protégé of

Ayatollah Ali Khamenei who went on to become Iran's president, then Supreme Leader. It was Kamyab, Soleimani said, who spurred him to 'revolutionary activities'. After the overthrow of the Shah of Iran in 1979, he joined the Islamic Revolutionary Guard, established to prevent a military counter-coup toppling the new government. It was then he got his only formal military training, which lasted just two months.

He was sent first to help suppress a Kurdish separatist uprising in the north-west of Iran, and later served throughout the brutal Iran–Iraq War, taking part in most major military operations. This gave him a taste for the battlefield, which he described as 'mankind's lost paradise'.

After the war, he concentrated on combating drug trafficking along the Afghan border. Success there led to him being appointed head of the Quds Force, which takes its name from the Arabic for Jerusalem. The elite unit's founding pledge is to take control of that city. While its role was extraterritorial, he had considerable influence at home, winning the ear of Khamenei who described him as a 'living martyr'.

He was also part of a group of Revolutionary Guard commanders who wrote a letter warning reformist President Mohammad Khatami to put down student protests or risk their intervention. Police moved in to crush protests, as they would again a decade later.

'He was more important than the president, spoke to all factions in Iran, had a direct line to the Supreme Leader and was in charge of Iran's regional policy,' said Dina Esfandiary, a fellow at The Century Foundation think tank. 'It doesn't get more important and influential than that.'

Despite his shadowy activities, he became a well-known public figure with the government projecting him as a pious patriot and national champion. He enjoyed genuine popularity in Iran, despite many Iranians' suspicions of the security forces. There was even talk of him running for president, though he denied political ambitions.

Although an outspoken enemy of the US, he joined the fight against the Taliban following 9/11, though pulled out of the informal alliance in 2002 when President Bush named Iran as part of the 'axis of evil' in his State of the Union address. During the height of the US war in Iraq in 2006, for example, when Iranian-armed and -trained militias were planting lethal roadside bombs targeting US troops, the Bush administration debated how to confront Soleimani and his operatives in Iraq. That same year he oversaw the conflict in Lebanon during the Israel–Hezbollah War. His ground forces were also supported by US airstrikes in the battle against ISIS, after he assumed personal control of the Iranian intervention in the Syrian civil war, supporting the government of Bashar al-Assad.

After his assassination there was a debate about whether his killing was legal under international human rights law. For his funeral thousands turned out chanting 'death to America, death to Israel'. On 8 January 2020, the Iranian military launched ballistic missiles at two US bases in Iraq in retaliation. As there were no reported American casualties, the US made no response. However, the following month it was revealed that over a hundred US troops had suffered traumatic brain injuries in the attack.

Although the assassination of Soleimani removed one of the US's most determined foes, it did little to ease the conflict in the Middle East. Indeed it threatened war between the US and Iran, an outcome that may yet inevitably happen.

2

JAMAL KHASHOGGI 2018

A Gulfstream jet with tail markings HZ-SK1 touched down at Istanbul's Atatürk Airport at 3.13am on 2 October 2018. It had come from Riyadh, the capital of Saudi Arabia. Nine members of the Saudi security forces disembarked and checked into two Istanbul hotels not far from the Saudi consulate.

Dissident Saudi Arabian journalist Jamal Khashoggi, a fifty-nine-year-old columnist for the *Washington Post* and a prominent critic of Crown Prince Mohammed bin Salman, aka MBS, arrived at the consulate at 1.14pm. Son of a well-connected family, Khashoggi was an unlikely dissident. His grandfather, Mohammed Khaled Khashoggi, was personal physician to King Ibn Saud, the founder of Saudi Arabia, a status that allowed the family to achieve prominence. Mohammed was the father of the late billionaire arms dealer Adnan Khashoggi, who was the middleman in the Iran–Contra scandal in the 1980s. Adnan was once a neighbour of Donald Trump and sold him a $200-million yacht. Mohammed's daughter was Samira. She married Mohamed al-Fayed, the former owner of Harrods, making Jamal first cousin to Dodi al-Fayed who died alongside Princess Diana in her fatal car crash in Paris in 1997.

In the mid-1980s, Jamal was writing for English-language newspapers such as the *Saudi Gazette* and *Arab News*. Then as editor of *Al Madina*, one of Jeddah's oldest newspapers, from 1991 to 1999, he covered foreign news – travelling to Algeria, Kuwait and Sudan, and reporting on the First Gulf War. He became well known for his interviews with Osama bin Laden, then head of the mujahideen in Afghanistan. From this it was clear he had connections to the Saudi intelligence service.

In 1999, Khashoggi became the deputy editor-in-chief of *Arab News*, the biggest English-language daily in the country, and a key interlocutor for Western journalists dealing with the Saudi royal family. Four years later he became the editor-in-chief of the Saudi Arabian daily *Al Watan* but was dismissed by the Saudi Arabian Ministry of Information because he had allowed a columnist to criticise the founding father of Wahhabism, the state religion of Saudi Arabia.

He went into voluntary exile in London as media adviser to Prince Turki al-Faisal, then ambassador in London but formerly the head of Saudi intelligence from 1977 to 2001. Khashoggi was permitted to return to Saudi Arabia as editor of *Al Watan* in 2007 but was dismissed a second time three years later.

Khashoggi was hired by a new news channel in Bahrain backed by Saudi Arabian billionaire Prince Al-Waleed bin Talal. However, it was closed down by the Bahraini government on its first day after airing an interview with a member of the opposition. Al-Waleed bin Talal was detained by Crown Prince Mohammed bin Salman on allegations of corruption in 2017. Khashoggi himself fell out with MBS for criticising his conduct of the war in the Yemen and his crackdown on dissidents. Eventually he was barred by the

Saudi authorities from publishing or appearing on television after criticising US President-elect Donald Trump, a political ally and business associate of MBS. In June 2017, after a series of arrests, Khashoggi fled Saudi Arabia with only two suitcases and found refuge in the US where he wrote a monthly column for the *Washington Post*. He also pledged $30,000 towards a social media protest against the Saudi regime, which included sending untraceable SIM cards to activists in Saudi Arabia.

In self-imposed exile in Virginia, Khashoggi planned to marry thirty-six-year-old PhD student Hatice Cengiz and needed copies of divorce papers from his previous wife. Hatice was a Turkish national and they planned to marry in Turkey. So the Saudi ambassador in Washington DC, Prince Khalid bin Salman bin Abdulaziz Al Saud, MBS's brother, directed Khashoggi to pick up the paperwork at the consulate in Istanbul, assuring him he would be safe. Khashoggi visited the consulate on Friday, 28 September 2018, but the divorce papers were not ready and he was told to return the following Tuesday, 2 October. This gave the Saudis four days to plan how to get rid of the troublesome journalist.

By the time Khashoggi entered the consulate at about 1pm on 2 October, a second Gulfstream jet, tail markings HZ-SK2, had landed at Attatürk Airport. Like the first, it carried passengers who were military personnel or intelligence officers, all of whom were close associates of Mohammed bin Salman. They had entered the consulate around noon.

Fearing there may be trouble, Khashoggi was accompanied to the consulate by his fiancée Hatice who waited outside. She was told that if he did not emerge in an hour, she should call a friend and fellow journalist who had the ear of the Turkish government.

When Khashoggi entered the consulate, he was ushered to the second floor of the building and into the office of the consul general Mohammed al-Otaibi. Waiting in nearby rooms were the fifteen men who had arrived on the Saudi jets. Among them were Maher Abdulaziz Mutreb, a colonel who was attached to the Crown Prince's security detail, and Salah Muhammed al-Tubaigy, the head of forensics in the kingdom's General Intelligence Directorate. Turkish employees of the consulate had been given the afternoon off and the consulate's CCTV had been disabled.

Not long after Khashoggi entered the consul general's office, Mutreb came in. He told Khashoggi that he had to return to Saudi Arabia. Khashoggi refused. There followed a Skype call to Saud al-Qahtani, one of the Crown Prince's closest advisors. Khashoggi was then told he would be taken back to Saudi Arabia by force, if necessary. Khashoggi warned that someone was waiting outside for him with instructions to inform the authorities if he did not reappear.

During the following seven minutes, Khashoggi was beaten and tortured. He was held down while his fingers were cut off – a punishment that the Crown Prince ordered for writers who criticised him. Khashoggi was injected with a drug to silence him and throttled. Then he was dragged into another room where he was dismembered on a meeting table while still breathing. This was done by Tubaigy – the forensic scientist who specialised in conducting autopsies and was equipped with a bone saw for the purpose.

Tubaigy relished his work. He put on headphones and is heard to say to his colleagues: 'When I do this job, I listen to music. You should do that too.'

'It is like *Pulp Fiction*,' a Turkish official told the *New York Times*.

The whole thing was videotaped so that MBS could see that his orders had been carried out. Khashoggi's fingers would also be delivered to him as further proof. What happened to the rest of his body is open to conjecture. It has never been found.

Some two hours after Khashoggi entered the consulate, six vehicles left. Two arrived at the residence of Mohammed al-Otaibi, the Saudi consul general, five hundred yards away at 3.09pm. One of the vehicles, a Mercedes Vito van with tinted windows, pulled into the garage there. Turkish employees at the residence had also been told to leave hastily that day. Khashoggi's remains may have been burnt in a barbeque pit there.

At 6.20pm one of the Saudi jets took off heading for Cairo. After spending twenty-five hours on the ground there, it flew on to Riyadh. The Saudi men from the first flight were seen leaving their hotels around 8pm that evening. Their plane left Istanbul at 10.35pm. It made a stop about 170 miles to the east in Nallihan, Turkey. It then skirted the border between Iraq and Iran, favouring the Iraqi side, and crossed the Persian Gulf, landing in Dubai at 2.30am. The following morning, it flew on to Riyadh. Thirteen passengers departed on these flights – six in one group, seven in the second.

At 4pm on 2 October, Hatice Cengiz alerted the Turkish authorities, who expressed their concern. The following day, Al Jazeera, the TV station based in Qatar, reported that Jamal Khashoggi had been abducted. The Saudi authorities issued a statement denying he was being detained, saying he 'visited the consulate and exited shortly thereafter'.

In the face of protests from the Turkish government, the police were allowed into the consulate, but not before a specialist Saudi team had given the building a thorough clean. The Saudi authorities eventually admitted that Khashoggi had been killed. While it was clear to the world that he had been murdered on the orders of the Crown Prince, renegade intelligence officers were blamed. Eleven Saudi nationals were charged. Following a trial behind closed doors in Riyadh, five – including Mutreb and Tubaigy – were sentenced to death.

The United Nations rapporteur on summary executions, Agnès Callamard, described the sentence as a mockery of justice as Jamal Khashoggi's death was an 'extrajudicial execution for which the state of Saudi Arabia is responsible' yet its masterminds walk free. Meanwhile MBS and President Trump still talk on the phone. Later it was revealed that the American administration was making a secret deal to supply Saudi Arabia with nuclear technology and, during the 2016 election, Donald Trump was privately setting up companies in Saudi Arabia to support the luxury beach resort MBS was building on the Red Sea coast.

3

KIM JONG-NAM 2017

Born in 1971, Kim Jong-nam was the eldest son of Kim Jong-il, who succeeded his father Kim Il-sung as Supreme Leader of North Korea in 2009. However, it seems Kim Jong-nam did not want to succeed his father in the socialist world's most enduring political dynasty. After being educated in Switzerland, he preferred to enjoy the decadent pleasures offered by the Western world, rather than confining himself to the socialist paradise of the world's last hard-line Communist state.

Kim Jong-nam's mother, Song Hye Rim, was a leading actress at the North Korea Film Studio who divorced her husband to live in secret with heir apparent Kim Jong-il. When Kim Jong-nam returned to North Korea at the age of eighteen, he found himself and his mother sidelined as his father had taken a second wife and new mistresses and had transferred his affections to the children he had by them. Kim Jong-nam was never mentioned in the North Korean media and only a handful of the Communist Party elite knew of his existence, though he was responsible for a number of IT projects.

In 1995, he began making clandestine visits to Japan. This came to the attention of the world in 2001 when Kim Jong-nam and his entourage, bedecked in diamond-encrusted Rolex watches and toting Louis Vuitton bags, were stopped at Narita Airport, reportedly en route to Disneyland in Tokyo. Kim was travelling on a forged Dominican Republic passport bearing the name Pang Xiong, which means 'Fat Bear' in Chinese. It then came out that he had entered the country at least three times in late 2000. A hostess at the exclusive gentlemen's club Soapland in Tokyo's Yoshiwara district remembered Kim's $350-per-hour visits. She also recalled a dragon tattoo on Kim's back. Tattoos are usually taboo in North Korea, though in South Korea they are the distinctive marking of criminal gangs. Kim Jong-il was furious with his son. After being deported from Japan, Kim Jong-nam went gambling in Macau.

Kim's mother died in 2002 and another of Kim Jong-il's mistresses, Ko Yong-hui, who had borne him three children, began campaigning for her two sons to succeed their father. Kim Jong-chul and Kim Jong-un were promoted both to the public and, more importantly, to the military who had a stranglehold on power in North Korea.

While Kim Jong-chul was considered too effeminate for leadership, the twenty-six-year-old Kim Jong-un was created a four-star general and named as the Dear Leader's successor. When Kim Jong-il made a state visit to China the following year, Kim Jong-un was left in charge in the North Korean capital Pyongyang.

When Kim Jong-il died on 17 December 2011, Kim Jong-un took over. Kim Jong-nam visited Pyongyang briefly, but did not stay for the funeral. It was thought that this was to prevent any speculation about the succession. Even so Kim Jong-un issued a standing order to have his half-brother killed. According to South Korea's intelligence a North Korean spy, jailed by South Korea in 2012, confessed to planning a hit-and-run on him in China. Kim Jong-nam wrote to Kim Jong-un begging for his life.

'Please withdraw the order to punish me and my family,' he said in the letter. 'We have nowhere to hide. The only way to escape is to choose suicide.'

Kim Jong-nam stayed out of politics. However, while emphasising that he had no wish to take over, in the book *My Father, Kim Jong-il, and Me* by Japanese journalist Yoji Gomi, he predicted that the North Korean regime would collapse unless reforms were made. He also said that Kim Jong-un would fail as president because 'he has a lack of experience, he's too young, and he didn't have enough time to be groomed'. Around the same time Kim Jong-nam's son called the North Korean regime a 'dictatorship' on a Finnish talk show. Given that North Korean officials have been executed for slumping in their chairs at meetings, such comments would easily qualify as capital offences.

Kim Jong-un's death threats could not be discounted. His uncle and political adviser Jang Song-thaek was a reformer. He was executed for treason, along with his supporters and, reportedly, members of his family, including children and grandchildren, so all traces of his existence were expunged.

On 6 February 2017, Kim Jong-nam travelled to Malaysia on a passport in the name of Kim Chol, a pseudonym he used frequently. On 9 February, he was on Langkawi Island, a tourist resort off Malaysia's west coast, where he met a US national. The Japanese daily paper *Asahi Shimbun* reported that this was an intelligence agent and that a large amount of data had been transferred from Kim Jong-nam's laptop. In June 2019, reports surfaced that Kim Jong-nam had been acting as a CIA informant since his half-brother took power.

While still in favour with his father, Kim Jong-nam had audited the state-run industries, often leading to the execution of factory managers, and while abroad he managed the Kim family's accounts, which amounted to billions of dollars.

Michael Madden, who runs the blog 'North Korea Leadership Watch', said that he had ties with Office 39, a department that seeks foreign income for the Kim regime through illicit means. There were rumours that China hoped to install Kim Jong-nam as leader in Pyongyang if Kim Jong-un fell from power. Meanwhile China saw Kim Jong-nam as useful leverage. This gave the authorities in North Korea even more reason to kill him.

Kim Jong-nam was passing through Kuala Lumpur International Airport on 13 February on his way back to Macau. At 9am he was attacked by two women in the departure lounge. They covered his face with a cloth laced with liquid. This turned out to be the banned nerve agent VX which North Korea, not a signatory to the 1993 Chemical Weapons Convention, was thought to have stockpiled.

He felt dizzy and the police took him to the airport clinic. He died in the ambulance on the way to hospital. In his backpack was $100,000 in cash and four North Korean passports in the name of Kim Chol.

The two women left the scene in a taxi. Later, twenty-eight-year-old Doan Thi Huong, a Vietnamese, and twenty-five-year-old Siti Aisyah, an Indonesian, were arrested and charged with murder, which carried a mandatory death sentence. Four North Koreans were also accused of orchestrating the plot but fled Malaysia shortly after the attack and have never faced trial.

The two women claimed that they were playing a prank for a reality TV programme at the behest of four North

Koreans. They had been recruited in early 2017 while working as escorts, Doan in Hanoi and Siti in Kuala Lumpur. They said they were told that they had been selected to take part in a Japanese comedy show on YouTube, where they would perform pranks by smearing lotion on people's faces.

Siti said she was paid hundreds of dollars to carry out the prank at various malls in Kuala Lumpur as practice before she was brought to the airport where Kim Jong-nam was picked out as the next target for the TV show. Both Siti and Doan denied knowing who he was, nor knowing what they were doing was dangerous. However, after the attack, Doan was seen rushing to the bathroom to wash her hands.

After determining that the regime had 'used chemical weapons in violation of international law or lethal chemical weapons against its own nationals', the US imposed additional sanctions on North Korea. South Korea also blamed the North for the assassination of Kim Jong-nam.

However, South Korean President Moon Jae-in met Kim Jong-un in April 2018 to sign the Panmunjom Declaration, pledging to convert the Armistice Agreement ending the Korean War in 1953 into a full peace treaty. They had another meeting in May, while on 12 June Kim Jong-un met President Trump in Singapore to discuss nuclear disarmament. A further meeting between Kim Jong-un and President Moon took place in September.

Doan Thi Huong and Siti Aisyah spent two years behind bars – in adjoining cells – before they were sent back to their respective countries. The prosecution withdrew the charges against Siti, while Doan was sentenced to three years and four months in jail after she pleaded guilty to voluntarily causing hurt by dangerous means to Jong-nam. An appeal by the prosecution was thrown out.

'Doan and I grew very close over the course of the trial,' said Siti. 'I always gave my support to her, and she always gave her support to me. When I cried, she would always console me. And when she cried, I would do the same for her. I think of her as my own sister.'

While the North Korean regime has never formally confessed to the assassination, in late 2018 they reportedly expressed 'regret' to Vietnam, a strategic ally, for involving one of their citizens.

Meanwhile Kim Jong-un continued ordering the gruesome execution of those who opposed him. Reports emerged in 2020 that he threw one of his generals into a tank of flesh-eating piranhas after being accused of planning a coup. The un-named general had his arms and torso cut open with knives before being tossed in, according to sources. It was thought that Kim Jong-un drew inspiration from the 1977 James Bond movie *You Only Live Twice* where villain Helga Brandt is devoured by piranhas as a punishment for not killing 007.

4

JO COX 2016

Thankfully political assassination is a rare thing in the UK. Since the 1812 assassination of Spencer Perceval – the only prime minister to have been killed in office – only seven sitting MPs have been murdered, six of them by Irish Republicans. Following the 1998 Good Friday Agreement, political violence was thought to have become a thing of the past. But on 16 June 2016, forty-one-year-old Jo Cox, the Labour MP for Batley and Spen, was gunned down and stabbed in her constituency by a deranged Neo-Nazi white supremacist. It was the first murder of an MP since the assassination of Ian Gow, Conservative MP for Eastbourne. He was killed in 1990 by the Provisional IRA who exploded a bomb under his car outside his home in East Sussex.

Jo Cox was born Helen Joanne Leadbeater in Batley in 1974 and brought up in nearby Heckmondwike, which is also in the constituency of Batley and Spen in West Yorkshire. Her mother, Jean, was a school secretary and her father, Gordon, was a factory worker in Leeds. She read social and political science at Cambridge, the first in her family to go to university. It was not an experience she enjoyed.

'I never really grew up being political or Labour. It kind of came at Cambridge where it was just a realisation that where you were born mattered. That how you spoke mattered... who you knew mattered,' she said. 'I didn't really speak right or know the right people. I spent the summers packing toothpaste at a factory, working where my dad worked, and everyone else had gone on a gap year. To be honest my experience at Cambridge really knocked me for about five years.'

Her university experience led her to join the Labour Party. After graduating, she worked for Oxfam, becoming head of policy, and was an adviser to Labour MP Joan Walley, Gordon Brown's wife Sarah and then Glenys (now Baroness) Kinnock. By the end of the 1990s she was head of campaigns for the pro-European pressure group Britain in Europe. After further studies at the London School of Economics, she built a career working for charities including Save the Children and the NSPCC. Her work took her to some of the world's most dangerous war zones.

'I've been in some horrific situations – where women have been raped repeatedly in Darfur, I've been with child soldiers who have been given a Kalashnikov and kill members of their own family in Uganda,' she said. 'In Afghanistan I was talking to Afghan elders who were world weary of a lack of sustained attention from their own Government and from the international community to stop problems early. That's the thing that all of that experience gave me – if you ignore a problem it gets worse.'

In 2014, she was selected from an all-women shortlist to fight the safe Labour seat of Batley and Spen at the 2015 election after the previous MP, Mike Wood, retired. She increased the Labour majority by two thousand votes.

Arriving in Westminster she told the *Yorkshire Post*: 'Having gone through that experience of being in a Cambridge college, surviving it and building myself up, meant that coming here was a walk in the park and a lot of the same people are here.'

In parliament, she joined the Communities and Local Government select committee and used her maiden speech to urge the government to live up to its rhetoric about building a 'Northern Powerhouse', urging more regional devolution and increased funding for local authorities. She also established and became co-chairman of a new all-party parliamentary group on Syria, chaired the Labour Women's Network and was a senior adviser to the Freedom Fund, an anti-slavery charity.

She lived with her husband Brendan and two young children, Lejla and Cuillin, on a converted barge moored at Tower Bridge and, in her spare time, was a keen mountain climber.

Jo Cox was one of the thirty-six MPs to nominate Jeremy Corbyn as a candidate in the 2015 Labour leadership election, though she upset the Corbynite wing of the party by voting for the Blairite Liz Kendall. In May 2016, she warned that Corbyn could face a leadership challenge if Britain voted to leave the EU because of his failure to mobilise voters for the Remain campaign.

'I want to see those Labour voters come out and vote Remain,' she said. 'If they don't, and we leave... Ultimately there are many of us who think that Jeremy needs to take responsibility.'

In the run-up to the 2016 EU referendum, she was getting out of a car to meet constituents at a routine surgery in Birstall when she was confronted by fifty-two-year-old unemployed gardener Thomas Mair. Yelling 'This is for Britain,' 'keep Britain independent' and 'Britain first,' he shot her twice in the head and once in the chest with a sawn-off .22 Weihrauch bolt-action hunting rifle. Wounds to her hands showed Jo had raised them to try to defend herself.

She was then stabbed fifteen times, including in the heart and lungs, with a seven-inch blade. The attacker then kicked her as she bled to death. Despite emergency surgery at the scene, she died in the back of the ambulance. The gun and the knife were later found in Mair's backpack. Blood on the handle of the knife contained a major DNA profile matching that of Jo Cox and a minor DNA profile of Mair. Her blood was also found on the barrel of the gun.

The attack was witnessed by retired mine rescuer Bernard Carter-Kenny who had run to Cox's assistance. Mair turned and stabbed him in the stomach. Bleeding profusely, Carter-Kenny staggered across the road and found safety in a shop. Bloodstains around a cut on the gilet he was wearing were also found to contain the MP's DNA. Carter-Kenny survived and was awarded the George Medal for bravery.

Mair walked calmly away from the attack. He disappeared behind a pub, took off his jacket and swapped his white baseball cap for a black one. The authorities were already on their way. Shelly Morris, who also witnessed the attack, had called 999.

She said she saw a man with a large steak knife with a jagged blade, which he wielded in a 'stabbing motion'. The attacker stood over a figure and fired a gun twice, according to her account.

Mair was arrested leaving the scene by PCs Craig Nicholls and Jonathan Wright. They were awarded the Queen's Gallantry Medal.

According to Detective Superintendent Nick Wallen of the West Yorkshire Police, Mair was a 'loner in the truest sense of the word. This is a man who never held down a job, never had a girlfriend, never any friends to speak of.' Nor was he on any watch list. He had never had 'so much as a conversation' with the police.

When the police searched the semi-detached council house where Mair had been living alone since the death of his grandmother three years earlier, they found Nazi regalia, far-right books and instructions for making bombs. He had collected newspaper cuttings about Anders Breivik, the far-right terrorist who killed seventy-seven people in Norway in 2011 and searched the internet for, among other things, accounts of the murder of Ian Gow. He also drew inspiration from David Copeland who planted nail bombs aimed to kill black, Asian and gay people in London in 1999.

Mair stole the bolt-action rifle he used from the boot of a sports utility vehicle in August 2015. The stock and most of the barrel had been removed, leaving it just twelve inches long, so it could easily be hidden under his clothes. He carried out online research into .22 ammunition, reading one page that offered an answer to the question: 'Is a .22 round deadly enough to kill with one shot to a human's head?' He also bought a replica British Army World War II dagger.

Remanded in Westminster Magistrates' Court, when asked what his name was, he said: 'My name is death to traitors, freedom for Britain.'

He refused to plead and the judge entered a not-guilty plea on his behalf and remitted him for trail at the Old Bailey. There, on 14 November 2016, Thomas Mair was convicted of Cox's murder, grievous bodily harm for stabbing Bernard Carter-Kenny, being in possession of a firearm with intent and the possession of a dagger. He was sentenced to life imprisonment without the possibility of parole.

After the murder, President Barack Obama spoke to Jo's widower Brendan Cox from Air Force One. A White House statement said: 'President Obama offered his sincere condolences on behalf of the American people to Mr Cox and his two young children, as well as to her friends, colleagues and constituents. The president noted that the world is a better place because of her selfless service to others, and that there can be no justification for this heinous crime, which robbed a family, a community and a nation of a dedicated wife, mother and public servant.'

Prime minister David Cameron and Labour leader Jeremy Corbyn united to pay tribute to Labour MP Jo Cox in the West Yorkshire town where she was killed. It was one of the few things they could agree on.

5

OSAMA BIN LADEN 2011

In August 2010 a trusted aide of Osama bin Laden received a phone call. He had no idea that simple act of answering his phone would lead US intelligence to the location of his boss who, since 9/11 in 2001, had been the world's most-wanted terrorist.

The phone call was made to Abu Ahmed al-Kuwaiti, aka Arshad Khan. He was outside a walled compound called Waziristan Haveli in Abbottabad, north-east Pakistan. American intelligence had been looking for bin Laden for nine years. He was savvy enough to know that he could not use any form of electronic communication which would be bound to come to the attention of the NSA, the American National Security Agency which collects signals intelligence. So messages had to be carried by a courier.

When the CIA captured al-Qaeda's third in command and operations leader Khalid Sheikh Mohammed in 2003, he had given up the code names of several of bin Laden's couriers. The following year, interrogation of Khaled Sheikh Mohammed's successor Abu Faraj al-Libi also yielded the name of Arshad Khan. The CIA believed that if they could track him down he would lead them straight to bin Laden.

In August 2010 the phone call to Arshad Khan was picked up by the NSA. Looking closer they noticed that there were no telephone lines coming in and out of the compound at Abbottabad. Nor was it connected to the internet. Few people went in or out and they burnt all their trash. The CIA began to suspect that bin Laden was hiding there in plain sight, but there was no way to be sure. They continued to watch the place for eight months before, in February 2011, they reported to President Barack Obama that the compound contained a 'high-value target, very possibly Osama Bin Laden'. The president then gave the order to go in.

On Sunday, 1 May 2011, as the clock approached midnight local time, four helicopters flew out of Bagram Air Base in south-eastern Afghanistan and crossed over the border into Pakistan. They were headed for the city of Abbottabad, which is seventy miles to the north of Pakistan's capital Islamabad.

The four helicopters, two Sikorsky UH-60 Black Hawks and two Boeing CH-47 Chinooks, maintained a low altitude over the Hindu Kush mountains to avoid being detected by radar. The Black Hawks had also had their rotors and stabilisers modified for additional stealth. They had to ensure that they would not be detected.

The four helicopters held a contingent of seventy-nine Special Forces Commandos and one sniffer dog. When told 'We think we found Osama bin Laden, and your job is to kill him', they began to cheer. On point were twenty-four members of an elite Navy SEALs team called SEAL Team 6, which up to this point had never officially existed. They had spent two weeks training on a full-size replica of the compound, but now they faced the real thing. Their target, they had been told, was Osama bin Laden, founder of al-Qaeda, the terrorist group responsible for the attacks on the United States on September 11, 2001 when almost three thousand people lost their lives.

Equipped with night-vision goggles and M4 rifles with laser sights, they checked their gear as the compound came into view. Its walls ranged from ten-feet high to eighteen feet in places. Inside there were two buildings – a three-storey house with a single-storey guest house just to the south. The first team would land in the yard to the west of the main house. A second team would land on the roof. At least, that was the plan. As the first Black Hawk helicopter was coming in to land in the yard, the second stalled as it flew over the compound walls and was forced to make a 'hard landing', but all twenty-four SEALs scrambled out of their helicopter unharmed.

One team approached the guest house. As they neared the door they were met by Arshad Khan, bin Laden's courier. Armed with an AK-47 assault rifle, he opened fire. The SEALs returned fire and, after a brief exchange, Arshad Khan was shot dead. This was the only armed resistance the SEALs would face on their mission.

The other team surrounded the main building. After blowing out the windows and doors, they entered the ground floor. Inside the SEALs came face to face with Tariq Khan, Arshad's brother. He was killed with a single shot. The team moved quickly through the ground floor, clearing each room, then headed for the stairs. On their way up to the first floor a young man charged down the stairs towards the SEALs. He was quickly eliminated. This turned out to be Khalid bin Laden, Osama bin Laden's twenty-two-year-old son. After clearing the first floor, the SEALs moved up to the top floor.

As they reached the landing, they caught the first glimpse of their target. Osama bin Laden was standing just inside the doorway of his quarters. He scuttled back into the room as bullets struck the door frame. The SEALs charged into the room. They were confronted by one of bin Laden's wives, who tried to get between them and her husband. She was quickly put down with a shot to the leg. Two more shots were fired. The first shot struck bin Laden in the chest; the second hit him in the head. SEAL Team 6 immediately radioed in: 'Geronimo EKIA.' Geronimo was the code name for bin Laden, while EKIA is the acronym for Enemy Killed In Action.

The SEALs did not pause for a moment; they continued their sweep of the top floor, room by room, until they could be sure that the compound and the remaining occupants were secure. There were several women and children in the main building, most belonging to the family of Tariq Khan, but there was also bin Laden's twelve-year-old daughter Safia, who was injured by flying debris.

The entire raid lasted just thirty minutes, with the assault taking only seven minutes. The majority of the time was spent searching both buildings for weapons stashes and intelligence information. The SEALs recovered a wealth of electronic equipment, including DVDs, SIM cards and computer hard drives. They also recovered two handguns and three AK-47 assault rifles. The SEALs then prepared bin Laden's body for transportation.

The remaining residents of the compound were secured with zip ties and left for the Pakistani authorities to pick up. The SEALs then made their way back to the helicopters. The Black Hawk that had made the 'hard landing' was badly damaged and unable to fly. The decision was taken to destroy the craft to ensure that none of the classified equipment aboard, especially the modified stealth systems, could be recovered. The downed aircraft was packed with explosives which were detonated with a controlled explosion. They then called in one of the supporting Chinooks to pick up the remaining SEALs and bin Laden's body, and take them to USS *Carl Vinson*, an aircraft carrier stationed in the North Arabian Sea, off the south coast of Pakistan.

Once aboard ship, bin Laden's identity was confirmed by a DNA test against samples previously taken from his extended family – several of them lived in the United States. His body was then washed and wrapped in a white sheet in accordance with Islamic practice. It was put in a weighted bag. Islamic last rites were given in Arabic and bin Laden was buried at sea less than 24 hours after his death.

On the other side of the world in Washington DC, President Barack Obama had been watching the whole raid unfold in the White House situation room. Vice President Joe Biden and Secretary of State Hillary Clinton were there, along with the top brass and the director of the CIA, Leon Panetta.

'Once those teams went into the compound I can tell you that there was a time period of almost twenty or twenty-five minutes where we really didn't know just exactly what going on,' Panetta later commented. 'We had some observation of the approach there, but we did not have direct flow of information as to the actual conduct of the operation itself as they were going through the compound.'

Then they received radio confirmation from the SEALs' team leader: 'Geronimo EKIA.' The tense silence in the situation room was then broken by President Obama.

'We got him,' he said.

At around 10.30pm Eastern Daylight Time, a newsflash came up on television, announcing that an address to the nation was about to be given by the president. Newspapers across the world were told to hold the front page. At 11.30 pm, almost fifty-seven million people tuned in to see the president deliver his speech from inside the White House.

'Today, at my direction, the United States launched a targeted operation against that compound in Abbottabad, Pakistan,' he said. 'A small team of Americans carried out the operation with extraordinary courage and capability. No Americans were harmed. They took care to avoid civilian casualties. After a firefight, they killed Osama bin Laden and took custody of his body.'

Nine years, seven months and nineteen days after 9/11, the world's longest and most expensive manhunt was over and Osama bin Laden was dead.

6

BENAZIR BHUTTO 2007

Daughter of the former president of Pakistan, Zulfikar Ali Bhutto, founder of the Pakistan People's Party who was executed after a military coup in 1977, Benazir Bhutto had survived a long and controversial political career. After her father's death, Benazir took over the leadership of the PPP and was frequently jailed by the military government led by General Muhammad Zia-ul-Haq, who had ousted her father. She went into voluntary exile in Britain in 1984.

She returned to lead the PPP to victory in the 1988 election and served as prime minster until 1990, the first woman to head a democratic government in a Muslim nation. After being dismissed by the president on corruption charges, she became leader of the opposition. When it came to corruption, the new government was little better and the PPP was re-elected in 1993. Bhutto became prime minister again, only to be dismissed a second time three years later. Serving a second term as leader of the opposition, she lost the election in 1998. Fearing prosecution, she went into exile in Dubai and was sentenced to five years' imprisonment *in absentia*.

It is clear that she knew the dangers when she returned to Pakistan in 2007 to compete in the elections the following year. Her brother Murtaza, a political rival, had been assassinated in 1996, possibly with the connivance of her husband Asif Ali Zardari. There had also been a series of suicide bombings in 2006–07, but Bhutto was seen as a person who could bring back some domestic stability.

When she returned to Pakistan on 18 October 2007, she rode from the airport into Karachi in an armoured truck with two thousand PPP workers surrounding it, preventing any other vehicles or people approaching it. She spent eight hours on the open roof of the truck waving to supporters. Just ten minutes after she climbed back inside, two bombs went off just a few feet away. She was uninjured, but over a hundred people were killed and many more wounded. This was clearly a warning that worse was to come.

She had discussed obtaining additional protection from the American security firm Blackwater and the British company ArmorGroup International. However, visas were denied. President Pervez Musharraf said that the Pakistani security services were more than adequate to protect her. Later, a United Nations' investigation into Bhutto's subsequent murder noted that Musharraf's government failed to provide comparable measures for her as it had for two other former prime ministers.

On 27 December, Benazir Bhutto left Islamabad to attend a rally in Rawalpindi in an armour-plated Toyota Land Cruiser. At the front of the speeding motorcade was a blue police van and a black Mercedes safety car. Behind came another police pickup, five pickups carrying her bodyguards and jeeps carrying leading members of the PPP.

At around 3pm, she arrived at Liaquat Bagh, the park where the rally was being held, and entered through a back gate reserved for her. Only her car and the black Mercedes were allowed through. The other vehicles were stopped. Even her own bodyguards were not allowed to enter the park.

When she appeared on the platform, the crowd roared, yelling '*Jiye Bhutto!*' – 'long live Bhutto' and '*wazir-i-azam Benazir*' – 'prime minister Benazir'.

In a fiery speech, she declared: 'This government cannot control the situation. This is your country and this is my country. And we have to save it! All my family have sacrificed for this cause. And we must work together.'

She left the park around 5pm in the backseat of her armoured car. While police had been frisking everyone entering the park even after they passed through metal detectors, crowds had been allowed to gather unchecked around the back gate. As her car emerged they swarmed around it. Unusually, it was not surrounded by a phalanx of her young security guards, who called themselves the Martyrs for Benazir.

Bhutto was exhausted, but she could not resist the chants of the crowd. As the car drove towards the main road, she poked her head out of the open sunroof. A gunman ran up to her car, peppering it with automatic-weapon fire. She was hit in the head and neck by the bullets and died almost instantly. Then he blew himself up with a suicide bomb. At least twenty others lost their lives in the blast.

Photographer John Moore, who was taking pictures of Bhutto, said: 'I heard several shots ring out – I think three – and she went down. The timing was right with the shots; that's when she was killed, right there. I raised my camera and started shooting photographs and that's when the blast happened.'

Bhutto's secretary Naheed Khan was in the car with Benazir. She did not realise what had happened to start with when Bhutto slumped back into her seat.

'I thought she might have become unconscious because of exhaustion,' Khan said. 'She was in my lap and then suddenly I saw blood on my hands.'

Babar Awan, a leading lawyer and PPP official, was in the black Mercedes behind.

'The cars were bumper to bumper,' he said. 'I rolled down the window of my side to keep an eye on Benazir. Then I heard a few shots and moments later there was a blast. I was the first to see her corpse. There was a bullet wound on her neck just below her left ear. On the forehead there was another wound with scattered shrapnel pieces. I could not say whether it was the entry or exit point of the bullet. But it was very powerful.'

The cause of death immediately became a matter of controversy with the Interior Ministry insisting that there were no gunshot wounds and that death was as a result of a neck fracture sustained when she ducked or fell into her vehicle, hitting her head on the sunroof catch as she dodged the fusillade. Later it was reported that the cause of death was a skull fracture. There was no formal post-mortem and she was buried the following day. The scene of the attack was cleared before any forensic examination could be carried out.

There were violent protests at her death, especially in her home province of Sindh. Demonstrators torched a train, buses, banks, a prison and police checkpoints. Major roads were blocked with burning tyres and shops were boarded up. Over a hundred people were killed in the unrest, which included running gun battles between rioters and the police.

The Pakistani authorities claimed that the assassin had been a teenage boy from South Waziristan, a stronghold of the Taliban. They claimed to have proof that the attack had been masterminded by Baitullah Mehsud, leader of the Pakistani Taliban. Mehsud denied the accusation, but the CIA said he had a motive – he believed that Bhutto's pro-American and secularist agenda would undermine the Pakistani Taliban's control of South Waziristan and hinder the growth of Sunni Islamist radicalism. Al-Qaeda commander Mustafa Abu al-Yazid claimed responsibility for the assassination, saying: 'We terminated the most precious American asset which vowed to defeat the mujahideen.'

Bhutto's supporters continued to blame the government – especially allies of President Musharraf. A UN investigation later concluded that 'Ms. Bhutto's assassination could have been prevented if adequate security measures had been taken'.

Internationally there was condemnation of the assassination of Benazir Bhutto. Indian prime minister Manmohan Singh praised Bhutto's efforts to improve India–Pakistan relations. The UN Security Council held an emergency meeting and unanimously condemned the assassination. UN Secretary General Ban Ki-moon, European Union President José Manuel Barroso and US President George W. Bush expressed the hope that Pakistan would continue on its path to democracy. Bush condemned the assassination as a 'cowardly act by murderous extremists' and encouraged Pakistan to 'honour Benazir Bhutto's memory by continuing with the democratic process for which she so bravely gave her life'.

Benazir Bhutto left instructions that her husband Asif Ali Zardari and her nineteen-year-old son Bilawal should take over the leadership of the PPP as co-chairmen. After the parliamentary election in March 2008, the PPP formed a coalition government with the Pakistan Muslim League. Zardari won the 2008 presidential election, but he relinquished presidential power to the prime minister and parliament, and a constitutional amendment was passed turning Pakistan back into a parliamentary democracy.

In 2017, an anti-terrorism court in Rawalpindi convicted two policemen of abetting the assassination. One of them, the Deputy Inspector General Saud Aziz, was also blamed for not ordering a post-mortem. They were sentenced to seventeen years. In a landmark ruling, the court also declared ex-President Pervez Musharraf, who had gone into exile in 2008, an absconder in the case.

Educated at Harvard and Oxford – where she was friends with Theresa May, later British prime minister – Benazir Bhutto was a pro-Western liberal. Since her death Pakistan has continued to shelter Islamic terrorists, particularly those seeking refuge from the fighting in neighbouring Afghanistan. She had also sought to improve relations with India, something that has eluded Pakistani politicians ever since. Both countries are armed with nuclear weapons and the disputed province of Kashmir remains one of the world's flashpoints.

7

ALEXANDER LITVINENKO 2006

Murder victim Alexander Litvinenko was buried in a lead-lined coffin. When the Russian dissident died in London in 2006, it was discovered that his body was full of polonium-210, a rare, expensive and dangerous radioactive element practically impossible to obtain unless, of course, you own a nuclear reactor.

As a young man Litvinenko had been a high flier in the KGB. He also excelled in the Federal Security Service, or FSB, which replaced the KGB after the collapse of the Soviet Union in 1991. He worked in the Division of Economic Security, then at the Anti-Terrorist Centre where he ran undercover agents and amassed intelligence on organised crime, kidnappings, assassinations and the criminal links of the police, politicians and businessmen.

Through his work in counter-intelligence he met oligarch Boris Berezovsky. A former mathematics professor, when the Soviet Union crumbled, Berezovsky went into the automobile industry, selling cars with the protection of a Chechen crime outfit that fought with rival Slav gangs for control of Moscow. When there was an assassination attempt on Berezovsky in 1994, Litvinenko was sent to investigate and they became firm friends.

This did not endear him to his boss at the FSB Vladimir Putin, especially when Litvinenko claimed he too had been given orders to assassinate Berezovsky. Going public, Litvinenko appeared at a press conference revealing the conspiracy to kill Berezovsky and fellow dissident intelligence officer Mikhail Trepashkin, who had successfully sued the FSB for corruption. As a result, Litvinenko was dismissed from the FSB. Putin said: 'I fired Litvinenko and disbanded his unit... because FSB officers should not stage press conferences. This is not their job. And they should not make internal scandals public.'

Evading arrest, Litvinenko and his family fled to Turkey where he applied for asylum at the US embassy. When this was denied, he flew to the UK where he was granted asylum in 2001. Five years later, he naturalised as a British subject.

Berezovsky had also fled to the UK and Litvinenko joined him in his campaign against Putin. Litvinenko also worked for MI6, though in the tradition of the service they will not confirm or deny this. However, in the inquiry after Litvinenko's death, it was revealed that he had been put on the payroll in 2003, given an encrypted phone and was assigned a handler called 'Martin'.

In his book *Blowing Up Russia*, Litvinenko claimed the Russian security services were complicit in a series of apartment block bombings in 1999 that killed more than three hundred people as part of a coup to bring Putin to power as president. After several chapters were published in *Novaya Gazeta*, the deputy editor-in-chief Yuri Shchekochikhin, who had picked up the manuscript in Zagreb, was poisoned and died after three months in a coma.

Litvinenko also asserted that FSB agents trained al-Qaeda leaders in Dagestan and were involved in the 9/11 attacks.

In 2002, he was convicted *in absentia* in Russia and sentenced to three and a half years in prison for corruption, and Trepashkin, then in jail, warned him that an FSB unit had been assigned to assassinate him.

One former colleague begged him to return to Russia, saying he had nothing to fear. Another phoned him to say: 'Do you think you are safe over there in England? Well, you're dreaming. Just remember what happened to Trotsky.'

In a series of newspaper articles, Litvinenko claimed that the FSB were complicit in the 2002 Moscow theatre siege, the 2004 Beslan school massacre and numerous other terrorist attacks. According to Litvinenko, former prime minister of Italy and president of the European Commission Romano Prodi had also worked for the KGB. However, perhaps his most damaging allegation was that Vladimir Putin, then president of the Russian Federation, had ordered the assassination of dissident journalist Anna Politkovskaya. There were wilder accusations – that Putin was involved in drug running, even that he was a paedophile.

On 1 November 2006, Litvinenko had lunch with Italian lawyer and security consultant Mario Scaramella at Itsu, a sushi restaurant in Piccadilly. Previously Litvinenko had provided him with intelligence for an Italian parliamentary commission. In return Scaramella gave him an FSB hit list with his name on it. Litvinenko then rushed to Berezovsky's office in Mayfair to show him, but Berezovsky had gone to watch CSKA Moscow play Arsenal at the Emirates stadium.

At 4.30pm, Litvinenko met two former KGB officers, Andrei Lugovoy and Dmitry Kovtun, in the Pine Bar of the Millennium Hotel in Mayfair. Later Litvinenko told his wife Marina that, at the meeting, he had drunk tea that did not taste too good. It was cold and he had only taken three or four sips.

It was later discovered that the tea was laced with the highly radioactive substance polonium-210 and the dose he had ingested was far in excess of the known survivability levels.

That evening Litvinenko fell ill. Suffering from diarrhoea and vomiting, he retired to bed. As his condition grew worse, his wife called an ambulance. At the A&E department of Barnet General Hospital, he registered under the pseudonym 'Edwin Carter'. The doctors diagnosed food poisoning from bad sushi. When he told them that he thought he had been poisoned by the KGB, they called for a psychiatrist. But when he told them who he really was, they called Scotland Yard.

Litvinenko's hair began falling out and Professor John Henry, the leading toxicologist at St Mary's Hospital, was consulted. He said that hair loss was a symptom of exposure to thallium, the principal ingredient of a rat poison banned in the UK but still available throughout the Middle East.

Escorted by armed police, Litvinenko was transferred to University College Hospital. There Professor Henry soon concluded that, while Litvinenko's thallium level was around three times greater than normal, this was not high enough to account for his symptoms. He suggested that radioactive thallium might have been used. This was thought to have been used in an assassination attempt on KGB defector Nikolai Khokhlov in 1957. However, when he checked, Professor Henry discovered that radioactive thallium emitted gamma rays, which would easily have been detected with medical equipment. What they should be looking for, he concluded, was a radioactive substance that emitted alpha particles.

A sample of Litvinenko's urine was sent to the Atomic Weapons Research Establishment at Aldermaston. They discovered polonium-210 and sent a warning that Litvinenko's body would be dangerously radioactive.

Knowing he was about to die, Litvinenko allowed himself to be photographed by the press. 'I want [the] world to see what they did to me,' Litvinenko said. In a final statement, he blamed Vladimir Putin for his impending death.

On 23 November, Alexander Litvinenko died of heart failure. His body was later found to contain more than two hundred times the lethal dose of the radioactive element polonium-210. Detectives from Scotland Yard found they could trace three trails of radioactive polonium – belonging respectively to Litvinenko, Lugovoy and Kovtun. Passengers on board the planes Lugovoy and Kovtun had flown back to Moscow on were warned to contact the Department of Health. Meanwhile the UK Atomic Weapons Establishment traced the source of the polonium to the Ozersk nuclear power plant, near the city of Chelyabinsk in Russia.

The British government requested the extradition of Lugovoy to face charges relating to Litvinenko's death. The request was denied. Kovtun was under investigation by the German authorities for suspected plutonium smuggling, but Germany dropped the case in 2009.

There can be little doubt why Litvinenko was killed. Two days after he died, representative Sergey Abeltsev told the Russian Duma: 'The deserved punishment reached the traitor. I am confident that this terrible death will be a serious warning to traitors of all colours, wherever they are located. In Russia, they do not pardon treachery. I would recommend citizen Berezovsky to avoid any food at the commemoration for his accomplice Litvinenko.'

After US security analyst Paul Joyal alleged that Litvinenko had been killed as a warning to all critics of the Putin government, he was shot outside his home in Maryland. Surviving several assassination attempts, Boris Berezovsky was then found dead in suspicious circumstances in his house at Sunninghill near Ascot in Berkshire on 23 March 2013. The verdict: Suicide.

As regards Litvinenko, Dmitry Kovtun and Andrei Lugovoy denied any wrongdoing, but a leaked US diplomatic cable revealed that Kovtun had left traces of polonium in the house and car he had used in Hamburg.

In a case remarkably similar to that of the assassination of Litvinenko, former Russian military intelligence officer and British spy Sergei Skripal and his daughter Yulia Skripal were poisoned in Salisbury, England, with a Novichok nerve agent on 4 March 2018. Developed in Russia, Novichok is thought to be one of the deadliest nerve agents ever produced.

Sergei Skripal had been an officer for Russia's Main Intelligence Directorate, the GRU, and worked as a double agent for Britain's Secret Intelligence Service from 1995 until his arrest in Moscow in December 2004. Convicted of high treason, he was sentenced to thirteen years in a penal colony in 2006. He was released and settled in England in 2010 after a spy swap. Yulia remained in Russia and was visiting her father in 2018. One theory was that the Russian secret services had somehow tricked her into carrying the deadly poison.

Britain maintained that the poisoning had been carried out by the Russian secret services and that it was likely to have been ordered by Russian President Vladimir Putin himself. Sixty Russian diplomats were expelled from Britain. The Russians responded in kind. More than twenty other countries expelled Russian diplomats in support of the UK. Russia claimed that Britain had the means and the motive to murder Skripal. Again Russia refused to extradite two former Russian military intelligence officers who had visited Salisbury that day and were thought to be responsible.

The murder of Litvinenko was a distant echo of the assassination of Bulgarian dissident Georgi Markov. After he fled the country in 1969, he went to work for the BBC. On 11 September 1978, he was walking across Waterloo Bridge, London Bridge when a Bulgarian Secret Service agent fired a pellet of ricin from a specially modified umbrella into the back of his leg. There was no known antidote to ricin at the time and he died.

8

YITZHAK RABIN 1995

Prime minister of Israel Yitzhak Rabin was elected to a second term in 1992 on a platform embracing an Israel–Palestine peace process that offered a two-state solution if the Palestinians took steps to actively prevent terrorism and acknowledged Israel had an unconditional right to exist.

Rabin had once been a national hero. He had fought in Israel's war for independence in 1948. He then became chief of the general staff. In that position he oversaw Israel's rout of Arab armies in the Six Day War in 1967. He remained a military officer at heart even after entering politics, always more comfortable talking with generals about security matters than interacting with other politicians and alienating him from the people. This had dire consequences.

In 1974, he succeeded Golda Meir as leader of the Labor Party and served a first stint as prime minister, leaving office in 1977 under the cloud of a minor financial scandal dating from earlier service as ambassador in Washington.

Then in 1992, more seasoned at age seventy, he led his party to victory over Likud prime minister Yitzhak Shamir, a former Stern Gang terrorist whose antagonistic relations with the United States led the administration of George H.

W. Bush to withhold loan guarantees for Israel. Over the next three years, Rabin led his country through the first steps of implementing the Oslo agreement.

Rabin did not share the belief held by many Israelis that the possession of the territory conquered in the Six Day War in 1967 was a fulfilment of Jewish destiny. He argued that Israel needed parts of the West Bank for security purposes, not because of any sacred status of the land itself. He said that clinging to territories inhabited by Arabs would mean Israel losing its Jewish majority and turning it into an apartheid state – a term few Israelis dared to use at the time. He had little time for the Jewish settlers there, who in turn saw him as a threat.

Rabin signed several historic agreements with the Palestinian leadership as part of the Oslo Accords guaranteeing the Palestinian people's right to self-determination. In 1994, Rabin was awarded the Nobel Peace Prize together with long-time political rival Shimon Peres and Palestinian leader Yasser Arafat. Rabin also signed a peace treaty with Jordan that year.

Conservatives opposed the Oslo Accords with the leader of the Likud Party and future prime minister Benjamin Netanyahu warning that Israeli concessions would encourage Palestinian extremism. However, the Oslo II Accord, establishing a Palestinian interim self-government in parts of the West Bank and Gaza, passed the Knesset on 6 October 1995 only with the support of Arab-Israeli members.

Likud organised anti-Oslo rallies. At one, posters depicted Rabin in a Nazi uniform in the crosshairs of a gunsight. Netanyahu was also seen marching in front of a mock coffin labelled 'Zionism' and claiming Rabin 'illegally conspired' with the Palestinian Liberation Organization to 'undermine democracy', while the mob responded by shouting 'death to Rabin'. Head of the General Security Service Carmi Gillon asked Netanyahu and the protesters to moderate their language. Gillon had also uncovered a plot to assassinate Rabin; nevertheless Rabin refused to wear a bulletproof vest or use the armoured car that had been offered to him.

Left-wing supporters of the Oslo Accords organised their own rallies. After addressing one of these pro-Oslo gatherings in Tel Aviv on 4 November 1995, Rabin was walking down the steps of the city hall towards his car when a right-wing ultra-Orthodox law student named Yigal Amir fired three shots at him at close range.

Born in 1980 to an Orthodox Yemenite Jewish family, Amir's father was a sofer or religious scribe who taught in the synagogue on the Sabbath and supervised the kosher killing of chickens. Amir declined the exemption from military service then available to most ultra-Orthodox and, after completing high school, did a stint in the Israeli Defence Force in a Hesder unit that combined military service with study of the Torah. Even though he was in a religious platoon, his comrades saw him as a religious fanatic.

While in the army his radicalism acquired a more activist tone. He disdained as too passive the teachings of his strict Haredi upbringing which said that God alone determines the fate of the Jews. Instead he thought that Jews needed to take the initiative in figuring out God's will and implementing it through their own actions. When he saw Rabin shake hands with Arafat on television he concluded that Rabin was a traitor. In Amir's eyes, he was handing over land promised by God to the Jews to the Palestinians and concluded that something must be done about it.

At first he tried to recruit a militia from fellow students at Bar-Ilan University. His aim then was to disrupt the nascent peace process through attacks and sabotage in Palestinian areas. He participated in anti-Oslo rallies and led marches in Hebron on the West Bank supporting the Israeli settlers there.

He then began discussing assassinating Rabin with his brother, who suggested killing the prime minister with a homemade bomb. Yigal thought long and hard about a religious justification for killing Rabin. He settled finally on a Talmudic principle called *rodef*, which made it possible for a bystander to kill someone who themselves were intent on killing an innocent victim. According to Amir, this applied to Rabin as he was in effect killing Jewish settlers. He also considered Rabin to be a *moser* – a person who turns Jews over to a hostile authority. For them the penalty was death.

Amir then was inspired by American-born physician and settler Baruch Goldstein who massacred twenty-nine Palestinian worshippers and injured over a hundred more in a suicide attack on a mosque in Hebron in 1994. Within weeks, Israeli public opinion swung against the idea of forcible removal of settlers. Some rabbis pronounced that it was permissible for Israeli soldiers to disobey orders for any such removal, and Rabin had to back down on the eviction of settlers from Hebron.

To Amir, this demonstrated the power of a lone gunman to disrupt the peace process. The rabbi conducting Goldstein's funeral declared him to be a martyr. He also issued a statement confirming that Rabin was a *redof* and a *moser*. Amir later told the commission investigating the assassination: 'If I did not get the backing and I had not been representing many more people, I would not have acted.'

At demonstrations it was common to hear protesters chanting: 'Rabin is a murderer.' Rabin and his administration were compared to the Jewish organisations who co-operated with the Nazis during World War II. These sentiments were even expressed by top echelons of the opposition Likud Party.

Amir spoke openly about killing Rabin with Avishai Raviv who posed as a right-wing radical but was in fact working for the Israeli internal security services. However, he did not report it as he did not think that Amir would follow through.

Meanwhile Amir lost his girlfriend Nava Holtzman, a law student whose Orthodox Ashkenazi family objected to her having a relationship with someone from a Mizrahi background. She then married one of his friends which sent Amir into a deep depression.

A month before the assassination, there was a huge antigovernment demonstration at Zion Square in Jerusalem while the Knesset was considering the Oslo II agreement. Amid the chants of 'death to Rabin' and the burning of pictures of the prime minister, other pictures were distributed through the crowd depicting Rabin's head atop the body of a dog or showing him in a Nazi uniform.

While Netanyahu looked on, demonstrators marched on the Knesset and, when the prime minister's driver attempted to bring his limousine to the Knesset, the crowd attacked the car.

Even so, security at the pro-Oslo rally in Tel Aviv on 4 November was surprisingly lax. Amir was waiting by Rabin's official car. He shot Rabin twice, puncturing his lung. A third shot injured Yoram Rubin, a security guard. Amir was seized by Rabin's bodyguards with the gun in his hand. Rabin was rushed to nearby Ichilov Hospital at the Tel Aviv Sourasky Medical Center, where he died on the operating table forty minutes later. When Amir was told of Rabin's death he said he was satisfied that the work of God had been done.

At his trial he expressed no regret. Amir was sentenced to life imprisonment for murder, plus a further six years for injuring the security guard. He was later sentenced to another eight years for conspiring in the assassination with his brother Hagai Amir and Dror Adani, a friend.

Netanyahu was among those who said that Yigal Amir must never be released from prison. Nevertheless Amir had succeeded in bringing the peace process to a halt. It has never recovered and the conflict between Israel and Palestine has continued ever since.

9

JUVÉNAL HABYARIMANA 1994

The twentieth century was particularly rich in atrocities. In the last decade of the century alone, revolt in Chechnya, revolution in the Congo, civil war in Sierra Leone and 'ethnic cleansing' in the Balkans all yielded rich pickings. But there is one name that chills the blood like no other. It conjures images of bodies, fly-blown, bloated, uncountable. That name is Rwanda.

Rwanda is a small country in central Africa, not much bigger than Wales. But while the Land of My Fathers has a population of three million, in 1990 there were nearly eight million souls crammed into Rwanda, making it the most densely populated country in Africa. The conflict in Rwanda was between the Tutsi, who make up 14 per cent of the population, and the Hutu, who make up 85 per cent. The other 1 per cent are Twa hunter-gatherers who, in less politically correct times, were known as pygmies.

In fact, the Tutsis and Hutus are not distinct races. They do not have separate languages or cultures. However, the Tutsis were cattlemen while the Hutu were agrarian farmers, so their rivalry was akin to the range wars that broke out in America's Old West in the late nineteenth century where ranchers fought the encroaching homesteaders.

However, as cattle were a form of convertible currency in central Africa, the Tutsis became the wealthy elite and the division between Tutsis and Hutus became institutionalised in the caste system – rather like the division between Norman and Saxon in post-conquest England. But in Rwanda there was no Robin Hood.

Then along came the Germans. In 1890, Rwanda was colonised as part of German East Africa. They naturally co-opted the Tutsi whose well-established administrative system would run the country for the colonial power. Race theory was all the rage in Europe at the time. The Tutsis were tall and slim, with straight noses and long fingers – more European-looking than the Hutu, who were shorter and had broad noses and stubby fingers. The Germans also seized on folklore that the Tutsis had originally come from Ethiopia and had taken over the country from the Hutus – in other words, they were colonisers themselves. This is almost certainly not true. No one knows who got there first – though it is known that the Twa were there before either the Tutsi or Hutu.

If the Tutsis had once been Ethiopian, they had once been Christians. Or so the Catholic Church reasoned. So the first duty of the missionaries they sent was to re-Christianise the Tutsi. Saving the souls of the Hutu came later. Church schools also dedicated themselves to educating Tutsi children as they would become the administrators. The poorer Protestant churches mopped up the Hutu. This further entrenched the Tutsi–Hutu divide.

In 1916, the Belgians took over all these easy assumptions – and the country. The Hutu were then press-ganged into forced labour in a system of slavery only abolished in 1927. In the late 1950s, the wind of change started through Africa. In Rwanda, the call for independence came from the Hutu. Seeing which way the wind was blowing, the Belgians quickly dropped the Tutsis. The Tutsi king was assassinated while visiting Burundi. An uprising in the north left fifteen thousand Tutsis dead. Thousands more fled to neighbouring Uganda, Zaire, Tanzania and Burundi.

A Hutu named Grégoire Kayibanda became the first president of an independent Rwanda in 1962. His aim was to overturn the feudal system that favoured the Tutsis. Rather than abandon the old racial theories, he used them for his own ends. The identity cards introduced by the Belgians in the 1930s were retained. These specified whether the holder was a Tutsi, Hutu or Twa. Your ethnic designation could only be changed if you paid a huge bribe.

Tutsis were dubbed *inyenzis* or cockroaches and removed from all positions of authority, except in the Catholic Church. They looked to the exiled Tutsis for their salvation. However, Kayibanda was maintained in power by Belgian paratroopers. In 1963, Hutu peasants turned on the Tutsis, massacring twenty thousand and sending another hundred thousand fleeing into Burundi.

Fresh attacks on the Tutsis destabilised the government and, in 1973, Major General Juvénal Habyarimana seized power on the promise of ending ethnic strife. He did. In a way. He declared that not only Tutsis would be excluded from power, but also any Hutus who had been 'infected' by Tutsis – in other words, anyone Habyarimana did not like. He and his chums ruled the country with an iron hand – and with an army which he increased from five thousand to thirty-five thousand men.

But under the surface, the conflict was simmering. Rwandan women have one of the highest fertility rates in the world and, despite the massacres and exile of hundreds of thousands of Tutsis, the population swelled from 2.8 million in 1962 to over 7.5 million in 1990. There was an acute shortage of land. Hutus, who had occupied the land of exiled Tutsis, feared the return of the *inyenzi*. And Habyarimana argued that the Tutsi refugees in neighbouring countries would have to stay there because Rwanda was, in effect, full up.

However, the exiled Tutsis had not been sitting on their hands. In Uganda, they had joined the National Resistance Army, which overthrew the regime of Tito Okello who, in turn, had ousted Milton Obote, the leader who had brought independence. They were battle hardened and had seen how a well-organised army could seize political power. In 1986, Tutsi ex-NRA officers formed the Rwandan Patriotic Front. And in 1990, the fifteen-hundred-strong RPF invaded.

Habyarimana's army clearly outnumbered them by over twenty to one, but his forces were inexperienced and poorly motivated. It was only the intervention of Zaire and then France that kept Habyarimana from being routed. A ceasefire was called and the two sides sat down to peace talks which dragged on for three years.

Meanwhile, other Rwandans, alienated by the corruption of the Habyarimana regime, seized the opportunity to form new political parties. Finding himself outmanoeuvred politically, Habyarimana began organising his own fiercely loyal militia. It was called the *interahamwe* – which means 'those who stand together'. Its men were well equipped, well trained and well paid.

Although Habyarimana distanced himself from the *interahamwe*, it could essentially do what it liked. And what it liked was bumping off Habyarimana's political opponents. Over two thousand dissidents were killed at his behest. When killers were caught, they were pardoned. This meant that Habyarimana could maintain the appearance of democratic government by allowing other parties into the government with no danger of losing power. He even promised a multi-party election, which he did not deliver. In the meantime, he could fire opposition politicians from his administration at will. By this time Habyarimana's cronies – known as the *Azaku* – ran everything in the country, including drugs, prostitution and protection rackets, not things they were likely to give up without a fight.

The RPF began to see that the peace talks were getting them nowhere. They attacked the Rwandan capital Kigali. While Habyarimana was maintained in power by French troops, neighbouring countries were growing worried that the conflict in Rwanda might destabilise the whole region. They forced Habyarimana and the RPF back to the negotiating table. A power-sharing deal was hammered out. A six-hundred-man RPF battalion was to be stationed in Kigali to protect Tutsi politicians and the French-trained Presidential Guard – which was essentially Habyarimana's hit squad – was to be disbanded.

However, during the handover the World Bank blocked all funds. Bankrupt, the country was on the brink of anarchy. The *interahamwe* ruled the streets, setting up its own roadblocks in downtown Kigali to harass and rob Tutsis. The *Azaku* were desperate to hold on to their ill-gotten gains. Habyarimana's in-laws, who had grown wealthy under his rule, owned a radio station which began pumping out anti-Tutsi propaganda. Meanwhile Habyarimana stalled on implementing the power-sharing deal.

The secretary general of the Organization of African Unity, along with the heads of states of Tanzania, Uganda, Kenya and Burundi, summoned Habyarimana to a meeting at the Hotel Kilimanjaro in Tanzania. They insisted that he implement the power-sharing deal. Under immense pressure he gave in.

Habyarimana had flown to the Hotel Kilimanjaro meeting in a French Mystère Falcon given to him by President Mitterrand. On 6 April 1994 he was giving the president of Burundi a lift home when his sleek jet was blasted out of the sky by three hand-launched heat-seeking missiles. Habyarimana did not get home in one piece but get home he did. His plane was just passing over the outskirts of Kigali when it was hit and Habyarimana's charred remains landed in the gardens of his splendid new presidential palace. This sparked the all-out genocide. Within a hundred days, a million Rwandans would be dead and half the country's population displaced.

The world stood by shocked as no one, not even the UN, stepped in to stop the massacre. When Tony Blair became Britain's prime minister in 1997, he led a call for intervention in countries where governments were killing their own people. This led to NATO taking action in the former Yugoslavia, British intervention in the civil war in Sierra Leone and the invasion of Iraq.

10

GIOVANNI FALCONE 1992

On 3 September 1982, tough anti-Mafia laws were passed in Italy. These gave two investigating magistrates named Giovanni Falcone and Paolo Borsellino cause for optimism. Both had been born in Palermo. They had worked in the Mafia strongholds of Monreale, Agrigento and Trapani before being transferred back to Palermo. There Falcone worked in the bankruptcy section of the prosecutor's office and became an expert in forensic accounting.

Borsellino concentrated on prosecuting the killers of Emanuele Basile, a captain in the carabinieri who had been gunned down after issuing fifty-five warrants for drug charges to members of the Bontade and Inzerillo families, though the suspects had walked free after the judge declared a mistrial. Borsellino's boss, Rocco Chinnici, was so frightened for his safety that he took Borsellino off Mafia investigations. But it was Chinnici himself who was killed, along with his two bodyguards and the concierge of his block when a car bomb blew up outside. His replacement, Antonino Caponnetto, let Falcone and Borsellino work together and share information with other investigating magistrates. Then, in 1984, Bettino Craxi came to power in Rome and the new minister of justice allowed them to buy computers to deal with the huge amounts of financial data they had to handle.

Falcone was moved into the investigation office, where he began investigating Rosario Spatola, who was a cousin of both Salvatore Inzerillo and New York Mafia boss John Gotti, who was about to take over the Gambino family. He was able to prove that the Spatola Construction Company was a front for drug smuggling. Going through five years of bank records by hand, he managed to jail the rest of the Spatola family, obtaining seventy-four convictions in all. His cases depended only on financial records, so there were no witnesses who could be intimidated, and he only prosecuted cases that could be heard before a tribunal of three judges, so there were no jurors who could be bought.

With additional evidence from informers, 475 defendants were then to face justice in the so-called Maxi Trial. It was to take place in a special courtroom bunker the size of a small sports stadium built near Ucciardone prison in Palermo. Built in reinforced concrete, it was surrounded by barbed wire and guarded by three thousand troops, plus a tank. Inside there were thirty cages, each big enough to house twenty defendants. In the well of the court were a dozen tables for the lawyers and witnesses. And overlooking the whole thing, behind bulletproof glass, was a public gallery with room for a thousand spectators.

The trial went on for twenty-two months. In all, 344 of the defendants were found guilty and sentenced to a total of 2,665 years in jail, not counting the nineteen life sentences that had been handed down to the most important bosses in Sicily, including Michele Greco and – *in absentia* – Totò Riina and Bernardo Provenzano.

Riina was keen to take his revenge. Giovanni Falcone had been transferred to Rome. On 23 May 1992, he and his wife were paying a visit to their holiday home in Palermo. They travelled in secret on a government plane and were met at the airport by a police escort. But as the convoy headed down the autostrada towards the town of Capaci, a bomb in a culvert under the motorway exploded, killing the policemen in the lead car and Falcone and his wife in the car following. It was detonated by Giovanni Brusca – who was then given the nickname *Lo Scannacristiani*, 'the man who kills Christians'.

Brusca had experimented repeatedly with explosives and detonating devices. Trees had been pruned to give a clear view of the highway. On the evening of 8 May, Brusca and others arranged thirteen barrels loaded with about four hundred kilograms of explosives onto a skateboard placed in a drainage tunnel under the road. This was in place when, on 23 May, a lookout at the airport saw Falcone arrive, then followed his car, staying in touch with Brusca by mobile phone.

At the sight of Falcone's car, Brusca activated the remote control that caused the explosion. The first car was hit by the full force of the explosion and thrown from the road surface into a garden of olive trees a few metres away, instantly killing agents Antonio Montinaro, Vito Schifani and Rocco Dicillo. The second car, carrying Falcone and his wife, crashed into the concrete wall, throwing Falcone and his wife, who were not wearing seat belts, through the windscreen.

At the news, there were cheers among the inmates of Ucciardone prison and someone phoned the Palermo newspaper *Giornale di Sicilia* saying the bombing was a 'wedding present for Nino Madonia' – he was the eldest son of the Madonia family who had been married in the chapel at Ucciardone earlier that day.

For the public though, it was a killing too many. As pictures of the bomb site made the front pages of newspapers around the world, the Italian parliament called for a day of mourning and suspended their session until after the funeral. Forty thousand people turned out in Palermo for the service. A general strike was called, closing all stores and businesses. People hung sheets out of their windows bearing anti-Mafia slogans and the politicians who turned up were berated as 'murderers' and 'accomplices'.

Borsellino had been moved to Marsala in the west of Sicily. Nearly two months after the death of Falcone, on 19 July, he was going to visit his mother in Palermo. A car bomb had been placed outside her home. It exploded killing Borsellino and his six bodyguards.

Seven thousand troops had to be sent to Sicily to keep order. The following January, the carabinieri arrested Totò Riina as he was being driven, unarmed, through Palermo, where he had been living for the previous twenty-three years as a fugitive.

Stories vary about his capture. Baldassare Di Maggio had been acting head of the San Giuseppe Jato clan while Riina's hitman Giovanni Brusca and Riina's father Bernardo were in jail. When Brusca was released, Di Maggio feared that he was going to be eliminated, even though he had committed numerous murders for Riina. Riina tried to reassure him that he was not going to be thrown away like 'a used orange'. But Di Maggio knew that Riina was at his most dangerous when he was being charming and fled. He was picked up on minor charges in the northern Italian city of Novara. Still convinced Riina was going to kill him, he turned *pentito*.

The alternative is that Riina was shopped by Bernardo 'The Tractor' Provenzano so that he could seize compromising material held in Riina's apartment.

Riina had already been given two life sentences. He was tried and convicted of ordering many murders including those of Falcone and Borsellino, along with Provenzano who was tried *in absentia*. Still at large, Provenzano became Sicily's boss of bosses. He sought to eliminate Giovanni Brusca by killing or co-opting his allies. Then in 1996, Brusca was arrested. He had also been sentenced to life *in absentia* for the murder of Falcone and Borsellino. In court, he admitted to planting the bomb under the motorway from the airport and detonating it by remote control.

Nino Gioè, who was with Giovanni Brusca when he killed Giovanni Falcone, showed a genuine change of heart in prison. This may have been because some of his conversations had been bugged by the police, so he had inadvertently broken the *omertà*. He stopped shaving and cleaning his clothes. Those around him feared he was about to break. On 23 July 1993, he hanged himself in his cell. In his suicide note, he wrote: 'This evening I will find the peace and serenity that I lost some seventeen years ago [when he was 'made']. When I lost them, I became a monster. I was a monster until I took pen in hand to write these lines... Before I go, I ask for forgiveness from my mother and from God, because their love has no limits. The whole of the rest of the world will never be able to forgive me.'

Riina was unrepentant and died in jail in 2017. After forty-three years living as a fugitive, Provenzano was captured in 2006. He died in jail in 2016. In May 2019 it was revealed that John Gotti, then head of the Gambino crime family in New York, had sent one of their explosives experts to

Sicily to help. In 1992, Gotti was convicted of five murders, conspiracy to commit murder, racketeering, obstruction of justice, tax evasion, illegal gambling, extortion, and loan sharking. He was sentenced to life in prison without parole. He died in jail in 2002.

In Italy, the Maxi Trials had significantly dented the power of the Mafia. Both Falcone and Borsellino were awarded the Italian '*Medaglia d'oro al valore civile*' (Gold medal for civil valour). Palermo International Airport has been named Falcone–Borsellino Airport in honour of the two judges and hosts a memorial of the pair by the local sculptor Tommaso Geraci. There are other monuments commemorating Falcone around Italy, as well as one at the FBI's National Academy in Virginia to honour his contribution to the 'Pizza Connection' case where independently owned pizza parlours were used as fronts for narcotics sales distributing $1.65 billion of heroin imported from south-west Asia, via Sicily, to the US between 1975 and 1984. Seventeen racketeers were jailed, significantly damaging the strength of the Mafia in the US too.

11

OLOF PALME 1986

Sweden was traditionally seen as a peaceful and law-abiding country where politicians and celebrities could walk the streets unmolested. But this came to an end on 28 February 1986, when prime minister Olof Palme was shot dead on the streets of Stockholm on his way back from the cinema with his wife. The assassin has not been found. Palme was prominent in international politics and a number of conspiracy theories have grown up around his death.

Born in the Östermalm district of Stockholm on 30 January 1927, Olof Palme was the son of a politically conservative, Lutheran family. But after compulsory military service he enrolled at the University of Stockholm where he joined the Social Democratic Party (SAP). He also studied at Kenyon College in Ohio where he wrote his senior honour thesis on the United Auto Workers union. Palme said his time in America opened his eyes to racism.

Back in Sweden, he came to prominence as president of the Swedish National Union of Students. In that capacity, he travelled around Europe and the Third World, witnessing extreme poverty at first hand. This, he said, made him aware of the consequences of colonialism and imperialism.

After university Palme was recruited by Tage Erlander, the social democrat prime minister of Sweden. In 1955, Palme had become leader of the Swedish Social Democratic Youth League, the youth section of the Social Democratic Labour Party.

Two years later, at the age of thirty, he was elected to parliament. As a member of the Agency for International Assistance (NIB), he sought to provide educational aid to Third World countries. In 1963, he became a member of the cabinet and held a number of influential government posts, including minister for transport communications and minister of education, which brought him into conflict with students over university reform.

In 1969, he was elected as leader of the Social Democratic Party and succeeded Tage Erlander as prime minister. In that role, he made a number of constitutional changes reining in the power of the monarchy. With close ties to the labour movement, he became unpopular with the business community and by expanding social welfare he gave Sweden the highest tax rates in the Western world. Internationally he was a leader in the non-aligned movement. Championing revolutionaries in the Third World, he was the first Western leader to visit Cuba after Fidel Castro took over.

Losing office in 1976, he went to work for the United Nations, trying to broker a peace agreement to end the Iran–Iraq War. This proved impossible. Nevertheless he earned a reputation as an internationally respected statesman. In 1982 he became prime minister of Sweden again and continued his programme of social democratic reforms. Abroad, he was critical of apartheid and of the dictators Francisco Franco of Spain and António de Oliveira Salazar of Portugal, as well as Leonid Brezhnev in the Soviet Union and Gustáv

Husák in Czechoslovakia. He made more enemies with his condemnation of America's bombing of Hanoi during the Vietnam War. This led to a freezing of relations with the US.

On 28 February 1986, he and his wife made an impromptu visit to the cinema without a bodyguard. This was not unusual. He made a point of living as much as possible like an ordinary person; he did not want the fact that he was running the country to come between him and his countrymen. His was a familiar face on the streets in central Stockholm.

At 11.21pm, Olof and Lisbet Palme were walking down Sveavägen, one of Stockholm's busiest streets, when a tall man in a dark coat walked up behind them. The man put one hand on Palme's shoulder, and with his other hand he shot Palme twice in the stomach. Another round grazed Lisbet before the gunman fled up a flight of eighty-nine steps that links the main street with a road above.

A passing taxi driver stopped to help, calling the emergency services on his cab radio. Two young girls who were sitting in a car nearby ran over to help the injured couple while waiting for an ambulance to arrive. Six minutes later it was speeding the victims to the nearest hospital, but it was too late to save the fifty-nine-year-old Palme. He was pronounced dead on arrival. It was later determined that a bullet had severed his spinal cord and that he had died before hitting the ground. Lisbet was treated for her injury and survived.

Sweden was traumatised by the news of his assassination. This was the first killing of its kind in modern times and the country prided itself on its peaceful way of life. Palme was loved by many. His predecessor Tage Erlander called him 'the greatest political talent Sweden has seen this century'. Others despised him. Some on the left distrusted him for being from aristocratic stock, while aristocrats considered him a class traitor. Paranoid extremists on the Swedish right claimed he was a Soviet spy. *Contra*, a popular conservative magazine, sold dartboards featuring a caricature of his face.

On the night of the killing, when word of Palme's death reached Claes Löfgren, a journalist for the Swedish national broadcaster SVT, he was in a restaurant. When the diners heard the news, Löfgren said some people in the restaurant cheered and toasted.

Internationally, Palme was remembered as a great statesman who had campaigned tirelessly on behalf of the poor, both in Europe and in the Third World. During the Vietnam War, he had been a leading spokesman for peace. During the 1980s, when the right-wing governments of Ronald Reagan in America and Margaret Thatcher in Britain were in the ascendancy, he had remained a staunch advocate of social democracy. His radical policies had made him many enemies, both abroad and at home. He was accused of being in league with the Soviet Union when he was seen not to protest strongly enough when Soviet submarines ventured into Swedish waters. In fact, before he met his death, he had made arrangements to visit Moscow to address this issue.

The first man to be arrested for Palme's assassination was right-wing extremist Victor Gunnarsson. However, there was little evidence to show that he had anything to do with the murder and he was released. The next suspect was John Stannerman, a right-wing agitator who was later convicted of a racist murder. However, Stannerman – later known as John Ausonius, or 'The Laser Man' because of the laser gun that he used – had a cast-iron alibi as he had spent the night of the murder in a prison cell.

The police then followed up a lead given to them by the security services that linked the assassination to a group of

Kurdish activists living in Sweden. The investigation was led by Hans Holmér, the head of the Stockholm police force, but it proved another dead end. Meanwhile, the police and security forces were coming under intense criticism for prolonging the investigation and getting nowhere. Holmér was later dismissed as a result.

It was eighteen months before the police came up with a plausible suspect. Christer Pettersson, a petty criminal, alcoholic and drug addict, was picked up in December 1988. Aged forty-two, he was a drifter with a history of mental illness and violent crime. In 1970, he had killed a youth with a bayonet and had served time. When he was arrested, Palme's wife, Lisbet, identified him as the killer of her husband, but she admitted she had not seen him fire or hold a gun. Nor was it clear why Pettersson had attacked the prime minister. He appeared to have no political or other motive for the assassination, and his actions did not seem to have been pre-meditated.

In July 1989, Pettersson was convicted of murder and sentenced to life imprisonment. However, the verdict began to be questioned when it emerged that the two judges in the case had recommended that he should be acquitted, while six lay assessors had voted for him to be convicted. Only three months after the trial, the Court of Appeal overturned Pettersson's conviction and he was freed. To this day, it remains unclear whether Pettersson was involved in the assassination. Before he died in September 2004, he was reported to have confessed to the murder, but still did not explain why he had done it.

The assassination of Olof Palme remains officially unsolved. As a result it has continued to generate many conspiracy theories. Pettersson's reported confession has prompted calls for the case to be reopened, but the Swedish state prosecutor has ruled that, unless there is fresh forensic evidence about the gun, the case cannot be brought to court again. Meanwhile, the assassination has been variously blamed on supporters of the apartheid regime in South Africa, arms traders and freemasons, all of whom – according to the conspiracy theorists at least – had reasons to want Palme out of the way.

A week before his murder, Palme had made an important speech to the Swedish People's Parliament on the evils of apartheid. The address had been attended by several leading figures of the anti-apartheid movement, including Oliver Tambo, president of the African National Congress. In it, Palme announced: 'Apartheid cannot be reformed, it has to be eliminated.'

A decade later, in 1996, a former South African policeman named Eugene de Kock alleged that Palme's assassin was a man named Craig Williamson, a former colleague of his in the South African police force. According to de Kock, Williamson was also a spy. Williamson's boss, Johannes Coetzee, then announced that the actual murderer was Anthony White, a former Selous Scout from Zimbabwe, formerly Rhodesia. Next, a colleague of White's, Peter Caselton, identified Swedish mercenary soldier Bertil Wedin as the real assassin. Swedish police travelled to South Africa but could not come up with any evidence to sustain these allegations.

The claims that Palme had been murdered by a secretive group of arms dealers, businessmen and freemasons because of his well-known opposition to the arms trade proved equally difficult to substantiate. The real reason for the assassination of Olof Palme, one of the most distinguished yet controversial politicians in Swedish history, remains a mystery. However, his death removed a powerful presence from the international stage.

12

INDIRA GANDHI 1984

In June 1984, the Indian Army had been sent into the Punjab to remove militant Sikh Jarnail Singh Bhindranwale and his armed followers from the Gold Temple in Amritsar, one of the most important pilgrimage sites of Sikhism. Over five hundred were killed in the operation which proved divisive. Afterwards, Indira Gandhi, who had then been prime minister of India for four years, discussed the possibility of her assassination with her son Rajiv and his wife Sonia, and wrote out instructions for her funeral. She also talked about the risk to her life with her fourteen-year-old grandson, Rahul. Rahul and his sister Priyanka had been sent to boarding school in 1982, but they were then brought home and enrolled in day schools in Delhi as Indira was worried about their safety. She told them not to play beyond the garden gate which led to the path connecting her house at 1 Safdarjung Road to her Akbar Road office next door. The compound was now a prison for all its inhabitants.

On 11 October, Indira's sense of foreboding heightened when she heard that Margaret Thatcher had narrowly escaped being blown up in an IRA bomb attack during the Conservative Party conference in Brighton. Unlike Mrs

Thatcher, Indira was no stranger to assassination and violent death. She phoned Mrs Thatcher to console the British leader.

The daughter of India's first prime minister Jawaharlal Nehru, Indira had taken the Gandhi name from her husband, Indian freedom fighter, politician and journalist Feroze Gandhi who died in 1960. Running for re-election in 1984, she made a campaign speech in Bhubaneshwar on the night of 30 October. In it she said: 'I am here today, I may not be here tomorrow... Nobody knows how many attempts have been made to shoot me... I do not care whether I live or die. I have lived a long life and I am proud that I spent the whole of my life in the service of my people. I am only proud of this and of nothing else. I shall continue to serve until my last breath and when I die, I can say, that every drop of my blood will invigorate India and strengthen it.'

The following day, back in New Delhi, she was up and dressed at 6am. She had donned a vibrant saffron-coloured sari with a hand-woven black border. Her first appointment was a television interview with actor Peter Ustinov who was making a documentary about Indira for the BBC. In the afternoon, she was to meet the former British prime minister James Callaghan and, in the evening, she would host a formal dinner for Princess Anne.

After breakfast, two make-up artists set to work preparing her for the Ustinov television interview, which would be filmed at her Akbar Road office. Originally it was scheduled for 8.30, but there had been some trouble with the equipment and the interview had been put back to 9.20. While the cosmeticians applied powder and blusher, Indira chatted with her personal physician, Dr K. P. Mathur, who looked in on her most mornings. Among other things, Indira joked about

Ronald Reagan's heavily made-up face when he appeared on television and they speculated about the seventy-three-year-old Reagan's lack of grey hair.

It was a crisp, sunny day when Indira emerged from her house at 9.10am. The trees and plants in her garden had been washed clean by the summer monsoon and the air was clear. She set off down the garden path that connected her home to her Akbar Road office with Constable Narain Singh beside her, holding a black umbrella to shield her from the sun. Her personal secretary and confidante R. K. Dhawan followed a few steps behind. He was followed by Indira's personal servant, Nathu Ram. Sub-inspector Rameshwar Dayal brought up the rear.

At the far end of the path, Indira saw her bodyguard, Beant Singh, standing at the wicket gate. A great bear of a man, Singh was a Sikh from the Punjab who had been one of Indira's security guards since she had returned to office in 1980. Nearby was a young, new constable named Satwant Singh who had yet to see Indira at close quarters. He was holding a Sten gun.

Indira was talking over her shoulder to Dhawan as she approached the gate, but she broke off to acknowledge her bodyguards with her hands raised and pressed together in the namaste greeting. Instead of returning the gesture, Beant Singh pulled out his revolver and pointed it at Indira. After a second or two of silence, Indira said: 'What are you doing?'

At that moment Beant Singh pulled the trigger. The bullet hit her in the abdomen. She instinctively raised her right hand to protect her face. Beant Singh fired four more shots into her at point-blank range. The bullets entered her armpit, chest and waist. Five feet away stood Satwant Singh, immobilised with fear until Beant Singh shouted at him to shoot. He did as he was ordered and pumped twenty-five bullets into her body.

Indira spun round from the impact before falling in a heap on the path. Only Rameshwar Dayal, in the rear, reacted quickly. While Satwant Singh was still emptying his Sten gun, Dayal rushed forward, but was hit in the thigh and leg. Indira's other companions formed a frozen tableau behind her body. Dhawan, who had narrowly missed the second volley of bullets, stood rooted to the spot. Slowly he came out of his trance, crept forward and crouched over Indira. Another security man named Dinesh Kumar Bhatt came running from the Akbar Road office and Nathu Ram rushed back to Indira's house to get the doctor on duty, Dr R. Opeh.

Both Beant Singh and Satwant Singh dropped their guns. Beant Singh said in Punjabi: 'I have done what I had to do. Now you do what you have to do.'

At this, Constable Narain Singh lunged forward and tackled Beant Singh, bringing him to the ground. Commandos from the Indo-Tibetan Border Police came running from the guardroom nearby and overpowered Satwant Singh.

By this time Dr Opeh had arrived on the scene and was attempting to give Indira mouth-to-mouth resuscitation. Indira's political adviser M. L. Fotedar, who had been in the house, shouted for a car to take Indira to hospital. A white Ambassador was brought round and R. K. Dhawan and Dinesh Bhatt laid Indira's limp body on the back seat. Dhawan and Bhatt then got into the front seat next to the driver. The car was just about to leave when Sonia Gandhi came running down the path in her dressing gown, crying: 'Mummy! Oh my God, Mummy!'

She pulled open the back door and jumped in next to her mother-in-law. The car sped off towards the All India

Institute of Medical Sciences three miles away through heavy traffic. No one spoke, while Sonia Gandhi cradled Indira's head in her lap. Her dressing gown was soon soaked in blood.

They reached the All India Institute of Medical Sciences at 9.32am. The Institute kept a supply of Indira's blood type, O Rh negative, and her medical records. But no one back at 1 Safdarjung Road had thought to telephone ahead to warn the hospital that Indira Gandhi was being brought in, critically wounded. The young house doctors on duty panicked when they recognised her. But one of them had the presence of mind to call the Institute's senior cardiologist and within five minutes a dozen of the hospital's top doctors were working on Indira. An endotracheal tube was pushed down her windpipe to pump oxygen into her lungs, while two intravenous lines were attached to start blood transfusions.

An electrocardiogram showed faint traces of a heartbeat and the medical team tried to massage her heart. But they could find no pulse and Indira's eyes were dilated, indicating she had suffered brain damage. Though it was clear that she was already dead, Indira was moved up to the operating theatre on the eighth floor. During a four-hour operation a team of surgeons tried to pull off a miracle. But the bullets had ruptured Indira's liver, perforated her small and large intestines, penetrated one lung, shattered bones and vertebrae, and severed her spinal cord. Of her internal organs only her heart was left intact. At 2.23 in the afternoon, five hours after being gunned down by men employed to protect her, Indira Gandhi was pronounced dead.

Back at the house, Beant Singh and Satwant Singh had been taken away by guards and behind closed doors Beant Singh was shot dead. Another man, Kehar Singh, was later arrested for conspiracy in the attack. Both Satwant and Kehar were sentenced to death and hanged in Delhi's Tihar Jail.

Indira Gandhi was cremated on 3 November at what became the Indira Gandhi Park near Raj Ghat, which was inaugurated by her son Rajiv Gandhi. Following her cremation, millions of Sikhs were displaced and nearly three thousand were killed in anti-Sikh riots. Rajiv Gandhi said of the carnage: 'When a big tree falls, the earth shakes.'

Indira Gandhi was succeeded in office by her son Rajiv. He too was assassinated by seventeen-year-old suicide bomber Thenmozhi Rajaratnam, a member of Sri Lanka's Tamil Tigers. The deaths of the two Gandhis, mother and son, led to the decline of the Congress Party and the rise of Hindu nationalist parties led by the Bharatiya Janata Party or BJP, whose leader Narendra Modi became prime minister in 2014.

13

BENIGNO AQUINO 1983

Benigno 'Ninoy' Aquino Jr was a Filipino politician who served as a senator from 1967 to 1972 after serving as governor of the province of Tarlac from 1961 to 1967. He led the opposition to Ferdinand Marcos, president from 1965, who ruled as a dictator under martial law from 1972 to 1981. In 1972, Aquino was arrested and jailed for seven years. Following a heart attack in 1980, he was allowed to travel to have medical treatment in the United States, where he stayed in self-imposed exile, settling in Boston and running a campaign against Marcos and for the return of democracy to the Philippines.

In 1983, the deteriorating political situation in his country and the declining health of President Marcos, who suffered from lupus, led Aquino to decide to return to the Philippines.

The Head of the Philippines Liberal Party said: 'Ninoy was getting impatient in Boston, he felt isolated by the flow of events in the Philippines. In early 1983, Marcos was seriously ailing, the Philippine economy was just as rapidly declining, and insurgency was becoming a serious problem. Ninoy thought that by coming home he might be able to persuade Marcos to restore democracy and somehow revitalize the Liberal Party.'

However, Aquino's passport had expired and the Ministry of Foreign Affairs had issued orders that it was not to be renewed. Despite the government's ban on issuing him a passport, Aquino acquired one with the help of Rashid Lucman, a former Mindanao legislator and founder of the Bangsamoro Liberation Front, a Moro separatist group against Marcos. It carried the alias Marcial Bonifacio – Marcial for martial law and Bonifacio after Fort Bonifacio where Aquino had been imprisoned. He eventually obtained a legitimate passport from a sympathiser working in a Philippine consulate through the help of Roque R. Ablan Jr, who was then a Congressman.

The Marcos government warned all international airlines that they would be denied landing rights if they tried to fly Aquino back to the Philippines. So Aquino took a circuitous route. He flew from Boston to Los Angeles, then on to Singapore where he met up with Muslim supporters. He then flew to Hong Kong, then on to Taipei. This was his final stopover as Taiwan – that is, the Republic of China – had broken off diplomatic relations with the Philippines so the government there was unlikely to inform Marcos of Aquino's movements.

In an interview at the Taipei Grand Hotel prior to departure, Aquino said he would be wearing a bulletproof vest when he landed in the Philippines, adding: 'It's only good for the body, but in the head there's nothing else we can do.'

On 21 August 1983, he took Taiwan's flag carrier China Airlines Flight 811 to Manila. Speaking aboard the plane, Aquino told reporters he was well aware of the risk he was taking.

'I suppose there's a physical danger because you know assassination's part of public service,' he said. 'My feeling is we all have to die sometime and if it's my fate to die by an assassin's bullet, so be it.'

As they approached Manila International Airport, he told journalists: 'You have to be very ready with your hand camera because this action can become very fast. In a matter of a three or four minutes it could be all over, you know, and I may not be able to talk to you again after this.'

Over a thousand armed soldiers and police had been sent to the airport ostensibly to provide security for his return. When his plane arrived at gate eight at 1.04pm, soldiers boarded the plane to arrest him. Instead of taking him down the jet-way into the airport building, he was taken down a service staircase and out onto the apron where a military vehicle was waiting to take him to prison.

A news camera filming the event recorded the words: '*Pusila! Pusila! Op! Pusila! Pusila! Pusila!*' – '*Pusila*' means 'shoot'. However, bright sunshine prevented the camera filming what happened next. There was a fusillade of shots. When the firing stopped, Aquino and a man later identified as Rolando Galman lay dead.

Two soldiers from the Aviation Security Command carried Aquino's body to a van, while another soldier continued shooting at Galman. It was officially recorded that Aquino had died before he reached Fort Bonifacio General Hospital. Aquino had on him his last formal statement that he was not able to deliver. It said: 'I have returned on my free will to join the ranks of those struggling to restore our rights and freedoms through non-violence. I seek no confrontation.'

Pablo Martinez, one of the convicted conspirators in the assassination, said that it was Galman who had shot Aquino, but that was not supported by other evidence in the case. He also said that Eduardo 'Danding' Cojuangco, a close adviser and personal friend to President Marcos, had ordered the assassination. The murder weapon, a Smith & Wesson .357 Magnum revolver, had been traced by Interpol back to a gun store in Bangkok.

Aquino lay in state for nine days with the bullet wounds that disfigured his face clearly on display. His mother said that she wanted the public to see 'what they did to my son'. His family returned from Boston the day after the assassination and thousands of supporters turned out for the funeral.

A mass was said by the Cardinal Jaime Sin, Archbishop of Manila, and the body was carried on a flatbed truck which wound through the streets of metropolitan Manila for twelve hours. More than two million people lined the streets for the procession and flags flew at half-mast.

Marcos set up a commission under former Court of Appeals Justice Corazon J. Agrava to investigate Aquino's assassination. A passenger named Rebecca Quijano testified that she saw a man running from the stairs towards Aquino and his escorts, pointing a gun at the back of his head. The post-mortem confirmed that he had been shot through the back of the head. She also said that the gunman had been wearing a military uniform.

The Agrava commission submitted two reports to Ferdinand Marcos. The majority report indicted several members of the Armed Forces including General Fabian Ver, Marcos's cousin and his most trusted general. The minority report, submitted by Agrava alone, cleared General Ver. It was thought that she had been intimidated by Marcos.

Twenty-five members of the military, including General Ver, were tried by a special court which acquitted all of them. Immediately after the decision, Marcos re-instated Ver. This was another nail in Marcos's coffin.

The assassination of Benigno Aquino unified the opposition to Ferdinand Marcos. It also brought the world's attention to his excesses, symbolised by his wife, former beauty queen Imelda's collection of over a thousand pairs of shoes. The Reagan administration kept its distance. The death of her husband thrust his widow, Corazon Aquino, into the spotlight. She became the figurehead of the anti-Marcos opposition. In February 1986, Marcos called a snap election which was marred by massive electoral fraud, violence, intimidation, coercion and disenfranchisement of voters. Corazon Aquino was the presidential candidate of the UNIDO opposition party. The official results maintained that Marcos had won the election, but the result was universally dismissed as fraudulent. Even the US Senate condemned the election.

Corazon called a People's Victory Rally, where she claimed that she was the real winner according to the election watchdog, the National Citizens' Movement for Free Elections. President Reagan sent American diplomat Philip Habib to defuse the situation, but Aquino refused his help.

Mass demonstrations followed with protesters offering civil resistance to the regime's violence. This became known as the People Power Revolution, or the Yellow Revolution after the Tony Orlando song 'Tie A Yellow Ribbon', which was about the return of an involuntary exile. There was an attempted military coup which Marcos thwarted, arresting its leaders. But there was little he could do about the demonstrations that involved over two million Filipino civilians, as well as several political, military and religious groups led by the Archbishop of Manila.

General Ver urged Marcos to allow him to fire on the demonstrators, but Marcos refused. On 25 February, Corazon

Aquino was inaugurated as president of the Philippines at Club Filipino. An hour later, Marcos held his inauguration at Malacañang Palace, the presidential residence. While troops held back protesters, Marcos called the White House, asking for advice. A USAF helicopter was sent to transport Marcos to Clark Air Base, the US stronghold north of Manila. From there he was flown to the US territory of Guam and went into exile in Hawaii where he died in 1989.

Once in office, Corazon Aquino ordered a new investigation into her husband's death. Sixteen defendants were found guilty and sentenced to life imprisonment. Some were pardoned, some had their sentences commuted and some died in jail. The alleged gunman Pablo Martinez was released in 2007 on humanitarian grounds, while the last of the convicts was released in 2009.

In 1987, Manila International Airport was renamed Ninoy Aquino International Airport in his honour. The spot where he was killed is marked by a brass plaque and 21 August is commemorated as Ninoy Aquino Day.

The Philippines has remained a democracy since and Benigno Aquino's son Benigno Aquino III became president in 2010.

14

ANWAR SADAT 1981

Anwar Sadat was the president of Egypt who was awarded the Nobel Peace Prize, along with Israeli prime minister Menachem Begin, in 1978 for brokering peace between the two nations, recognising the legitimate rights of the Palestinian people and establishing an autonomous self-governing authority on the West Bank and in the Gaza Strip. With the Egypt–Israeli Peace Treaty the following year, Egypt became the first Arab state to recognise Israel's right to exist.

PLO Leader Yasser Arafat said: 'Let them sign what they like. False peace will not last.' Egypt was suspended from the Arab League and various jihadist groups, such as Egyptian Islamic Jihad and al-Jama'a al-Islamiyya were outraged at what they saw as caving into Israel. They plotted Sadat's assassination in 1981.

Sadat was born to a poor family in Mit Abu Al-Kum, Al-Minufiyah, forty miles north of Cairo, in 1918. He had twelve sisters and brothers, one of whom was a pilot killed in the Yom Kippur War in 1973. Sadat grew up at a time when Egypt was effectively a British colony. The British and French controlled the Suez Canal, so Egypt earned no money from its greatest asset. This caused great resentment.

Incidents in his youth convinced Sadat that the British control of Egypt must be brought to an end. In one, a man named Zahran, who came from a small village like Sadat's own, was hanged for taking part in a protest where a British officer had been killed. Interested in politics, Sadat studied the lives of great statesmen, particularly Kemal Atatürk, who had brought down the Ottoman Empire and liberated the Turkish people and went on to make reforms and modernise the country. Sadat also admired Mahatma Gandhi, who had toured Egypt in 1932, giving speeches about the use of non-violent action and civil disobedience to throw off the British. But Sadat went on to admire Adolf Hitler on the principle: my enemy's enemy is my friend.

A bright student, Sadat enrolled in the British-run Royal Military Academy in Cairo, where he studied military tactics. He graduated as a signals officer in 1938, and was posted to the Sudan, where he met Colonel Gamal Abdel Nasser, the future president of Egypt. Sadat and other young officers formed the Free Officers Movement whose aim was to overthrow the British puppet King Farouk.

During World War II, Sadat was imprisoned by the British for seeking help from the Nazis. During his time in jail, he taught himself English and French. He went on to join other revolutionary movements, including the Muslim Brotherhood, the fascist Young Egypt and the Iron Guard of Egypt.

In 1952, members of the Free Officers Movement mounted a successful coup, ousting King Farouk and the British colonists. A public relations minister in the Nasser regime, Sadat announced news of the revolution on the radio. The Egyptian revolution inspired other Arab nationalists, particularly those in Libya, Syria and Saudi Arabia.

Four years later, Nasser nationalised the Suez Canal. Along with the newly formed state of Israel, Britain and France declared war on Egypt. However, they were forced to withdraw under pressure from the United States and Egypt retained control of the Suez Canal. Under the leadership of Nasser and his right-hand man Sadat, Egypt established itself as an independent and non-aligned country, though it accepted aid from the Soviet Union.

Sadat became a minister of state, president of the National Assembly and vice president. When Nasser died in 1970, Sadat succeeded him. In 1973, he led Egypt into the Yom Kippur War, known in the Arab world as the October War. During the war the Egyptian Army crossed the Suez Canal and secured part of the Sinai Peninsula that had been in Israeli hands since the Six Day War in 1967. This made him a hero in Egypt and throughout the Arab world.

However, it was clear to Sadat that periodic wars with Israel and the continuing animosity between the two countries seriously damaged the Egyptian economy. He attempted to build a peace settlement with Israel, the first Arab leader to do so. In 1978, he negotiated the Camp David Accords with Israeli prime minister Menachem Begin. The following year, they received the Nobel Peace Prize. However, there were those who felt that he was betraying Egypt's role as independent leader of the Arab peoples and ignoring the interests of the Palestinian people. In the view of many Muslims, Sadat had sold out to the Israelis purely to benefit Egypt, forgetting the plight of other Arabs.

Although making peace with Israel returned the rest of the Sinai to Egyptian control, Sadat became extremely unpopular domestically. He began to suppress dissident voices, imprisoning hundreds of members of Muslim and

Coptic organisations. The leader of al-Jama'a al-Islamiyya, also known as 'The Islamic Group', the imam Omar Abdel-Rahman, aka 'The Blind Sheikh', issued a fatwa against him. Abdel-Rahman was later convicted for his role in the bombing of the World Trade Center in 1993 and is now serving a life sentence in the US.

Sadat's treaty with Israel had led to peace but not prosperity and the president's popularity sank further. To counter his critics, Sadat held a series of referendums on his policies, which he kept winning with more than 99 per cent of the vote. No one was convinced by the results. Egyptian Islamic Jihad began collecting weapons and recruiting army officers with the aim of fomenting a revolution. When this was discovered, there were further round-ups of dissents and, in July 1981, there was religious violence in poorer parts of Cairo. Men, women and children were slaughtered. Plans to assassinate Sadat were already in hand.

On 6 October 1981, Sadat attended a victory parade in Cairo to commemorate the eighth anniversary of Egypt's crossing of the Suez Canal. During the ceremony, a group of soldiers, who were members of the Egyptian Islamic Jihad, managed to penetrate the security cordon around Sadat who was distracted by Egyptian Air Force Mirage jets flying overheard. An army truck full of dissident soldiers stopped next to the stand where the president was inspecting the troops. The assassination squad dismounted. Thinking it was part of the parade, Sadat waited for them to salute. Instead, the soldiers opened fire and threw grenades. Their leader, Lieutenant Khalid Islambouli, ran towards the president, shouting 'Death to the Pharaoh!' and fired at him at close range.

As Sadat fell to the ground, his security guards returned fire at the assassins. In the shoot-out that followed, seven onlookers were killed and twenty-eight wounded. Those who died included the ambassador for Cuba and a Greek Orthodox priest. The vice president and Sadat's successor, Hosni Mubarak, was injured in the hand. Sadat was rushed to hospital where eleven surgeons tried to save his life. Two hours later, he was declared dead.

The leader of the assassins Khalid Ahmed Showky Al-Islambouli was a soldier who had graduated from the Military Academy with distinction. His brother Mohamed, who was also arrested, was a member of a religious fundamentalist group that had ordered the murder. Curiously Khalid was only at the parade because he was taking the place of another soldier who away making the pilgrimage to Mecca.

Khalid Al-Islambouli and the other assassins were tried by court-martial. Found guilty of murder they were sentenced to death and executed by firing squad in April 1982. The Iranians named a street in Teheran after Islambouli as Sadat had been a supporter of the Shah. However, he was mourned in many countries and his funeral was attended by a record number of international dignitaries, including four presidents of the United States – Ronald Reagan, Gerald Ford, Jimmy Carter and Richard Nixon. Also present was Boutros Boutros-Ghali, who was later to become head of the United Nations.

Hosni Mubarak returned Egypt to the Arab League and, with Saudi Arabia, continued with efforts to resolve the Israeli–Palestinian conflict by allowing a Palestinian state. However, the peace process made little progress. Nevertheless the Arab League moved its headquarters to Cairo.

Egypt was a member of the allied coalition during the 1991 Gulf War; Egyptian infantry were some of the first to land in Saudi Arabia to remove Iraqi forces from Kuwait.

This brought with it financial benefits. However, President Mubarak spoke out against the 2003 invasion of Iraq, arguing that the Israeli–Palestinian conflict should have been resolved first and saying that the war would cause 'a hundred bin Ladens'.

Mubarak managed to hold onto power for thirty years, only stepping down at the Egyptian Revolution in 2011. He stood trial for failing to prevent the killing of peaceful protesters during the revolution. Sentenced to life imprisonment, he suffered a series of health crises. After a trial, he was eventually freed on appeal in March 2017. He died three years later.

He had been succeeded in office by the commander-in-chief Mohamed Hussein Tantawi, until an election in 2012 led to the inauguration of Mohamed Morsi, a member of the Muslim Brotherhood. He was removed from office by General Abdel Fattah el-Sisi in a coup d'état.

15

JOHN LENNON 1980

John Lennon was shot dead in the entranceway to the Dakota building, his home in New York, on 8 December 1980. Having involved himself in politics – particularly in his opposition to the war in Vietnam – he was seen as a martyr by his many fans worldwide. Before he was murdered he had become practically a recluse and had undergone long periods of creative inactivity. Nevertheless after his death his reputation grew. He came to be seen as one of the seminal figures of popular music in the twentieth century. As a figurehead for the peace and love movement spawned in the 1960s, he attracted a loyal following among new generations of fans.

Born in Liverpool on 9 October 1940, John Lennon was the son of a merchant seaman and grew up in a working-class area of the city. This was key as sailors brought rock and roll and rhythm and blues records, particularly those by African American artists, across the Atlantic from the US.

His parents, Julia and Alf, split up when he was five. Left to cope on her own, Julia sent John to live with his aunt Mimi. He continued to see his mother, but their relationship was troubled. However, she played him Elvis Presley records and taught him to play the banjo. The first tune he mastered was 'Ain't That A Shame' by Fats Domino. This gave him a distinctive style when he eventually picked up a guitar, another present from his mother.

From an early age, he was a rebel and a troublemaker. At Quarry Bank High School, he formed the skiffle group, The Quarrymen, at the age of fifteen. They also took up rock and roll and it was through The Quarrymen he met Paul McCartney. When Lennon was seventeen, his mother was killed in a car accident and he had to go to the morgue to identify the body. This was said to have scarred him emotionally for life.

After failing his O levels, Lennon was accepted by the Liverpool College of Art. He dressed as a Teddy boy and was thrown out before his final year for his rebellious behaviour. In the meantime, he had formed a band called The Silver Beetles with Paul McCartney and George Harrison.

The band's name was soon shortened to The Beatles when they went on to tour in Germany. During a residency in Hamburg, they developed their distinctive sound. Later, they were joined by drummer Ringo Starr. Local music-shop owner Brian Epstein took over their management and steered them to worldwide success.

Crucial to their popularity were the songs written by Lennon and McCartney. These began with the bright, melodic pop of the early 1960s and grew into introspective psychedelia later in the decade. The Beatles became one of the most influential bands of their time, not only musically. They championed the new 1960s counterculture, taking drugs and becoming involved in the transcendental meditation movement. Their opinions were sought on every question under the sun. Lennon used this as an opportunity to express his controversial beliefs, often in a humorous vein. But when he said The Beatles were 'more popular than Jesus' the Christian church took offence. The Beatles' records were burnt and Lennon was roundly condemned by members of the establishment.

Lennon's personal life also became the subject of controversy after he divorced his first wife Cynthia Powell, the mother of his son Julian, and married Japanese artist Yoko Ono. Many fans of The Beatles felt that Ono's influence on Lennon was a negative one. Lennon began to include his wife in every aspect of the band's recording work, and she became a constant presence everywhere he went. Ono's influence, and other issues to do with leadership of the group, put Lennon's relationship with The Beatles under strain. There followed a series of acrimonious disputes with Paul McCartney and the band broke up in 1970.

After that Lennon recorded as a solo artist and with Ono. Together, they recorded experimental albums and conducted a series of attention-grabbing public protests, including lying in bed surrounded by posters for peace. They were regarded by certain sections of the media as laughably eccentric but were an inspiration to youth.

They moved to New York, but when they took against the war in Vietnam, the administration of Richard Nixon undertook a four-year campaign to deport him. It failed. Following the birth of his second son, Sean, Lennon was granted permanent residency in the US. In 1980, Lennon returned to the studio, recording the album *Double Fantasy* to the delight of his fans.

During the 1960s, Lennon had been asked how he thought he would die and had replied that he expected to be 'popped off by some loony'. As it turned out, these words proved prophetic.

On Saturday, 6 December 1980, twenty-five-year-old Mark Chapman checked into the YMCA on 63rd Street, just off Central Park West in New York City. Born in Texas on 10 May 1955, he had grown up in Decatur, Georgia. Afraid of his abusive father, he believed he was king of 'little people' who lived in the walls of his bedroom. An overweight child he had been unpopular at school and began skipping classes and taking drugs. Nevertheless, he went on to become a committed Christian and youth worker at the behest of his first girlfriend. In despair after the relationship failed, he dropped out of college and moved to Hawaii where he planned to kill himself. When his suicide attempt failed, he was diagnosed with clinical depression. His parents divorced and his mother joined him in Hawaii.

He travelled around the world, then married a Japanese American travel agent, Gloria Abe. Things went well for a couple of years until he lost his job and he began drinking heavily. His behaviour became increasingly eccentric and he developed an obsession with John Lennon and J. D. Salinger's novel *The Catcher in the Rye*. When Chapman heard that John Lennon had a new record out he felt compelled to meet his idol. He had been a long-time fan of The Beatles but had condemned Lennon for blasphemy when he said they were more famous than Jesus. After Lennon released the single 'Imagine', he told his prayer group: 'Imagine, imagine if John Lennon was dead.' The hypocrisy of 'Imagine' also annoyed him. His wife Gloria said: 'He was angry that Lennon would preach love and peace, but yet have millions.'

The Saturday he arrived in New York, Chapman spent several hours outside the Dakota building, holding a copy of *Double Fantasy* and waiting for Lennon. When he did not appear, Chapman returned to the YMCA for the night. Next day, he moved to the nearby Sheraton Hotel, then returned to the Dakota. Once again Lennon failed to show. Chapman bought a copy of *Playboy* magazine featuring an interview with John Lennon to pass the time. That night he called an escort agency. When the call girl arrived he told her he merely wanted to talk to her, just as Holden Caulfield, the protagonist of *The Catcher in the Rye*, had done. He paid her $190 when she left at 3am.

Next morning he woke at 10.30am, took out the hotel Bible, opened it at the beginning of the Gospel of St John and wrote in the word 'Lennon' after 'John'. Then he picked up his copy of *Double Fantasy* and a gun he had bought in Honolulu, and headed off to the Dakota building, picking up a new copy of *The Catcher in the Rye* from a bookstore on the way.

Once at the Dakota building he became so engrossed in the book that he did not notice Lennon entering the building. He continued his vigil, chatting with other Lennon fans who had gathered there. Soon after lunchtime, a fellow fan spotted Lennon's five-year-old son Sean coming out with his nanny. Chapman shook the child's hand. During the course of the afternoon he saw other celebrities including Lauren Bacall and Paul Simon coming in and out of the building. Around six o'clock, John Lennon came out with Yoko Ono. They were heading for their recording studio. Chapman asked Lennon to sign the album he was holding. Lennon did so graciously and asked: 'Is that all you want?'

Chapman said later that part of him was satisfied with this. He had got his autograph and wanted to go home to Hawaii and get on with his life. However, another part of him had a much darker purpose and he continued to wait outside the Dakota building.

At around 10.50pm John and Yoko returned from the recording studio in their white limousine. She got out first and he followed. According to Chapman's own account given to the police a few hours later: 'He walked past me, and then a voice in my head said, "Do it, do it, do it" over and over again, saying "Do it, do it, do it, do it", like that. I pulled the gun out of my pocket. I handed it over to my left hand. I don't remember aiming. I must have done it, but I don't remember drawing the bead or whatever you call it. And I just pulled the trigger steady five times.'

Lennon recoiled from the gun, but four of the five bullets hit him. Even so he managed to run up six steps into the concierge's station in the building. There he said: 'I'm shot.' Then fell face down. He was rushed in a police car to St Luke's Roosevelt Hospital, but died soon after his arrival.

Meanwhile Chapman stayed where he was, reading *The Catcher in the Rye*. When the police arrived, he put his hands in the air and said: 'I acted alone.'

As the news of the shooting spread, thousands of fans gathered outside the hospital. The following day the whole world seemed to be in mourning on a scale not seen since the assassination of President Kennedy.

At his trial Mark Chapman pleaded guilty to murder. Convicted, he was sentenced to life imprisonment. Although eligible for parole in the year 2000 he has not been released, partly because it was feared that he himself might be murdered.

16

PARK CHUNG-HEE 1979

The president of South Korea from 1963 to 1970, Park Chung-hee is credited with transforming the country from a backward rural economy into a modern industrial state. After serving as chairman of the Supreme Council for National Reconstruction, he became president after a military coup. On 26 October 1979, he was assassinated by Kim Jae-gyu, the chief of the Korean Central Intelligence Agency. Other KCIA officers shot his bodyguards. However, it remains unclear whether the assassination was a spontaneous act of passion by an individual or part of a pre-arranged attempted coup by the intelligence service. Kim claimed that Park was an oppressive dictator and that his act was one of patriotism designed to return democracy to South Korea.

Park Chung-hee was born in Gumi, a small town in the backward province of North Gyeongsang, on 14 November 1917 when Korea was under Japanese rule. His boyhood hero was Napoleon. He also admired Japan for its rapid modernisation after the Meiji Restoration of 1868 and for *Bushido*, the Japanese warrior code.

He attended school in the city of Daegu. After teaching for a while, he entered the Changchun Military Academy of the Imperial Army of Manchukuo, the Japanese puppet state. He adopted the Japanese name Takagi Masao and during World War II served as aide-de-camp to a regimental commander, using Korean turncoats to suppress Korean armed resistance.

Following the Japanese defeat, Park aligned himself with the left and rebelled against the Korean government of Syngman Rhee who was installed by the Americans in 1948. He narrowly escaped being put to death. Later, he joined the South Korean Army, rising to become Chief of Operations Staff. The increasing authoritarian Syngman Rhee was forced from office in 1960 and replaced by a democratic government which was overthrown by a military coup the following year. In 1963, the military government was replaced by a civilian administration under Park who had won the election as leader of the Democratic Republican Party.

He took over the Supreme Council for National Reconstruction, arresting its former head. Park persuaded the US Army not to interfere as he set about transforming South Korea from an underdeveloped, peasant economy into a modern industrialised state. While criticised for his dictatorial methods, under his government, the incomes of ordinary people increased massively. Many escaped the grinding poverty of rural areas, moving to towns and cities where they had access to jobs, housing, education and medical facilities. The rise in the standard of living was rapid, and South Korea's transformation is still regarded as an economic miracle, albeit at the expense of democracy.

Despite the country's increasing prosperity, Park made himself unpopular, particularly by resuming friendly relations with Japan who had been a brutal oppressor after annexing the peninsula in 1910. While Park argued that without economic aid from Japan, as well as from America, the country could not rebuild itself, the people had bitter memories of the Japanese occupation. After waning in the polls, he took the controversial step of altering the country's constitution in 1972 to make himself a virtual dictator. He banned all forms of opposition and his regime grew more and more oppressive as the years went by. Dissidents were regularly imprisoned and tortured. Elections were still held, but they were anything but free and fair, and South Korea became a byword for human rights abuses.

Opposition grew and on 15 August 1974 there was an attempt to assassinate him. Park was giving a speech to more than a thousand people at the National Theatre in Seoul to mark the country's Liberation Day when a gunman ran down the centre aisle of the theatre, firing a pistol at the stage. Park was protected by a bulletproof lectern, but a stray bullet hit his wife Yuk Yeongsu in the head. He continued his speech while his wife and a seventeen-year-old girl who was also hit were rushed to hospital. Both died.

The assassin tried to flee, but security guards opened fire on him, wounding him. Once captured, he was identified as Mun Segwang, a twenty-two-year-old Korean living in Osaka, Japan. A member of the Korean Youth League, who opposed the Park regime, he had travelled to South Korea on a false Japanese passport. Later he told the authorities that he had been instructed to kill the president by North Korean agents he had met in Japan. The assassination had been ordered by Kim Il-Sung, he said. However, the matter remains a controversy to this day. Mun Segwang was convicted of the murder of Yuk Yeongsu and executed.

Five years later, on 26 October 1979, there was another attempt on the president's life which proved successful. The assassin was Kim Jae-gyu, once trusted head of security forces in the state, formerly a close friend of the president. He had opposed Park Chung-hee's dictatorial style of leadership, standing against him in elections and narrowly escaping being imprisoned before Park changed the constitution to secure his position.

The assassination took place during a meeting at a safe house in Seoul called to discuss opposition to the regime, in particular student riots that had taken place in Pusan. According to some sources, Kim Jae-gyu was afraid of losing his job because of the disturbances. An argument broke out between Kim and the president's bodyguard, Cha Chi Chol, who had replaced Kim as the president's right-hand man.

After the disagreement Kim walked out of the meeting. Returning with a gun, he opened fire on Cha Chi Col. When Cha took cover behind some furniture, Kim shot Park in the chest, then dragged Cha out of his hiding place and shot him in the stomach. He then shot Park in the head and continued firing until he was sure both men were dead. A gunfight ensued between the president's bodyguards and Kim's men. Five were killed.

Details of the assassination were suppressed, but the country was thrown into chaos. The military under the leadership of General Chun Doo-hwan seized power. Kim Jae-gyu was convicted of murder and put to death on 24 May 1980.

Little was said about the assassination. However, two decades after the event, Kim Jae-gyu's widow, Kim Young-hee, presented the special commission for democratisation with a petition, asking them to collect new information on the case. According to some sources, Kim Jae-gyu kept a diary in prison while awaiting his trial. In it he claimed that he wanted to end the tyranny of the regime and restore democracy to the country. It also showed that he was a devout Buddhist who expressed an indifference to wealth, position and power. It also seems that several high-ranking figures in the country had petitioned for his release, including several Catholic priests and political leaders. A thousand people, including some prominent members of the opposition, had organised a campaign to try to stop the execution. After Kim's death, his supporters erected a national monument to him in Gyeonggi Province.

Meanwhile, Park Chung-hee's daughter, Park Geun-hye, led a campaign to discredit Kim Jae-gyu, saying that he had killed the president for his own political ends. He was the head of the Central Intelligence Agency, which was known for its brutality in suppressing those who wanted to restore democracy to South Korea. The assassination of the president set back any democratic agenda in South Korea's politics for many years at a time when it was beginning to gain ground. In the year Park Chung-hee was assassinated, there had been a record number of protests and demonstrations against his regime, which was why the fateful meeting had been called in the first place.

After the assassination, General Chun Doo-hwan imposed martial law, closed universities, banned political activities and further curtailed the press. Special forces were sent to the city of Gwangju to suppress the democratisation movement there. Chun and his government held South Korea under a despotic rule until 1987, when a Seoul National University student, Park Jong-chul, was tortured to death. This ignited the June Democracy Movement around the country. Elections were called but Roh Tae-woo, the leader of Chun's Democratic Justice Party, won by a narrow margin. The following year, Seoul hosted the Olympic Games which were widely regarded as successful and a significant boost for the country's global image and economy.

South Korea was formally invited to become a member of the United Nations in 1991. The transition of Korea from autocracy to modern democracy was marked in 1997 by the election of Kim Dae-jung, who was sworn in as president on 25 February 1998. While Park Chung-hee is still seen as a controversial figure, he is credited for the 'Miracle on the Han River' that laid the foundations of South Korea's current prosperity. In a 2015 South Korean Gallup poll on the greatest president in South Korean history, Park topped the chart with an approval rating of 44 per cent. On the other hand, in 2007, South Korea's National Intelligence Service admitted that its precursor, the Korean Central Intelligence Agency, undertook the kidnapping of the then opposition leader and future President Kim Dae-jung with the at least tacit backing of Park Chung-hee.

17

MARTIN LUTHER KING 1968

The assassination of Martin Luther King on 4 April 1968 came as no surprise. The night before he made a speech to a packed congregation at the Mason Temple in Memphis, Tennessee, predicting it and reaffirming that he was not afraid to die. In fact, he was prepared for it.

'I got to Memphis and some began to say the threats, or talk about the threats that were out. What would happen to me from some of our sick white brothers?' he said. 'Well, I don't know what will happen now. We've got some difficult days ahead. But it really doesn't matter with me now, because I've been to the mountaintop. And I don't mind. Like anybody, I would like to live – a long life; longevity has its place. But I'm not concerned about that now. I just want to do God's will. And He's allowed me to go up to the mountain. And I've looked over. And I've seen the Promised Land. I may not get there with you. But I want you to know tonight, that we, as a people, will get to the Promised Land. So I'm happy, tonight. I'm not worried about anything. I'm not fearing any man. Mine eyes have seen the glory of the coming of the Lord.'

The following evening, he was shot dead. The man convicted of his murder was James Earl Ray, a petty criminal and an outspoken racist. But there were many – including members of King's family – who did not believe that Ray was responsible and suspected that the FBI or the CIA were behind the killing. Whatever the truth, King's death spelled the end of an optimistic period in America, when people thought that the racial discrimination and economic inequality that had plagued the country for so long could be swept away by non-violent action.

Born Michael Luther King, the son of a Baptist minister in Atlanta, Georgia, on 15 January 1929, his parents later changed his name to Martin. From an early age, he decided to follow his father into the church. After studying at Morehouse College – a respected black college – and Crozer Theological Seminary, he received a doctorate from Boston University and became a pastor in Montgomery, Alabama. In 1953 he married Coretta Scott. They went on to have four children, who all became civil rights workers.

King built a large congregation and became an important voice for African Americans in the area. He vociferously condemned the Jim Crow laws of the Southern states, which forced black people to live separately from whites and take second place to them. A staunch supporter of desegregation, he made his views widely known, even though he knew he risked retaliation by white supremacists.

In 1955, when Rosa Parks famously refused to give up her seat to a white man and move to the back of the bus, King organised a boycott of the buses in Montgomery. Eventually the bus company was forced to change its rules. This meant King became a leading spokesman for the growing US civil rights movement, leading protests in Alabama's most populous city Birmingham. A follower of Mahatma Gandhi, he advocated civil disobedience and insisted that all direct action should be non-violent. Even so, he was frequently arrested. His life was already in peril from bomb attacks on the activists' headquarters.

Despite numerous threats, King went on to lead a huge civil rights march on Washington in 1963. On the steps of the Lincoln Memorial, he made his famous 'I Have a Dream' speech, saying: 'I have a dream that one day right there in Alabama little black boys and little black girls will be able to join hands with little white boys and white girls as sisters and brothers...

'I have a dream that my four little children will one day live in a nation where they will not be judged by the color of their skin but by the content of their character.

'I have a dream that one day this nation will rise up and live out the true meaning of its creed – we hold these truths to be self-evident: that all men are created equal.

'Let us not seek to satisfy our thirst for freedom by drinking from the cup of bitterness and hatred.

'I have a dream that one day on the red hills of Georgia the sons of former slaves and the sons of former slave-owners will be able to sit down together at a table of brotherhood.'

King was awarded the Nobel Peace Prize in 1964 and went on to campaign successfully for black people's voting rights before widening his focus to oppose poverty and the Vietnam War. This brought him fresh enemies within the administration, including FBI Director J. Edgar Hoover. FBI agents investigated him for possible Communist ties, recorded his extramarital liaisons and mailed King a threatening anonymous letter, encouraging him to commit suicide. But while he was one of America's leading political figures, they offered him no protection.

At 6pm on 4 April 1968, King was on the second-floor balcony of the Lorraine Motel where he was staying in

Memphis. A lone gunman in the bushes below shot at him. The bullet hit him in the jaw and broke several vertebrae as it travelled down his spinal cord. King was rushed to hospital where he died an hour later.

The police seemed clueless. However, two months later escaped convict James Earl Ray was arrested in Britain, travelling under a forged Canadian passport. He was quickly extradited to Tennessee to face murder charges. On 10 March 1969, Ray confessed to the murder of Martin Luther King and was sentenced to ninety-nine years in prison.

Ray then recanted his confession, saying that he had only pleaded guilty to escape the death penalty. He accused his brother, Johnny, and a Canadian smuggler named 'Raul' of the murder, hinting that there had been a conspiracy, but his account did not check out. The questions about King's death remained unanswered until, in 1997, the House Select Committee on Assassinations concluded that there may well have been a conspiracy, but all the evidence said it was Ray who had shot King. Ray continued to maintain that he had not done it until his death in prison on 23 April 1998.

Nevertheless rumours persisted. Martin Luther King's son Dexter was convinced that his father had been killed by FBI agents and made strenuous efforts to prove his theory. He pointed out that ballistic tests conducted could not prove that the rifle found at the scene with Ray's fingerprints on it was the murder weapon. While Ray had been a burglar, there was no record of violence on his file. He was not a good enough marksman to hit his target. Nor did he have the intelligence or the courage to pull off the assassination.

According to one theory, the mastermind behind the assassination had been FBI assistant director Cartha 'Deke' DeLoach. Ray had been lured to Memphis to take part in a bank robbery and had been put up in a rooming house next door to King's hotel that evening while an FBI gunman hiding in a shrubbery nearby shot King. Afterwards, the FBI had planted the murder weapon, a Remington rifle, and framed Ray for the murder.

Dexter King met with Ray in 1997, shook his hand and publicly pledged his support for a retrial. Later, King's widow Coretta Scott King launched a civil suit against Memphis bar owner Loyd Jowers and 'other unknown conspirators'. The jury found againt Jowers, but the King family were only awarded a symbolic sum of $100. In later investigations, Jowers was cleared of any involvement. While no hard evidence has been found to link the FBI or the CIA to the assassination of Martin Luther King, there remain important questions about the FBI's harassment of King while he was alive.

At the time, news of King's assassination provoked race riots across the country. Dozens of people were killed, and thousands of people injured. Five days after the assassination, a new Civil Rights Act was signed into law by President Lyndon B. Johnson. This also comprised a Fair Housing Act. The fight against racial discrimination was far from over and many civil rights activists abandoned King's policies of civil disobedience and non-violence. Some, notably members of the Black Panther Party, began to advocate armed struggle.

The day after the death of Martin Luther King, the militant Stokely Carmichael called for forceful action, saying: 'White America killed Dr King last night. She made it a whole lot easier for a whole lot of black people today. There no longer needs to be intellectual discussions, black people know that they have to get guns. White America will live to cry that she killed Dr King last night. It would have been better if she had killed Rap Brown and/or Stokely Carmichael, but when she killed Dr King, she lost.'

Rap Brown himself said: 'If America don't come around, we're gonna burn it down.' In 2000, Brown was convicted of the murder of two deputies in Fulton County, Georgia and sentenced to life imprisonment.

18

ROBERT F. KENNEDY 1968

Just two months after the assassination of Martin Luther King, Robert F. Kennedy was also gunned down. At the time he was running for the Democratic nomination to become president of the United States. He had just split from the current administration and turned against the Vietnam War, the most contentious issue of the era. But on the night that King died, Kennedy was making a speech in a black ghetto of Indianapolis where he pleaded for reconciliation.

He reminded his audience that: 'Martin Luther King dedicated his life to love and to justice between fellow human beings. He died in the cause of that effort.' There would be some black people who would be 'filled with bitterness, and with hatred, and a desire for revenge.

'We can move in that direction as a country, in greater polarization – black people amongst blacks, and white amongst whites, filled with hatred toward one another. Or we can make an effort, as Martin Luther King did, to understand, and to comprehend, and replace that violence, that stain of bloodshed that has spread across our land, with an effort to understand, compassion, and love.'

He went on to speak of the 1963 assassination of his brother, John F. Kennedy, the first time he had done so in public.

Born on 20 November 1925 in Brookline, Massachusetts, Bobby Kennedy was the son of venture capitalist Joseph P. Kennedy who was US ambassador to the court of St James's from 1938 to 1940. During World War II, Bobby served in the navy. Afterwards, he studied law and worked in the Department of Justice, quitting in 1952 to manage his brother John's campaign for the US Senate.

He worked as counsel to Senator Joseph McCarthy who sought to unmask the numerous Communists and Soviet spies and sympathisers who, he claimed, had infiltrated the United States federal government, universities, film industry and elsewhere. Kennedy went on to work for the Senate Rackets Committee which investigated the activities of the Mafia and other mobsters, himself uncovering corrupt practices in the Teamsters' Union. He left the committee in 1959 to run his brother John's successful campaign for the presidency.

In the Kennedy administration, Bobby became attorney general and continued his war against organised crime. In May 1961, he sent five hundred federal marshals to protect the Freedom Riders who were attempting to forcibly integrate the buses and bus terminals in the South. Later he put an end to racial segregation in all forms of interstate travel. He also used federal authority to integrate universities in the South. Throughout his political career, he moved towards the liberal wing of the Democratic Party.

A close advisor to his brother, he played a key role in defusing the Cuban Missile Crisis which had brought the world to the brink of nuclear war. He came up with an inspired ploy to defuse the situation and negotiated a settlement with the Soviet ambassador. Robert was shattered by the assassination of his brother but stayed in post despite the animosity of the new president Lyndon B. Johnson. The following year, he was elected US Senator for New York.

Although John Kennedy's administration had got the US involved in Vietnam in the first place, Robert cooled to the war as it escalated under President Johnson. However, he supported Johnson's Great Society programme of social reforms and stifled his criticism to prevent splitting the Democratic Party.

As the situation in Vietnam worsened, Kennedy refused to join the 'Dump Johnson' movement. The Tet Offensive in January 1968 changed everything. Communist forces in Vietnam attacked thirty-six provincial capitals, sixty-four district towns, many villages and ten US military bases. Even the American embassy in the capital Saigon came under siege. Nevertheless President Johnson continued to insist that victory was near at hand. But the American people, who had watched the Tet Offensive nightly on newscasts, came to believe that the war was unwinnable. Kennedy had announced that he intended to run for president in 1968 against Johnson on 16 March, saying: 'I am today announcing my candidacy for the presidency of the United States. I do not run for the presidency merely to oppose any man, but to propose new policies. I run because I am convinced that this country is on a perilous course and because I have such strong feelings about what must be done, and I feel that I'm obliged to do all I can.'

Kennedy made this announcement from the same spot in the Senate Caucus Room where John F. Kennedy had announced his presidential candidacy in January 1960. Entering the race he risked splitting the anti-war votes with peace campaigner Senator Eugene McCarthy. But on 31

March, President Johnson made the surprise announcement that he would not seek, nor would he accept the nomination. The field was wide open.

At a speech in Kansas, Kennedy again reaffirmed his commitment to reconciliation, saying: 'I don't think that we have to shoot each other, to beat each other, to curse each other and criticise each other, I think that we can do better in this country. And that is why I run for President of the United States.'

In the primaries, Kennedy was running second to the incumbent vice president Hubert Humphrey, who still supported the war. Key was California's Democratic primary which was held on 4 June. Four hours after the polls closed, Kennedy claimed victory. Just after midnight, on 5 June, Kennedy went to the Ambassador Hotel on Wilshire Boulevard in Los Angeles to address his campaign workers in the Embassy Room ballroom.

He talked of healing the country's differences between blacks and whites, between the rich and poor, between old and young, and the split in opinion over the war in Vietnam, ending with: 'My thanks to all of you; and now it's on to Chicago, and let's win there!'

At that time, the Secret Service did not provide protection for presidential candidates. Kennedy's security was provided by former FBI agent William Barry and two unofficial bodyguards – Olympic decathlon gold medallist Rafer Johnson and former football player Rosey Grier. They had their work cut out as Kennedy relished direct contact with the public and the crowds pressed in on him.

Kennedy was on his way to another gathering of supporters elsewhere in the hotel when campaign aide Fred Dutton told him that reporters wanted a press conference. To get to the press area, Kennedy would cut through the kitchens behind the ballroom. Led by maître d'hôtel Karl Uecker, Kennedy weaved his way through the kitchen area, stopping to shake hands. Suddenly a lone assassin stepped out from behind an ice machine with a .22 revolver and fired three times from a range of about an inch, hitting Kennedy in the head.

He fell to the ground, while aides wrestled with the assassin, who tried to fire at Kennedy again. As the pistol was only of a small calibre, it was thought that Kennedy would survive. He was still talking, but when he was lifted onto a stretcher he lost consciousness.

Robert Kennedy was still alive when he reached hospital. Two bullets had entered his body through his armpit. One had exited through his chest. The other was lodged in the back of his neck. The third bullet was removed from his brain, along with bone fragments. But despite extensive neurosurgery, Kennedy was pronounced dead on 6 June, nearly twenty-six hours after the shooting. He was forty-two years old.

The killer, Sirhan Sirhan, was a twenty-four-year-old Palestinian. Diaries found at his home showed that he was obsessed with killing Robert Kennedy before 5 June 1968, perhaps because it was the first anniversary of the beginning of the Six Day War between Israel and its Arab neighbours. Sirhan believed that Kennedy was an avid supporter of Israel and sought to harm Palestinians.

Sirhan pleaded guilty on several occasions, but was subjected to a full trial nevertheless. He was convicted of murder and sentenced to death. This was commuted to life in prison without possibility of parole.

His gun had been obtained for him by his brother Munir Bishara Sirhan. Sirhan had said he wanted it to go to a shooting range. The purchase had been made covertly because it was illegal under Californian law for an alien to buy firearms. Sirhan had practised with it several times before the assassination.

With Kennedy dead Hubert Humphrey won the Democratic nomination, but he lost the election to Richard Nixon, who also promised to end America's involvement in the Vietnam War. He did so, but only after four years and another election. During that time, the war, race and the conflict between the generations has torn the country apart. These were all matters that Robert F. Kennedy had promised to reconcile.

Again, at his valedictory for Martin Luther King, he said: 'What we need in the United States is not division; what we need in the United States is not hatred; what we need in the United States is not violence or lawlessness; but love and wisdom, and compassion toward one another, and a feeling of justice toward those who still suffer within our country, whether they be white or they be black.'

The *American National Biography* says: 'Kennedy is best remembered for his thrilling presidential campaign in 1968 and its shocking conclusion. His place in history will probably turn on his role in helping save the human race from extinction during the Cuban Missile Crisis.'

19

HENDRIK VERWOERD 1966

Hendrik Verwoerd is remembered as the architect of apartheid, the system of racial segregation that divided South Africa until the election of Nelson Mandela in 1994. Although he defined apartheid as merely 'good neighbourliness', while prime minister of South Africa from 1958 to 1966, Verwoerd did everything he could to ensure the ascendancy of the whites at the expense of the blacks. Thousands were transported to Bantustans or 'homeland' areas, leaving the prosperous areas for those of European descent.

During Verwoerd's time in office, there were two attempts on his life, the second being successful. On 6 September 1966, he was stabbed to death by Dimitri Tsafendas, who was later declared to be mentally ill. However, his political motive was clear. He had been a lifelong Communist who had fought in the Greek Civil War. At the time, there were many in South Africa who believed Verwoerd to have been one of the country's great statesmen. However, since the end of apartheid, Verwoerd's legacy is generally seen as malign as it caused immense suffering to millions of black people which continues to this day.

Hendrik Frensch Verwoerd was born in Amsterdam in the Netherlands, on 8 September 1901. His father Wilhelmus was a religious man and sympathetic to the plight of the Afrikaners in South Africa after they had lost the Boer War to the British. In 1903, the family moved to South Africa. After ten years they moved to Bulawayo in Rhodesia, now Zimbabwe, where Wilhelmus became an evangelist in the Dutch Reformed Church. Four years later the family returned to South Africa, where Wilhelmus became a church minister in Brandtfort in the Orange Free State.

Hendrik was a very able pupil at the schools he attended, going on to study theology at the Stellenbosch University. Denied entrance to theology college, he switched to psychology and philosophy, gaining a masters, then a PhD. He was offered a scholarship at University of Oxford but turned it down because of his family's deep hostility to the British. Instead, he went to Germany where he studied under Dr Eugen Fischer, an anthropologist who advocated racial segregation and eugenics. While in prison Adolf Hitler read Fischer's work and expanded on these ideas in his own book, *Mein Kampf*.

In 1928, Verwoerd returned to Stellenbosch University, eventually becoming Professor of Sociology there. During the Depression he became involved in social work. This led him into politics. Committed to white supremacy, he campaigned for South Africa to throw off British rule and become a republic. In 1937 he became editor of the newspaper *Die Transvaler*, which supported Afrikaner nationalism. The newspaper denounced marriages between whites and blacks and protested against the arrival of Jews who were fleeing the Nazis.

During World War II, *Die Transvaler* was accused of being pro-Nazi by rival newspaper, the *Johannesburg Star*. Verwoerd sued the proprietor of the *Star* but lost the case in court. Once the war was over, Verwoerd's hostility to the British became even more intense. His newspaper famously ignored the visit to South Africa of the British royal family, merely decrying the traffic congestion caused by 'visitors from overseas'.

After the right-wing National Party came into power in South Africa in 1948, Verwoerd was elected to the South African Senate. He left his position as editor of *Die Transvaler* and began to work in politics full time. In 1950, he became a member of the cabinet as minister of native affairs. In that position he oversaw the establishment of the black 'homelands', or Bantustans, where over eighty thousand black Africans were displaced. Many were forced to move from mixed urban centres such as Sophiatown and Newclare to blacks-only townships such as Soweto. The National Party government, of which he was a member, passed the repressive Population Registration Act and the Group Areas Act in 1950, the Pass Laws Act of 1952 and the Reservation of Separate Amenities Act of 1953.

To ensure rigid segregation, Verwoerd wrote the Bantu Education Act that set up a separate education system for blacks with a curriculum limited to the basic skills of reading, writing and arithmetic. He maintained that black people would not need more than this since their role was to be confined to 'hewers of wood and drawers of water'. This meant that the educated white Afrikaners would have a permanent underclass who could provide manual labour.

Verwoerd justified this by saying: 'The Bantu must be guided to serve his own community in all respects. There is no place for him in the European community above the level of certain forms of labour. Within his own community, however, all doors are open'.

He became prime minister of South Africa in 1958. Then in January 1960, he announced that a referendum would be called on whether South Africa should become a republic. Only whites would be allowed to vote and the voting age was lowered from twenty-one to eighteen benefiting younger Afrikaans speakers, who were more likely to favour a republic. British prime minister Harold Macmillan visited the country and warned that the 'winds of change are blowing through Africa'. This confirmed that Britain was hostile to the idea of white minority rule. South Africa was declared a republic and withdrew from the Commonwealth.

South Africa's blatantly racist social system resulted in it being shunned by countries around the world. So Verwoerd tried to present apartheid in a new light. Black South Africans belonged to separate 'tribal nations' with their own homelands, where they could have equal political rights and develop their own culture in parallel with that of the whites. A more subtle argument than the previous Afrikaner theory that black people were inherently inferior to whites, this attracted more white followers to the cause of apartheid.

However, nothing could disguise the truth. Black people began to protest about the reality of life in the townships where they were forced to subsist in poverty. Under white masters their working conditions were harsh. They were subject to police brutality and unable to travel outside their designated areas freely. Clearly Verwoerd's 'separate but equal' policy was a charade.

This was brought home by the Sharpeville Massacre of 21 March 1960, when white policemen opened fire on a black crowd of protesters, killing many and injuring hundreds more. They had gathered to complain about the law forcing them to carry '*dompas*' or pass books. Verwoerd tightened his grip and outlawed political opposition to his policies. The African National Congress was banned and black leaders such as Nelson Mandela were imprisoned.

Unsurprisingly, Verwoerd became an extremely unpopular figure and there were many who wanted him out of the way. The first attempt on his life came on 9 April 1960, when Verwoerd was shot while opening the Union Exposition on the Witwatersrand, marking the fiftieth anniversary of the founding of the Union of South Africa. After he had made a speech a middle-aged man approached. Calling out Verwoerd's name, he fired a gun at him, at point-blank range. Two bullets hit Verwoerd in the face, one in his right cheek, one in his right ear. Colonel G. M. Harrison, the president of the Witwatersrand Agricultural Society, knocked the gun from the man's hand and he was overpowered by members of the audience. Verwoerd was rushed to hospital, where surgeons removed both bullets, leaving him pretty much unscathed. He returned to work less than two months after the shooting.

The would-be assassin was an English businessman named David Pratt who claimed he had been shooting 'the epitome of apartheid'. He was a member of the South African and British Liberal parties and was active in the British anti-apartheid movement. However, the courts found him to be insane and committed him to a mental hospital in Bloemfontein. Pratt hanged himself in October 1961, a few months after his incarceration. No inquest was held into his death and it was later found that many 'suicides' in custody during apartheid were murders by the police or security forces.

In the following six years, Verwoerd bolstered the system while sanctions were applied from outside. Then on 6 September 1966, Verwoerd came into the House of Assembly and took his seat. A moment later Dimitri Tsafendas, dressed in the uniform of a parliamentary messenger, walked over to the prime minister, pulled out a knife and stabbed him four times in the chest.

Four doctors who were members of parliament fought to save his life while they waited for an ambulance to arrive. Verwoerd was rushed to Groote Schuur Hospital, where he was pronounced dead on arrival. His lungs and heart had been punctured. The British satirical magazine *Private Eye* published a cover showing Zulus leaping in the air with the caption: 'Verwoerd – A Nation Mourns.'

Dimitri Tsafendas had been born in Mozambique on 14 January 1918 to a Greek father and a Mozambican woman of mixed race. In his youth he became a Communist and in 1939 joined the South African Communist Party. During World War II, he served as a seaman with the US merchant marine. In 1947, the US Immigration authorities deported him to Greece, which was embroiled in civil war. He fought for the Communists, who lost. He was jailed in Portugal and banned from Mozambique and South Africa for being a Communist.

The Portuguese eventually relented and allowed him to return to Mozambique, but he was jailed again for advocating the country's independence. In 1965, he managed to enter South Africa where his family had moved to. Although he was dark-skinned, he had been classified, under South Africa's race laws, as white. He applied to be re-classified as coloured as he had apparently fallen in love with a coloured woman and sex between the races was forbidden. It is not known whether this had any bearing on his motive for the assassination.

As with Pratt, the South African authorities found him to be insane. He was sent to a psychiatric hospital, where he remained until his death in 1999. By then, the apartheid system had been dismantled.

20

MALCOLM X 1965

Two days before he died, the charismatic Black Muslim leader Malcolm X told black film-maker Gordon Parks that the Nation of Islam – a militant black supremacist organisation he had broken with a year earlier – were trying to kill him. However, many believed that, like Martin Luther King, who was assassinated just a couple of years later, he had been killed by the FBI or the CIA because, in their eyes, he was a threat to the security of the nation, preaching a strong anti-white message and criticising American society as fundamentally racist.

Malcolm X was born Malcolm Little in Omaha, Nebraska, on 19 May 1925. His father Earl was a Baptist minister and a leading figure in Marcus Garvey's Back To Africa movement which advocated the repatriation of those of African descent. The family was harassed by the Ku Klux Klan. When Earl died in a streetcar accident when Malcolm was six, his mother Louise believed that he had been murdered by white racists.

After moving to Harlem in New York City in 1943, Malcolm X turned to petty crime as a drug dealer and pimp. He gained a reputation as a hard man, a ruthless hustler and snappy dresser. Appearing before the World War II draft board, he said: 'I want to be sent down South. Organize them n***** soldiers... steal us some guns, and kill us some crackers'. He was declared 'mentally disqualified for military service'.

At the age of eighteen, he was convicted for burglary, and sentenced to eight to ten years in prison. There he was introduced to the books of Elijah Muhammad, leader of the Nation of Islam. He wrote to Elijah Muhammad. Under his guidance he became a Muslim and changed his name to Malcolm X, rejecting 'Little' as a slave name. When he was released in 1952, the FBI already had file on him because he had written a letter to President Truman from prison expressing opposition to the Korean War and declaring himself to be a Communist.

He visited Elijah Muhammad in Chicago, then settled in Detroit and became a Muslim minister at the temple of the Nation of Islam there. He moved on to temples in Boston, Philadelphia and New York, expanding their membership each time. Meanwhile, the FBI kept their eye on him. He established temples in Springfield, Massachusetts; Hartford, Connecticut; and Atlanta, Georgia. Hundreds of African Americans were joining the Nation of Islam every month.

Elijah Muhammad had groomed his son-in-law Raymond Sharrieff to become his successor. However, Malcolm X was soon seen as a rival to Sharrieff, due to his intelligence, high level of commitment and generally magnetic character. In 1963, he came to the attention of the media when he said that the assassination of President Kennedy was a case of 'chickens coming home to roost', adding that 'chickens coming home to roost never did make me sad; they've always made me glad'. Meanwhile the Nation of Islam were sending their condolences to the Kennedy family and censured Malcolm, banning him from speaking in public for ninety days. It seemed that Elijah Muhammad was jealous of the amount of attention he was getting.

He turned against Elijah Muhammad when he refused to condemn police violence against members of the Nation of Islam and criticised him for conducting extramarital affairs with young secretaries. In 1964, he broke with the Nation of Islam to form his own movement, the Organization of Afro-American Unity.

On 26 March 1964, he met Martin Luther King for the first and only time in Washington DC, when they went to listen to the Senate's debate on the Civil Rights bill. Soon after Malcolm gave a speech called 'The Ballot or the Bullet'. In it, he advised black people to judiciously exercise their right to vote, but he cautioned that if the government continued to prevent African Americans from attaining full equality, it might be necessary for them to take up arms. Academics rate this as number seven in the top one hundred American speeches of the twentieth century.

At the Oxford Union in the UK he spoke in favour of the motion 'Extremism in the Defence of Liberty is No Vice; Moderation in the Pursuit of Justice is No Virtue'. The debate was televised by the BBC, bringing him to a broad audience outside the US.

While Malcolm was vilified in the American press for his anti-white statements, he began to modify his stance when he travelled around the world, especially to Africa, adopting a more integrationist perspective. After meeting anti-apartheid activists in South Africa, he became convinced that black and white people could work together to achieve political change. Making his Hajj to Mecca he said that seeing Muslims of 'all colours, from blue-eyed blonds to black-skinned Africans' interacting as brothers led him to see Islam as a means by which racial problems could be overcome. Embracing Sunni Islam, he changed his name to el-Hajj Malik el-Shabazz.

While he was in Africa, he complained that he was being followed by CIA agents. When he became seriously ill in Cairo, he believed that his food had been poisoned. Back in America the animosity between himself and Muhammad's followers grew more vitriolic. Muhammad himself told Louis X, later known as Louis Farrakhan and Muhammad's successor, that 'hypocrites like Malcolm should have their heads cut off'. Death threats were made against him. It was clear that his life was in danger either from the CIA or from the Nation of Islam. He told his wife that he was 'as good as dead'. The September 1964 issue of *Ebony* magazine showed him peering out of a window holding an M1 carbine.

A week before his assassination Malcolm X's house in Queens, New York was firebombed. He assumed that the Nation of Islam was behind the attack. The following day, 15 February, a speech he was making at the Audubon Ballroom in Harlem was disrupted when a scuffle broke out in the audience.

Six days later, on 21 February, Malcolm returned to the Audubon to make another speech. All the other speakers scheduled to appear had mysteriously cancelled. Before it was time for Malcolm to speak, a disturbance broke out in the audience of around four hundred. A man yelled: 'N*****! Get your hand outta my pocket! Don't be messin' with my pockets!' Then a smoke bomb went off at the back of the auditorium, causing widespread panic.

Malcolm X's bodyguards moved forward to calm the crowd. In the chaos, a black man came running towards the stage and shot Malcolm in the chest with a sawn-off shotgun. Two more men charged the stage, firing handguns. The three assassins then attempted to escape, but the angry crowd managed to capture one of them. He was later identified as Talmadge Hayer.

Malcolm X's bodyguard Gene Roberts attempted to resuscitate Malcolm, to no avail. He was pronounced dead at 3.30pm, shortly after arriving at Columbia Presbyterian Hospital. The post-mortem was performed by New York City's Chief Medical Examiner, Dr Milton Helpern. He found that 'the cause of death was multiple shotgun pellet and bullet wounds in the chest, heart and aorta'. Malcolm X had been hit by ten shotgun slugs and nine bullets.

Some 14,000 to 30,000 mourners turned up to view his body at the funeral home. The funeral was held in Harlem on 27 February 1965 at the thousand-seat Faith Temple Church of God in Christ. Loudspeakers were set up so the crowd outside could hear and a local television station carried the service live.

Delivering the eulogy, actor and activist Ossie Davis said: 'There are those who will consider it their duty, as friends of the Negro people, to tell us to revile him, to flee, even from the presence of his memory, to save ourselves by writing him out of the history of our turbulent times. Many will ask what Harlem finds to honour in this stormy, controversial and bold young captain – and we will smile. Many will say turn away – away from this man, for he is not a man but a demon, a monster, a subverter and an enemy of the black man – and we will smile. They will say that he is of hate – a fanatic, a racist – who can only bring evil to the cause for which you struggle! And we will answer and say to them: Did you ever talk to Brother Malcolm? Did you ever touch him, or have him smile at you? Did you ever really listen to him? Did he ever do a mean thing? Was he ever himself associated with violence or any public disturbance?'

Three members of the Nation of Islam were arrested for his murder – Talmadge Hayer, Norman 3X Butler, and Thomas 15X Johnson. All three men were convicted of first-degree murder and sentenced to life.

Ostensibly, Malcolm's death was a case of infighting between black radicals, but rumours began to circulate that, while the assassins may have been members of the Nation of Islam, they had been manipulated by government agencies. An investigation revealed that several members of the audience belonged to the New York Police Department's highly secretive Bureau of Special Services which collaborated with the FBI's controversial Counter-Intelligence Program COINTELPRO, set up to disrupt organisations the Bureau considered subversive. One of its undercover agents was Gene Roberts, Malcolm's bodyguard at the time of the killing. Four days after the assassination, one of Malcolm's senior followers, Leon 4X Ameer, said he was convinced his life was in danger. He was found dead, apparently from an overdose of sleeping pills. The story spread that he had been on the point of revealing evidence of government involvement in Malcolm's murder, and that the security forces had staged his apparent suicide.

While Talmadge Hayer was certainly guilty, there was evidence that his two co-defendants were not even at the Audubon Ballroom at the time of the assassination. The other killers escaped and have never been brought to justice. Hayer also asserted that he was not a member of the Nation of Islam and that he had been hired to commit the murder. The man who hired him was not a Muslim, he said. Perhaps he had been a government agent. Clearly J. Edgar Hoover and many others in the security forces would not have shed a tear for Malcolm X. Even the *New York Times* ran the headline 'The Apostle of Hate Is Dead'.

Earl Grant, one of Malcolm X's associates who was present at the assassination, later wrote: 'About five minutes later, a most incredible scene took place. Into the hall sauntered about a dozen policemen. They were strolling at about the pace one would expect of them if they were patrolling a quiet park. They did not seem to be at all excited or concerned about the circumstances. I could hardly believe my eyes. Here were New York City policemen, entering a room from which at least a dozen shots had been heard, and yet not one of them had his gun out! As a matter of absolute fact, some of them even had their hands in their pockets.'

Malcolm's family blamed Louis Farrakhan. In 1993, he said: 'Was Malcolm your traitor or ours? And if we dealt with him like a nation deals with a traitor, what the hell business is it of yours? A nation has to be able to deal with traitors and cutthroats and turncoats.'

Later he denied ordering the assassination of Malcolm X, but acknowledged that he 'created the atmosphere that ultimately led to Malcolm X's assassination'.

'I may have been complicit in words that I spoke', he said. 'I acknowledge that and regret that any word that I have said caused the loss of life of a human being.'

21

JOHN F. KENNEDY 1963

On 22 November 1963 President John F. Kennedy made a fateful trip to Texas to patch up a feud between Democratic governor John B. Connally and Democratic Senator Ralph Yarborough. Riding through Dallas in an open-topped car at 12.30 Central Standard Time, Kennedy and Connally were hit by sniper fire. They were rushed to Parkland Memorial Hospital. Connally survived, but Kennedy had suffered massive head wounds and was beyond saving. He had been president for just 1,037 days.

The Secret Service had been concerned that the motorcade might be a target for a gunman, but the president had wanted to visit Dallas as part of his re-election campaign and to raise funds for the Democratic Party. Everything went smoothly at first. Crowds lining the streets cheered and waved.

The motorcade had nearly completed its route when it pulled into Dealey Plaza. But as Kennedy's car passed the Texas School Book Depository a number of shots rang out. The president was struck in the shoulder and then by a bullet in the head. Connally was also hit.

A security man jumped on to the car to shield the president and his wife. By then it was too late. When they arrived at the hospital, it was clear that Kennedy was not going to survive. A priest was called, but by the time he arrived, the president had died. Meanwhile, Governor Connally was undergoing emergency surgery, and eventually pulled through.

That afternoon, Kennedy's body was driven to the presidential aeroplane. Since this was a murder, there should have been a forensic examination by the coroner before the body left the hospital. This was never done. On board Air Force One, Vice President Lyndon B. Johnson was sworn into office. The presidential party was then flown to Washington DC, where an autopsy was performed at Bethesda Naval Hospital.

A twenty-four-year-old employee of the Book Depository named Lee Harvey Oswald was arrested. He denied the crime, though there was substantial evidence against him. Two days later he was shot and killed by Jack Ruby, a local nightclub owner, in the basement of a Dallas police station.

Kennedy lay in state in the Capitol Rotunda while some 250,000 people filed past. He was given a state funeral in St Matthew's Cathedral in Washington. It was attended by ninety-two heads of state. Thousands packed the streets to pay their last respects. The caisson carrying his flag-draped coffin was followed by a riderless horse, symbol of a fallen leader. President Kennedy was buried in Arlington National Cemetery, where two of his children now lie beside him. The world mourned his passing – a youthful beacon of hope had been cruelly snuffed out.

A week after the assassination, a commission was set up under Chief Justice Earl Warren. The 888-page report of the Warren Commission, published on 24 September 1964, found that a lone gunman, Lee Harvey Oswald, was responsible. He had fired three shots at the president. The first had missed the motorcade. The second had wounded both Kennedy and the governor of Texas. The final shot had hit Kennedy in the head, killing him. But there were puzzling aspects to the 'lone gunman theory'. To both experts and the general public alike, it seemed unlikely that the same bullet could hit two people. This became known as the 'Magic Bullet Theory'. What's more, Lee Harvey Oswald had links to the Soviet Union.

Oswald had been born in New Orleans on 18 October 1939. His father had died shortly after his birth and, at the age of three, his mother had sent him to live in a children's home. She later remarried and he rejoined the family, but as a teenager, he showed behavioural problems.

He became a Marxist and, bizarrely, joined the US Marines. After he left the Marines, he defected to the Soviet Union, where he applied to become a citizen. When his application was rejected, he attempted suicide. He was then allowed to stay, married and had a child there. In June 1962, the family moved back to the US, eventually settling in Dallas. His wife later claimed that in March 1963 he had attempted to assassinate General Edwin Walker, a right-wing political figure.

On 14 October Oswald found a job at the Texas School Book Depository. On the day of the assassination, Oswald was seen at his workplace at 11.55am, and then again at 12.31pm. His landlady testified that he had come home after that, followed by a police car. When he was approached in the street by a police officer, J. D. Tippit, he pulled out a gun and fired several times before running away, leaving the officer dying on the sidewalk. Oswald was then seen slipping into a movie theatre without paying. The cops were called and he was soon under arrest.

In custody, Oswald revealed that he worked at the Book Depository. The police found that his handprint matched one on the rifle abandoned near the scene of the crime. Moreover, witnesses testified that they had actually seen Oswald shooting from the window. Oswald denied everything.

On 24 November 1963, Oswald was being escorted through the basement of Dallas Police Headquarters towards an armoured car that was to take him to the nearby county jail, when Jack Ruby, a Dallas nightclub owner, shot Oswald in the stomach from point-blank range. Oswald died soon afterwards.

This raised fresh questions. How had Ruby found it so easy to penetrate the security surrounding Oswald? Had he killed Oswald to prevent him from telling the truth about the killing? If the assassination has not been planned by the Soviet Union, was it the work of the Mafia? Ruby had connections to organised crime.

After serving in the US Army Air Force during World War II, Ruby had run several nightclubs in Dallas. Between 1949 and 24 November 1963, he had been arrested eight times on charges which included disturbing the peace, carrying a concealed weapon and permitting dancing after hours. He had been suspended by the Texas Liquor Control Board on several occasions. There was also evidence indicating he had been involved in illegal gambling, narcotics and prostitution, activities normally controlled by the Mob.

At first, Ruby claimed that he had shot Oswald out of sympathy for Kennedy's widow Jackie, then changed his plea to insanity. He was convicted of the murder and sentenced to death. His conviction was overturned on appeal, but he died of cancer while awaiting a new trial.

In 1976, the House Select Committee on Assassinations re-examined the evidence surrounding the assassination.

Evidence was collected from eyewitnesses and from people who had photographed, filmed or recorded the motorcade. Recordings of the gunshots indicated that there were possibly two gunmen and that the fatal bullet had been fired, not by Oswald, but by an unknown gunman hiding in an area known as the Grassy Knoll. But the committee was unable to identify the other gunman or the extent of the conspiracy.

What was certain was that the assassination of John Kennedy had robbed the world of an inspiring leader. In his inaugural address, he said: 'Let the word go forth from this time and place, to friend and foe alike, that the torch has been passed to a new generation of Americans – born in this century, tempered by war, disciplined by a hard and bitter peace, proud of our ancient heritage – and unwilling to witness or permit the slow undoing of those human rights to which this Nation has always been committed, and to which we are committed today at home and around the world.

'Let every nation know, whether it wishes us well or ill, that we shall pay any price, bear any burden, meet any hardship, support any friend, oppose any foe, in order to assure the survival and the success of liberty.'

During his short term in office, he had advanced the cause of civil rights for African Americans. After the Cold War confrontation in the Cuban Missile Crisis, he made peace overtures to the Soviet Union. And he had begun the space programme that resulted in men landing on the Moon. True, he sent military advisors to Vietnam, but there were indications that he would have pulled out if he had survived until the 1964 election. Instead, the war dragged on for another ten years, consuming millions of lives.

Since Kennedy's death his reputation has become tarnished. When his widow, Jackie Kennedy, married Greek shipping magnate Aristotle Onassis in 1968, Associated Press claimed that she had 'broken the spell'. It was also revealed that Kennedy was an insatiable womaniser, sharing the sexual favours of Marilyn Monroe with his brother Bobby. Another mistress was shared with a notorious Mafioso and Mafia money was thought to have secured his election in 1960.

22

NGO DINH DIEM 1963

Just three weeks before the assassination of President Kennedy, the president of South Vietnam, Ngo Dinh Diem, was murdered in Saigon. He had come to power in 1955, forming the Republic of Vietnam in the south of the country. The north was held by the Communists. Under the Geneva Accords ending the First Indochina War in 1954, there were supposed to be elections to unify the country. Diem refused to hold them. This precipitated the Second Indochina War, also known as the Vietnam War. He was murdered by the South Vietnamese military, possibly with the connivance of the Americans, in an attempt to prosecute the war more vigorously. However, it was subsequently found impossible to form a stable government in South Vietnam, which fell to the Communist North in 1975.

Diem had been born in a Catholic village near Hué City in central Vietnam in 1901. A hundred of his father's clan had been burnt alive in a church in an anti-Catholic riot led by Buddhist monks. His father had been studying in a Catholic school in British Malaya at the time. Returning to Vietnam, he worked as an interpreter for the French who were colonising Indochina, rising to become a counsellor to Emperor Thành Thái under the French colonial regime.

One of twelve children, Diem followed his elder brother into a seminary, but quit to attend a French lycée in Hué. Declining a scholarship to study in France, he enrolled at the prestigious School of Public Administration and Law in Hanoi, a French school that prepared young Vietnamese to serve in the colonial administration. During his career as a mandarin, Diem was known for his work ethic and incorruptibility, but he irritated the French by his frequent calls to grant more autonomy to Vietnam.

He became governor of Bin Thuan Province, where he helped the French suppress peasant revolts organised by the Communists. Under Emperor Bao Dai, he became interior minister, but quit when his calls for the French to allow a Vietnamese legislature were rejected, later denouncing Bao Dai as 'nothing but an instrument in the hands of the French'. Though under surveillance, he continued his calls for independence as a private citizen.

When Vietnam was invaded by the Japanese during World War II, he again called for an independent Vietnam, but was ignored. He was offered the position of prime minister under Bao Dai, but when he hesitated he found that the role had already been filled.

When the Japanese withdrew in September 1945, the Communist leader Ho Chi Minh proclaimed the Democratic Republic of Vietnam in the North and began fighting the French when they returned. Ho asked Diem to be his minister of the interior, but he refused and pursued his own non-Communist nationalist agenda. In 1950, the Communist Vietminh sentenced him to death *in absentia* and

Ho Chi Minh's cadres tried to assassinate him. He went into exile seeking American support.

When the French surrendered to Vietnamese forces at Dien Bien Phu, a conference was convened in Geneva. It decided that the Communists should hold the North, while Bao Dai should control the South until elections were held in 1956 to reunite the country. Diem became prime minster. Attempts were made by the military to oust him, but with American support he ousted the generals who opposed him.

Diem won a fraudulent referendum in 1955 and declared South Vietnam a republic with himself as president, while Bao Dai went into exile in France. The Communists sent an assassin who shot at him from close range but missed and was subdued before he could loose off another shot.

Diem rejected the Geneva Accords on the grounds that it was not possible to have free elections in the North. Fearing the spread of Communism, the US supported him, but forced Diem to hold legislative elections in 1959. He did so though the opposition were suppressed. Nevertheless, when US Vice President Lyndon B. Johnson visited Saigon in May 1961, he declared Diem to be the 'Winston Churchill of Asia'.

The Communists saw Diem as an American puppet and, in 1960, the government in Hanoi decided that the only way to reunify the country was by force. It established the National Liberation Front in the South. This was a front organisation that aimed to unite all the political opponents of the increasingly dictatorial regime of President Diem. He dubbed the NLF dismissively the Vietcong and cranked up repression in the countryside to counter the guerrillas, but only succeeded in increasing their numbers.

President Eisenhower had already given military aid to the Diem government in South Vietnam. Kennedy increased it.

He also sent a new elite corps of frontline troops who would wage the war against Communism – the Green Berets. At Diem's request, the US began spraying the defoliant Agent Orange on the forest to rob the Vietcong of their hiding places.

An attempted coup in 1960 failed to topple Diem. Then there was an attempt to assassinate Diem and his family in 1962 when two air force officers bombarded the Presidential Palace. Meanwhile Diem handed out weapons to Catholics to repel the Vietcong. Some Buddhist villages converted en masse to Catholicism in order to receive aid or to avoid being forcibly resettled into the Strategic Villages set up by Diem's regime.

Discontent grew among South Vietnam's Buddhist majority. A ban on displaying Buddhist banners provoked a protest in Hué, whose suppression resulted in the deaths of unarmed civilians. The Buddhists made five demands: freedom to fly religious flags, an end to arbitrary arrests, compensation for the Hué victims, punishment for the officials responsible and religious equality. Soldiers armed with tear gas and dogs were sent in to disperse protesters. When that failed, crowds were sprayed with chemicals, resulting in sixty-seven being hospitalised. Then in June 1963, a Buddhist monk set fire to himself in the middle of a busy Saigon intersection. The photograph went around the world, a potent image of the failure of the Diem regime.

Other monks followed suit. Over a thousand were arrested. Protests by the general population were brutally suppressed. High school students also took to the streets and children as young as five were sent to re-education camps. The US showed its disapproval of the treatment of the Buddhists when the American Ambassador Henry Cabot Lodge visited a pagoda.

In July 1963, Lucien Conein, a CIA operative, served as a liaison officer between Lodge and generals planning a coup against Diem, delivering $42,000 to the plotters after Kennedy's administration had asked the embassy to explore the possibility of regime change. The South Vietnamese army surrounded the Presidential Palace, telling Diem they were staging a phony uprising, only to crush it, reasserting presidential power. Instead they seized key installations.

When the real situation became clear, Diem refused to resign and go into exile. He eventually surrendered, but the US dithered about sending a plane to take him out of the country as it would implicate them in the coup. Before they could be arrested, Diem and his brother escaped from the palace, but were caught by renegade officers who shot and stabbed them. The leaders of the coup were horrified. It was announced on the radio that they had committed suicide. Kennedy was shocked when he heard what had happened and blamed himself for approving the cable that authorised the coup in the first place. Diem was buried in an unmarked grave in a cemetery next to the house of the US Ambassador.

A photograph of the dead brothers was circulated. They were dressed in the robes of Roman Catholic priests with their hands tied behind their backs. *Time* magazine ran the picture with the caption: '"Suicide" with no hands.'

Hearing of Diem's assassination, Ho Chi Minh said: 'I can scarcely believe the Americans would be so stupid.'

The North Vietnamese Politburo were prescient when they announced: 'The consequences of the 1 November coup d'état will be contrary to the calculations of the US imperialists... Diem was one of the strongest individuals resisting the people and Communism. Everything that could be done in an attempt to crush the revolution was carried out by Diem. Diem was one of the most competent lackeys of the US imperialists… Among the anti-Communists in South Vietnam or exiled in other countries, no one has sufficient political assets and abilities to cause others to obey. Therefore, the lackey administration cannot be stabilized. The coup d'état on 1 November 1963 will not be the last.'

The leader of the coup, General Duong Van Minh, took over as head of a military junta. General Nguyen Van Thieu won an election in 1967 and ruled until the fall of Saigon in 1975. Tran Van Huong was president for a week that April, then Duong Van Minh was president again for two days before going into exile. It was clear to observers the Diem's assassination had led to the collapse of the regime, the end of the first Republic of Vietnam and the Communist takeover of the whole country.

23

MEDGAR EVERS 1963

The struggle for African American civil rights in the 1960s was a bloody one. One of its many martyrs was Medgar Evers, field secretary for the National Association for the Advancement of Colored People in Mississippi. He was murdered on 12 June 1963 by a member of the Ku Klux Klan named Byron De La Beckwith who was acquitted by two all-white juries in the 1960s. It was not until 1994 that he was finally convicted and he spent the last three years of his life in jail.

Born on 2 July 1925 in Decatur, Mississippi, Medgar Wiley Evers was the son of a small holder. He and his four siblings had to walk twelve miles to attend a segregated school. Drafted into the US Army in 1943, he fought in the Battle of Normandy in June 1944 and the rest of the French campaign. At the end of the war, he was honourably discharged with the rank of sergeant.

Returning to Mississippi, he attended Alcorn Agricultural and Mechanical College, a segregated land-grant institution. Graduating with a bachelor's degree in business administration in 1952, he went to work as a travelling salesman for the Magnolia Mutual Insurance Company, a business founded, run by and serving African Americans. His job took him to impoverished areas of Mississippi. Aware of the poverty and oppression suffered by black southerners, he became an active volunteer in the Mississippi chapter of the NAACP.

In 1954, following the US Supreme Court ruling that segregated public schools were unconstitutional, Evers applied to enrol at the University of Mississippi Law School. This was an NAACP test case and Evers rejected on racial grounds.

To pursue the cause, he took the newly created and salaried position of field secretary of the NAACP in Jackson. His duties were bureaucratic – collecting and publicising information on civil rights abuses in Mississippi. However, angered by his treatment by Ole Miss, Evers helped organise boycotts and direct action to integrate beaches, parks and bus services, sometimes to the dismay of the conservative NAACP leadership.

He investigated the murder of Emmett Till, a fourteen-year-old black boy who was beaten, lynched and mutilated for allegedly whistling at a white woman. His murderers were acquitted by an all-white jury in 1955. Protected by the law against double jeopardy, the two men accused publicly admitted in a 1956 interview with *Look* magazine that they had killed Till. In 2008, the white woman concerned admitted that the testimony she had given was false.

Evers also acted as advisor to James Meredith in his quest to enrol as the first black student at the University of Mississippi. Denied admission twice, Meredith took the matter to the US Supreme Court who found in his favour. The Mississippi state legislature quickly passed laws denying Meredith admission. The governor of Mississippi was found in contempt and Attorney General Robert F. Kennedy sent five hundred US Marshals to accompany Meredith to his registration.

Such high-profile cases made Evers a target for white supremacists. Unlike Martin Luther King, Evers was not an advocate of non-violence in the face of white terrorism. He bought a rifle and kept it in his car to protect himself and his family. A race war was a real possibility in the South, he thought, if black people collectively created a real political movement to resist their oppression. If white structural racism was permanent, what other choice did African Americans have? He even considered demanding a separate all-black state, separating the races territorially.

His widow Myrlie said that her husband believed 'you must always be prepared for whatever comes our way. And we are talking about the guns, the arms, collecting what we would need to fight if by chance we ended up in a race war, which he felt could possibly happen... [If we] found ourselves in a separate part of America, how we would not be starved out, how we would be in a location where we would not be surrounded and wiped out at one time... He was thinking about building a nation of black people.'

On 28 May 1963, there was an attempt to run him over outside an NAACP office and a Molotov cocktail was thrown into the carport of his home.

In the face of growing militancy among black people and the violent obduracy of whites in the South, President Kennedy decided that he must address the nation on the matter of civil rights. On 11 June 1963, he went on television and said: 'If an American, because his skin is dark, cannot eat lunch in a restaurant open to the public, if he cannot send his children to the best public school available, if he cannot vote for the public officials who will represent him, if, in short, he cannot enjoy the full and free life which all of us want, then who among us would be content to have the color of his skin changed and stand in his place? Who among us would then be content with the counsels of patience and delay?'

As, for re-election the following year, Kennedy would need the support of white democrats in the South – the so-called Dixiecrats – this was judged to be the most courageous speech of his presidency. Mrs Evers watched it in bed with her three children. Her husband was out at a local church meeting with other activists. He returned home just after midnight with white T-shirts carrying the slogan: 'Jim Crow Must Go.'

Normally he was followed home by at least two FBI cars and one police car. That night he had no escort. Neither the FBI nor the local cops explained why they had not accompanied him that night. However, it was known that many members of the local police force were also members of the Klan.

Beckwith was lurking in the honeysuckle bushes across the road with a .30-06 bolt-action Winchester hunting rifle. The sound of Evers slamming the car door was followed rapidly by a burst of gunfire. Myrlie ran downstairs while the children assumed the position they had been taught to adopt if their house ever came under attack. By the time she reached the front door, Medgar's body was slumped in front of her.

'When Medgar was felled by that shot, and I rushed out and saw him lying there and people from the neighbourhood began to gather, there were also some whose color happened to be white,' said Myrlie. 'I don't think I have ever hated as much in my life as I did at that particular moment anyone who had white skin.'

A bullet had gone through Evers' back and exited through his chest. A few hours later, he was pronounced dead. News of his death spread rapidly through the black community in Jackson and a riot was narrowly averted.

President Kennedy wrote to Mrs Evers, saying: 'I extend to you and your children my sincerest condolences on the tragic death of your husband. Although comforting thoughts are difficult at a time like this, surely there can be some solace in the realization of the justice of the cause for which your husband gave his life. Achievement of the goals he did so much to promote will enable his children and the generations to follow to share fully and equally in the benefits and advantages our Nation has to offer.'

Medgar Evers was buried with full military honours in Arlington Cemetery and the NAACP honoured him posthumously with its 1963 Spingarn Medal, awarded annually for outstanding achievement by an African American and named after NAACP chairman Joel Elias Spingarn.

On the day of Evers' funeral, around a thousand black youths marched through Jackson, joined later by their elders. When police ordered them to disperse, scuffles broke out. The crowd chanted: 'We want the killer.'

Meeting their demand should not have been difficult. The rifle that was fired was traced to Beckwith, whose fingerprints were on its telescopic sight. Some witnesses reported seeing a man who fit his description in the area that night, as well as a car that looked like his white Plymouth Valiant. If that wasn't enough, he had openly bragged to fellow Klansmen about carrying out the shooting. Though it took several weeks, he was eventually arrested on the strength of this overwhelming evidence and charged with the murder. He was not brought to justice for another thirty years. Throughout the hearings he wore a Confederate flag pin.

After his untimely death Evers remained a symbol of the civil rights movement. The murder shocked both blacks and whites who began to see the extent to which racial violence was tolerated in the Deep South. It led President Kennedy to ask Congress to enact a new and comprehensive civil rights law, an action that committed the federal government to enforce racial equality throughout the United States. His murder also inspired Nina Simone to write the song 'Mississippi Goddam' which became an anthem of the civil rights movement.

Evers' name remains alive through the NAACP's Medgar Evers Fund, which provides financial assistance to improve housing, health care, education and economic opportunity for African Americans. A branch of the City University of New York was named Medgar Evers College in 1969. Myrlie Evers served as interim president of the NAACP in 1995.

24

PATRICE LUMUMBA 1961

When the Congo won its independence from Belgium, its colonial master, in 1960, the firebrand Patrice Lumumba became its first prime minister. However, the Belgian government had not given up its interests there and fomented a political crisis. There were rebellions against the government. After a few months, Lumumba was forced out of office and went on the run but was assassinated by Belgian forces on 17 January 1961. Since then the largest country in sub-Saharan Africa has changed its name several times and suffered a brutal dictatorship, civil war and inter-tribal violence.

Patrice Hemery Lumumba was born on 2 July 1925 in Onalua, Kasai Province, which at the time was part of the Belgian Congo, to a family of farmers. A member of the small Batetela tribe, his original name was Okit'Asombo, which means 'heir of the cursed or those who die quickly'. His principal rivals Moise Tshombe and Joseph Kasavubu were members of larger tribes from whom they derived their political power.

He attended a Protestant missionary school. With an interest in the Enlightenment ideas of Jean-Jacques

Rousseau and Voltaire, Molière and Victor Hugo, he wrote for a Congolese journal. Much of his work was anti-imperialist. Nevertheless he took Belgian citizenship. Moving to the capital Léopoldville, now Kinshasa, he found work as a postal clerk, joined the trade union and became regional president in 1955.

A highly intelligent man, he was interested in politics and joined the Belgian Liberal Party but was arrested and charged with embezzling funds. Convicted, he spent a year in prison, which helped to radicalise him. On his release he helped found the National Congolese Movement (Mouvement National Congolais, or MNC) on 5 October 1958. That December, he attended the first All-African People's Conference in Accra, Ghana, and the MNC joined the organisation.

In 1959, the Belgian government promised to give the Congo its independence within five years of the local elections that December. The nationalists feared that the Belgians were going to use the five years to install a puppet administration and decided to boycott the elections. There were riots. In October a clash in Stanleyville left thirty dead and Lumumba was arrested for allegedly inciting it.

The MNC changed tack, fought the elections and did well. The Belgian government convened a conference in Brussels to discuss political change. The MNC refused to attend unless Lumumba was there too. He was released and flown to Brussels. The conference decided that the Congo would become independent on 23 June 1960, following national elections in May. With Lumumba at its head, the MNC won the elections. He was asked to form a government and took power as prime minister on 23 June with Joseph Kasavubu as president.

It was clear that Lumumba's task was not going to be an easy one. In the ceremony marking independence, King Baudouin of Belgium gave a speech undermining it. He praised the great achievements of the Belgian monarchy and the Belgian people in civilising the Congo, despite the atrocities of the late nineteenth and early twentieth centuries when the indigenous population were forced by the most brutal methods to produce rubber. He talked of how the Belgians had liberated the Congolese from the Atlantic slave trade, forcing them into domestic slavery instead, how they had modernised the country, and he commented on how inexperienced the Africans were at governing themselves.

Lumumba was incensed and delivered an impromptu speech recalling the bitter struggle of the Congolese people to free themselves from the poverty and oppression of the colonial regime.

'For this independence of the Congo, although being proclaimed today by agreement with Belgium, an amicable country, with which we are on equal terms, no Congolese worthy of the name will ever be able to forget that it was by fighting that it has been won, a day-to-day fight, an ardent and idealistic fight, a fight in which we were spared neither privation nor suffering, and for which we gave our strength and our blood,' he said. 'We are proud of this struggle, of tears, of fire, and of blood, to the depths of our being, for it was a noble and just struggle, and indispensable to put an end to the humiliating slavery which was imposed upon us by force.'

The true history of his country, he continued, was that black people were forced to live in miserable conditions, while yielding their wealth and land to white overlords who treated them as inferiors. Those blacks who had dared to protest had been shot in cold blood by the authorities or exiled. Those days were now over, he said, and he called on his fellow citizens to build a strong country so that the Congo would be an inspiration to independence movements in the rest of Africa.

Not surprisingly, the Belgians were not best pleased with Lumumba's speech. *Time* magazine characterised it as a 'venomous attack'. In the West, many feared that the speech was a call to arms against the many Belgians who remained in the Congo. Indeed, a few days after independence, some army units rebelled because of the misgivings of their Belgian commander. Lumumba responded by Africanising the army, making former soldier Joseph Mobutu chief of staff, despite his alleged ties to Belgian and US intelligence services.

Europeans lived in fear. Some were killed. Others fled to mineral-rich Katanga Province, which seceded under Moise Tshombe with the support of the Belgian government who sent six thousand troops. The UN also sent a peacekeeping force, while Lumumba called on the Soviet Union for help. President Kasavubu then dismissed Lumumba from office, though the president was only supposed to have a ceremonial role.

Lumumba refused to go and tried to dismiss Kasavubu from office. Kasavubu then staged a coup with the support of sections of the military led by Mobutu, who in turn was supported by the Belgians and the CIA. He then seized power.

His life now in danger, Lumumba had no choice but to abandon his post. On 1 December 1961, he fled but was captured by Mobutu's men and charged with inciting the army to rebellion. The United Nations asked that Lumumba be properly treated according to the laws of the land, while the Soviet Union asked for Mobutu to be disarmed and that Lumumba be restored to power. Lumumba's supporters then began to threaten that, unless he was released immediately, there would be violence against all Belgians still living in the Congo. At the UN the Soviet Union refused to permit the UN to increase its peacekeeping force and several countries withdrew their personnel.

Lumumba was transferred to a prison in the Katanga amid rumours that he was being mistreated. Eventually, it was decided that Lumumba should be formally dismissed from his post, but allowed to return to his official residence, where he was placed under house arrest.

He escaped, but it was not long before Mobutu's troops caught up with him, capturing him once more. The UN refused to intervene and Lumumba was taken to Mobutu's residence, where he was publicly humiliated and beaten in front of the world's media. Lumumba was then returned to the custody of his enemy Tshombe.

There is some controversy about who ordered Lumumba's assassination, but there is little doubt that he was murdered by Katangan soldiers under the command of Belgian officers. What appears to have happened is that on 17 January 1961 Lumumba was led into the bush, where an army firing squad was waiting. Lumumba and two of his government aides were lined up and shot, one at a time, in front of Tshombe and other officials. The bodies were buried, but later disinterred and dissolved in acid.

Rumours of his assassination leaked out. The official announcement was that Lumumba had escaped and been murdered by hostile villagers. Many years later, documentation was found showing that Belgian soldiers had been present at his assassination. In 2002, the Belgian government issued a statement admitting 'partial' responsibility for Lumumba's murder and apologising to the Congolese people.

It was also revealed that during the 1960s, President Eisenhower had called on the CIA to murder Lumumba as he was considered a Communist threat to Western security. However, it seems they were beaten to it by the Belgians and the Katangans.

Under Mobutu, the Congo became the Democratic Republic of the Congo and later Zaire. Eliminating all political opposition, he established a one-party state. With the support of the US, Zaire was seen as a bastion against Communism. Mobutu became infamous as a tyrannical leader, heading the most corrupt regime in Africa that lasted for thirty-five years.

In 1996, the genocide in Rwanda spilled over into the Congo. Mobutu fled the following year and was replaced by Laurent Kabila. He was assassinated in 2001 and succeeded by his son Joseph Kabila. Disorder continued with ethnic violence and fighting over the country's mineral riches. Thousands were forced to flee their homes. Women were raped and millions of children died of starvation.

25

MAHATMA GANDHI 1948

Mohandas Karamchand Gandhi was the apostle of non-violence who used civil disobedience to gain independence for India from British colonial rule. After thirty years of struggle he succeeded. On 15 August 1947, the British granted India its independence. But just five months later he was assassinated by one of those he had liberated. As well as advocating non-violence, Gandhi also believed that people of all religious persuasions should have equal rights: Hindus were no more important than Muslims. This made him many enemies among radical Hindu political factions in India. On 30 January 1948, Hindu fanatic Nathuram Godse shot and killed him as he walked through the streets to attend a prayer meeting in New Delhi. His death was greeted by rioting. But over a million people joined the five-mile long funeral procession to mourn the loss of the man they called 'Mahatma', or 'great soul'. Jawaharlal Nehru, the first prime minister of the newly independent India, said: 'The light has gone out of our lives.'

Born in 1869 in Porbandar, western India, Gandhi travelled to London in 1888 to study law and was called to the bar at the age of twenty-two. Failing as a lawyer in

Bombay, he moved to South Africa on a one-year contract. Up until then, he had thought of himself as British first and Indian second and was shocked to face racial discrimination because of the colour of his skin. He stayed on to fight for Indian immigrants' rights there, later employing non-violent protest for the first time. During the Boer War he raised a unit of Indian stretcher-bearers and won the Queen's South Africa Medal.

On his return to India in 1915, he became involved in politics, and began to campaign on behalf of the Indian National Congress against the British government, encouraging Indians to buy Indian rather than British goods. He consistently advocated non-violent protest, but even so, became a thorn in the side of the British authorities and was imprisoned several times for his activities. However, during World War I, he helped recruit Indian volunteers for the British. In 1920, he became the leader of the Indian National Congress and on 26 January 1930 declared the Independence of India.

The British refused to recognise this but were prepared to negotiate. In 1931, he famously attended a political conference in Britain dressed only in the simple clothes of an Indian peasant to remind the world of the harsh poverty that most of his countrymen endured.

Gandhi opposed Indian involvement in World War II. His incarceration allowed the Muslim League to flourish under Muhammad Ali Jinnah. While Gandhi wanted a single united India, Jinnah insisted on a separate Muslim state that became Pakistan.

With Britain exhausted by the war, the new Labour government elected in 1945 relinquished India. Jinnah then got his way and the country was to be partitioned. This led to fourteen million people being displaced and anywhere from 200,000 to two million being killed.

Having co-operated with the British, Gandhi was accused of helping to partition the country, a thing he was fundamentally opposed to. He was also criticised for weakening the Hindus' political power through his belief in the equality of all religious faiths. And those who opposed him did not believe in non-violence.

On 20 January 1948, there was an assassination attempt on Gandhi. He was making a speech at Birla House in New Delhi when a grenade was thrown, causing the crowd to stampede. Once they had dispersed and Gandhi was alone, another grenade was to have been thrown, but the second assassin lost his nerve.

Ten days later, Gandhi was on his way to a prayer meeting at Birla House, the home of a prominent industrialist where he often stayed during his visits to New Delhi. At about five o'clock, people began to gather for the meeting. Gandhi arrived late at about twelve minutes past five. It was a cold evening and he was wearing a homespun shawl over his loin cloth. As he walked across the grass, accompanied by his followers, onlookers knelt or bowed their heads. One said: 'Gandhi, you're late.' This slowed his pace. Then, suddenly, a man wearing khaki pushed his way through the crowd. Several shots rang out and Gandhi fell to the ground, mortally wounded, his loincloth heavily stained with blood. A doctor rushed to the scene, but it was too late to save him. As Gandhi lay dying, the police took charge, dispersing the weeping crowds and carrying the body away.

At 6pm on All India Radio, it was announced that a lone gunman had shot Gandhi on his way to Birla House. He had been killed by three pistol shots to the chest. The killer was

Nathuram Godse, a Hindu activist who was thought to be connected to the militant Hindu organisation Mahasabha.

In an impromptu broadcast, Nehru said: 'Friends and comrades, the light has gone out of our lives, and there is darkness everywhere, and I do not quite know what to tell you or how to say it. Our beloved leader, Bapu as we called him, the father of the nation, is no more. Perhaps I am wrong to say that; nevertheless, we will not see him again, as we have seen him for these many years, we will not run to him for advice or seek solace from him, and that is a terrible blow, not only for me, but for millions and millions in this country.'

Godse had been seized by Herbert Reiner Jr, a thirty-two-year-old, newly arrived vice-consul at the American embassy in Delhi, who shoved him towards police guards. The crowd turned on him. To save him from the mob he was taken into custody and marched away.

Given the confusion of the assassination events, accounts of what Gandhi said as he lay dying differ. Some say that his last words were '*He Ram!*' (Oh God!), which may have expressed his spiritual commitment to God or, perhaps, were just an expression of surprise at being attacked. These words are inscribed on Gandhi's memorial tomb in New Delhi. Others believe that the Mahatma exclaimed 'Rama, Rama' and, as he fell, he put his hands together in the gesture of namaste, a religious gesture symbolising love, respect and connection to others.

According to some accounts, Gandhi died where he fell. Others say he was carried into Birla House, where he died about thirty minutes later as one of Gandhi's family members read verses from Hindu scriptures.

After his death, Gandhi was cremated on a funeral pyre, the Hindu custom. His ashes were collected in twenty urns which were taken around India and the ashes scattered on the waters of the country's great rivers, in accordance with Gandhi's wishes.

Godse and eight others went on trial for murder and conspiracy. The prosecution called 149 witnesses, the defence none. The court found all of the defendants except one guilty as charged. While he did not deny killing Gandhi, Godse sought to justify himself. He blamed Gandhi for partition and being indifferent to the suffering of Hindus. Godse was convicted and sentenced to death. Seven others were found guilty of conspiracy, including Godse's brother Gopal, who was given a life sentence. The president of the Mahasabha, Vinayak Damodar Savarkar, was also thought to be behind the assassination, but there was not enough evidence to link him to it.

Pleas for commutation of Godse's death sentence were made by Gandhi's two sons, Manilal Gandhi and Ramdas Gandhi, but were rejected by India's prime minister, Jawaharlal Nehru. On 15 November 1949, Godse was hanged in Ambala jail. It was not a quick and easy death. His neck did not snap, killing him instantly. Instead he was slowly strangled.

Today, Gandhi is remembered as the architect of Indian independence, and his philosophy of non-violence and civil disobedience has inspired freedom fighters around the world, including Martin Luther King, the Dalai Lama, Nelson Mandela and Steve Biko. But according to Gandhi himself, his teachings were nothing new, as he often stated: 'Truth and non-violence are as old as the hills.' He also pointed out: 'An eye for eye only ends up making the whole world blind.'

He even earned the respect of his old enemy Britain. Prime minister Clement Atlee said: 'Everyone will have learnt with profound horror of the brutal murder of Mr Gandhi and I know that I am expressing the views of the British people in offering to his fellow-countrymen our deep sympathy in the loss of their greatest citizen. Mahatma Gandhi, as he was known in India, was one of the outstanding figures in the world today... For a quarter of a century this one man has been the major factor in every consideration of the Indian problem.'

Albert Einstein added: 'He died as the victim of his own principles, the principle of non-violence. He died because in time of disorder and general irritation in his country, he refused armed protection for himself. It was his unshakable belief that the use of force is an evil in itself, that therefore it must be avoided by those who are striving for supreme justice to his belief.'

26

REINHARD HEYDRICH 1942

As head of the Reich Main Security Office, the combined security services of Nazi Germany, *SS-Obergruppenführer* Reinhard Heydrich was one of the most important men in the Third Reich. Hitler had made him head of the Final Solution, the murder of European Jews. But while most of the Nazi top brass were safely cosseted in Berlin or other secure locations, Heydrich had also been appointed acting Reichsprotektor of the Protectorate of Bohemia and Moravia. This meant he was to spend time in Czechoslovakia where he would be vulnerable, particularly as he drove around in an open-top car.

Heydrich was born in Halle in 1904. His father was strict and instilled German nationalism in his children. At school, Heydrich was teased for his rumoured Jewish ancestry. After the end of World War I, there were clashes between Communist and anti-Communist groups in Halle. At fifteen, he joined a paramilitary Freikorps unit. When order was restored, he joined an anti-Semitic party.

The hyperinflation in Germany between the wars ruined Heydrich's family. He joined the navy and was rapidly promoted. But he was dismissed for breaking off his engagement to marry Lina von Osten, a Nazi Party member. He joined the Nazi Party. Six weeks later, he was a member of the *SS*. The head of the *SS* Heinrich Himmler put him in charge of setting up a counter-intelligence division. Rumours of his Jewish heritage resurfaced, but by then Heydrich had enough power to quash them.

After Hitler came to power, Heydrich's renamed security service – the *Sicherheitsdienst* or *SD* – took over Munich's political police, then he became head of the Gestapo. In that role, he took part in the Night of the Long Knives, murdering any opposition to Hitler within the Nazi Party. In 1936, the Gestapo was given full powers to arbitrarily arrest, kill or send to a concentration camp anyone without judicial interference.

As head of the police, he organised the 1936 Berlin Olympics and the Nazi demonstrations in Austria which led to the Anschluss in 1938. He was also one of the organisers of Kristallnacht, a pogrom against Jews throughout Germany on the night of 9/10 November 1938. And he was the mastermind behind Operation Himmler, the staging of a supposed attack on a German radio station on the Polish border that gave Germany the pretext to invade Poland.

Promotions continued. After Hitler's invasion of Western Europe, Heydrich was in charge of neutralising opposition in occupied countries by arbitrary arrest and murder. Some 100,000 people were murdered in Poland alone. He also formed *Einsatzgruppen* who were sent into the occupied territories to round up Jews. They followed the German Army into the Soviet Union murdering Jews and Commissars as they went.

He organised the use of the railways to deport people to concentration camps, overseeing the construction of more of them. Then, on 20 January 1942, he chaired the Wannsee Conference where the 'Final Solution to the Jewish Question' – their mass murder – was agreed.

It was thought the Reich Protector of Bohemia and Moravia, Konstantin von Neurath, was too soft on the Czechs. On 27 September 1941, Heydrich was appointed his deputy, then von Neurath was sent on leave. Heydrich already had a formidable reputation, known variously as 'The Hangman', 'The Blond Beast', 'Himmler's Evil Genius', 'Young Evil God of Death' and 'The Man with the Iron Heart'. He would soon add to that 'The Butcher of Prague'.

His job was to crush resistance in Czechoslovakia and increase the output of arms and motor vehicles from the factories there. He declared martial law and arrested between four and five thousand people. Those who were not executed were sent to concentration camps.

Almost as soon as Heydrich was appointed Acting Protector, the Czech government in exile in London under Edvard Beneš decided that something must be done. His head of intelligence, František Moravec, approached Brigadier Colin Gubbins, who at the time was the Director of Operations in the British Special Operations Executive. They cooked up Operation Anthropoid and two hundred exiled Czechoslovakian soldiers were sent to one of the SOE's commando training camps in Scotland.

Two of them – Jan Kubiš, a Czech, and Jozef Gabčík, a Slovak – were selected to undertake the assassination and dropped in to Czechoslovakia. In Prague they did the detailed planning of the hit. Fearing reprisals, local resistance groups begged the government in exile to call off the operation. Beneš refused as the action would legitimise his government in British eyes.

At 10.30am on 27 May 1942, Heydrich started his daily commute from his home in Panenské Brežany, nine miles north of central Prague, to his headquarters at Prague Castle. He rode in a green, open-topped Mercedes 320 Cabriolet B, driven by *SS-Oberscharführer* Klein. Gabčík and Kubiš waited at a tram stop along the route where a tight curve would force the car to slow down. Another member of the party, Josef Valčík, was stationed around a hundred yards ahead to act as lookout.

As Heydrich's car approached Gabčík stepped out into the road and opened fire with a Sten gun. Heydrich ordered Klein to stop and stood up to shoot Gabčík. Kubiš then threw a briefcase containing a modified hand-grenade at the rear of the car. It detonated, ripping through the rear fender and peppering Heydrich with shrapnel and fibres from the shredded upholstery. Kubiš was also injured but with Gabčík continued shooting at the wounded Heydrich with pistols as he stepped out of the car. Stunned by the explosion, they missed.

Kubiš jumped on a bicycle to make his escape. Heydrich ran after him but collapsed from shock. He ordered Klein to chase after Gabčík. Klein cornered him in a butcher's, but Gabčík shot him twice, wounding him in the leg. Gabčík then jumped on a tram and the two assassins made it back to a safe house.

A Czech woman and an off-duty policeman went to Heydrich's aid and flagged down a delivery van which took him to Bulovka Hospital. There was major damage to his diaphragm, spleen and lung, as well as a fractured rib. The doctors there began treating him. Himmler sent his personal physician and other *SS* doctors.

After a week, Heydrich's condition appeared to be improving, but suddenly he fell into a coma and died at

4.30am on 4 June 1942. A post-mortem concluded he had died of sepsis, but its exact cause was a matter of conjecture.

Hitler ordered reprisals. He wanted ten thousand Czechs executed, but Himmler warned that indiscriminate killings might damage productivity. Instead some thirteen thousand people were arrested including friends and family of the assassins. Kubiš's girlfriend Anna Malinová was seized. She died in the Mauthausen–Gusen concentration camp. But still the assassins had not been caught.

A Gestapo report suggested they were hiding out in the village of Lidice. Hitler ordered its complete destruction. As a result, 199 men were killed and 195 women were deported to Ravensbrück concentration camp. Of the ninety-five children taken prisoner, eighty-one were later killed in gas vans at the Chełmno extermination camp, while eight were adopted by German families. The village of Ležáky was also destroyed, because a radio transmitter had been found there. The population were murdered. Both villages were burnt and the ruins of Lidice were levelled.

Further reprisals were threatened if the assassins had not been caught by 18 June. Karel Curda betrayed the safe house where the assassins had taken refuge for a bounty of one million Reichsmarks. It belonged to the Moravec family. When it was raided on 17 June, Marie Moravec killed herself with a cyanide tablet.

Alois Moravec was unaware of his family's involvement with the resistance. He was tortured along with his seventeen-year-old son Ata, who refused to talk until he was shown his mother's severed head in a fish tank and warned that his father's would be next. He revealed that Gabčík and Kubiš had moved on to the Karel Boromejsky Church. Ata Moravec was executed by the Nazis in Mauthausen on 24

October 1942, the same day as his father, along with Ata's fiancée, her mother and her brother.

Some 750 *Waffen-SS* troops surrounded the church. They tried to flush out the assassins with tear gas. When that failed they called in fire trucks to flood the basement. They failed to find Gabčík and Kubiš alive. They and other supporters in the crypt died either in the furious gun battle that ensued or by suicide.

Hitler attended Heydrich's funeral in Prague, posthumously awarding him the German Order and the Blood Order. The traitor Karel Curda was hanged for high treason in 1947, after attempting suicide.

Winston Churchill was so infuriated by the scale of the reprisals that he suggested levelling three German villages for every Czech village that the Nazis destroyed. Two years after Heydrich's death, Operation Foxley, a similar assassination plan, was drawn up against Hitler, but not implemented. That left Operation Anthropoid as the only successful government-organised assassination of a top-ranking Nazi.

The death of Heydrich did not halt the Holocaust. Ernst Kaltenbrunner, his successor at the RSHA (Reich Main Security Office), oversaw the building of the first three true death camps at Treblinka, Sobibór, and Bełżec. This project was named Operation Reinhard after Heydrich.

27

LEON TROTSKY 1940

Leon Trotsky was seen as one of the heroes of the Bolshevik Revolution in Russia. He was Vladimir Lenin's chosen successor but was pushed aside by the ruthless Joseph Stalin who became a bloodthirsty dictator as bad as Hitler. Trotsky was exiled, then assassinated by Stalin's agents.

On 20 August 1940, Trotsky was savagely attacked at his house in Coyoacán, Mexico by Spanish Communist Jaime Ramón Mercader, who had won his confidence. Mercader had an ice pick hidden in his coat. While Trotsky was reading, Mercader pulled it out and delivered a savage blow to his head, mortally wounding him. Bleeding profusely, Trotsky grappled with his assassin, but eventually collapsed and died. Dubbed an enemy of the people – a term he had used – Trotsky had been tried *in absentia* and sentenced to death in 1936. He was only rehabilitated in 2001, ten years after the collapse of the Soviet Union that he had helped create.

Trotsky was born Lev Davidovich Bronstein on 26 October 1879, by the old Julian calendar still in use in Russia, in the tiny village of Yanovka in the Ukraine, then part of the Russian Empire. He was Jewish – a key factor as Stalin was an anti-Semite. His father was a farmer who was unable to read or write, but the family were relatively well off and the young Bronstein was sent to Odessa to be educated at the age of eight. He enrolled in the University of Odessa to study mathematics at university. After being introduced to Marxism he helped organise the South Russian Workers' Union in the nearby town of Nikolayev and wrote Marxist pamphlets under the name 'Lvov'.

In January 1898 he was arrested and jailed for revolutionary activities. Exiled to Siberia, he escaped to join Lenin and other revolutionaries in London using a forged passport in the name of Trotsky, which he adopted as his revolutionary sobriquet. Under the pen name Pero – meaning 'pen' or 'feather' – he wrote for Lenin's revolutionary newspaper *Iskra – 'The Spark'*. However, at the Second Congress of the Russian Social Democratic Labour Party, he broke with Lenin, supporting the Mensheviks, who envisioned a gradual democratic route to a socialist state, against Lenin's Bolsheviks who believed that a dictatorship of the working classes should be established immediately, by force if necessary.

During the Russian Revolution of 1905, Trotsky returned to Russia to lead the St Petersburg Soviet of Workers' Deputies and organise strikes. He was arrested, tried and exiled. Escaping again in 1907, he settled in Vienna. With the outbreak of World War I, he moved to Switzerland, then Paris. Expelled from France and Spain for his anti-war stance, he moved to New York, where he worked on the socialist newspaper *Novy Mir – 'New World'*.

With the outbreak of the Revolution in February 1917, Trotsky returned to St Petersburg, then renamed Petrograd. Arrested in the crackdown in July, he became a Bolshevik in jail. Following the October Revolution which brought the Bolsheviks to power, he became People's Commissar for Foreign Affairs and led the peace talks with Germany at Brest-Litovsk. During the Russian Civil War he became Commissar for War and was responsible for the creation of the Red Army. His policy of recruiting former Tsarist officers as 'military specialists' brought him into conflict with Stalin.

After the end of the Civil War, Trotsky was seen as Lenin's number two. He founded the Comintern which aimed to foster world revolution. In 1921, the sailors at the Kronshtadt naval base who had backed the revolution in 1917 rebelled against the Communist Party's dictatorship, demanding 'soviets without Bolsheviks'. Trotsky led the force that put them down, shooting or imprisoning those captured.

When Lenin became ill and died in 1924, a bitter power struggle, both ideological and personal, took place between Trotsky and Stalin. Deceived about the date of Lenin's funeral, he was not present for the great state occasion, leaving Stalin centre stage. In January 1925, he was removed from the war commissariat. In October 1926, he was expelled from the Politburo. The following year he was dropped from the Central Committee, then expelled from the Party. In January 1928, he was exiled to Alma Ata in Kazakhstan. The following year he was banished from the Soviet Union altogether.

At first he settled in France, then Norway. Finally, in 1936, he found refuge in Mexico, where he continued to write about the progress of the Revolution, and to agitate against Stalin's increasingly vicious regime. Not surprisingly, Trotsky's activities made him extremely unpopular with Stalin and the Communist government in the USSR. It was not long before he began to receive visits from the NKVD, the Russian Secret Service, at his home in Coyoacán, a suburb of Mexico City. After a failed attempt to murder Trotsky in March 1939,

Stalin set up a special assassination squad to rid him of his troublesome critic.

On 24 May 1940, NKVD agent Iosif Grigulevich and Mexican painter David Alfaro Siqueiros sprayed Trotsky's house with gunfire. Trotsky's fourteen-year-old grandson was shot in the foot and one of Trotsky's bodyguards was abducted and murdered. Trotsky's other guards fended off the attackers. In response, Trotsky wrote an article called 'Stalin Seeks My Death' in which he said that another assassination attempt was inevitable.

Having failed to dispose of Trotsky by direct assault, the NKVD decided to proceed by stealth. One of their agents was Jaime Ramón Mercader. His mother, Caridad, had worked as a Soviet agent and Mercader himself had trained in Moscow as a saboteur and assassin. Posing as Canadian Frank Jacson, Mercader had travelled to Mexico City. His girlfriend, Sylvia Ageloff, a Jewish-American intellectual from Brooklyn who had known Trotsky in Paris, effected an introduction. Mercader gained the confidence of Trotsky, his family and entourage by feigning an interest in revolutionary politics.

On 20 August, he visited the house, pretending to have revised an article that Trotsky had previously corrected for him. He carried a coat with him, under which he had hidden a steel ice pick, the handle shortened so that it would be easier to conceal. The NKVD had perfected the use of the ice pick as a murder weapon. They had employed it several times before and it was held to be a quick and easy method of murder. Up the street, his mother Caridad and another NKVD agent were waiting for him in a getaway car.

Trotsky had not been very impressed with Jacson's political writings so far, telling members of his family that he considered him 'light-minded'. But out of politeness he agreed to look over the revised article again. The two men went to Trotsky's study, where Trotsky sat down to read the article. Mercader stood behind him. As Trotsky bent his head over the paper, Mercader raised the ice pick and brought it down on Trotsky's skull.

The blow was badly aimed. As blood gushed from Trotsky's head, he let out a blood-curdling scream and began to fight off his attacker. Hearing the commotion, Trotsky's bodyguards rushed in. Fatally wounded but still conscious, Trotsky told them not to kill Mercader, saying: 'He has a story to tell.'

A doctor was summoned and police surrounded the house. Trotsky was rushed to hospital and died the following day. It was perhaps a fitting end for a man who, as a young revolutionary, said: 'We must put an end once and for all to the Papist–Quaker babble about the sanctity of human life.'

Fearing their plot had failed, Mercader's mother and her companion fled. Trotsky's bodyguards handed Mercader to the Mexican authorities, but he did not reveal his true identity. He was tried, convicted and sentenced to twenty years under the pseudonym Jacques Mornard.

He did not deny the murder and told the court: 'I laid my raincoat on the table in such a way as to be able to remove the ice axe which was in the pocket. I decided not to miss the wonderful opportunity that presented itself. The moment Trotsky began reading the article, he gave me my chance; I took out the ice axe from the raincoat, gripped it in my hand and, with my eyes closed, dealt him a terrible blow on the head.'

He justified his actions by saying that he had wanted to marry Ageloff, but Trotsky had forbidden the marriage. A violent quarrel ensued.

'Instead of finding myself face to face with a political chief who was directing the struggle for the liberation of the working class, I found myself before a man who desired nothing more than to satisfy his needs and desires of vengeance and of hate and who did not utilize the workers' struggle for anything more than a means of hiding his own paltriness and despicable calculations,' he said.

In 1960, he was released and went to Cuba where he was welcomed by Fidel Castro's new socialist government. Returning to the USSR, he was presented with the country's highest decoration, Hero of the Soviet Union, by the head of the KGB. He died in Havana in 1978.

Trotsky's house in Coyoacán was preserved in much the same condition as it was on the day of the assassination and is now the Leon Trotsky Museum. His ashes are buried in the garden. Trotsky's political influence is still felt in the British Labour Party and elsewhere to this day.

28

HUEY LONG 1935

Huey P. Long – aka 'The Kingfish' – was one of the most controversial politicians in the American South. He avoided race-baiting and sought to improve the conditions of impoverished blacks as well as impoverished whites. A Democrat, he thought that President Franklin D. Roosevelt's 'New Deal' did not go far enough to alleviate the suffering of the poor during the Depression. He aimed to run for the presidency in 1936 but was gunned down on 10 September 1935.

Huey Pierce Long was born into a poor southern family in Winnfield, Louisiana, in 1893. At sixteen, he gained a scholarship to Louisiana State University, but his parents could not afford the books and living expenses for him to go there, so he found work as a travelling salesman instead. He did well and stayed at the best hotels but quit to study law. With no degree, he passed the Louisiana bar exam and set up a practice in Winnfield and then Shreveport.

In 1918, he came to prominence defending socialist state senator S. J. Harper, who had been charged under the Espionage Act for opposing America's intervention in World War I. Victory helped him win election to the Louisiana

Railroad Commission, later renamed the Public Service Commission. A champion of the common man, he fought the oil companies, vested interests and the conservative elite that ran the state and rose to become the commission's chairman.

Long ran unsuccessfully to become governor in 1924 but won a decisive victory in 1928. He channelled public money into roads, bridges, schools, hospitals and the state university, by increasing taxes on corporations and the rich, and limiting the power of the oil companies. He also created a state-wide political organisation which led opponents to call him 'dictatorial'.

Long countered this with the campaign slogan: 'Every man a king, but no one wears a crown.' Supporters dubbed him 'The Kingfish', a nickname drawn from the popular character in a radio show *Amos 'n' Andy*. According to Long, it meant: 'I'm a small fish here in Washington, but I'm the Kingfish to the folks down in Louisiana.' Among the sober politicians, Long cut a flamboyant character, and took to wearing a trademark white linen suit.

Despite criticism, Long continued his campaign to democratise public bodies, putting his own supporters in important municipal positions. In 1929 there was an attempt to impeach him on charges of bribery and misuse of state funds. He thwarted this by persuading fifteen state senators, enough to rob the opposition of the two-thirds majority required, to sign a round robin pledging that they would not convict. Unpopular with the rich and powerful, businessmen in the state accused him of embezzlement. That, too, proved unsuccessful.

In 1930, Long was elected to the US Senate, but refused to renounce the governorship and take his seat until the gubernatorial election in 1932, thereby ensuring that his ally Oscar K. Allen would replace him. Once in the Senate, Long made constant attacks on President Herbert Hoover's handling of the national economy at the onset of the Depression.

Next, Long rallied to the cause of Hattie Caraway who, with his help, became the first woman to be elected to Congress. He also backed Franklin D. Roosevelt in his campaign to become president of the United States. Roosevelt won, but Long quickly became disillusioned and attacked his government for failing to do enough to help the poor.

Although he was not a socialist, Long was critical of the inherited wealth, which excluded most Americans from positions of power, and felt that the government should pass legislation and impose taxes to make the situation more fairly balanced. Accordingly, he launched his 'Share Our Wealth Society', which campaigned for legislation that would limit large personal fortunes by levying a graduated capital levy tax that would be assessed on all persons with a net worth exceeding $1 million. Annual incomes would be limited to $1 million and inheritances would be capped at $5.1 million. Every family was to be guaranteed an annual family income of at least $2,000. An old-age pension would be given to everyone over sixty, and veterans should be paid a pension and get health-care benefits. And there should be free education and training for all students in all schools, colleges and universities.

Long was convinced that, if the government did not confront the problems of inequality, there would be revolution. He saw his plan as an alternative to revolution, saying: 'We haven't a Communist or Socialist in Louisiana.

Huey P. Long is the greatest enemy that the Communists and Socialists have to deal with.'

In an era when the Great Depression was making the lives of ordinary people a misery, Long's radical ideas proved popular. But he also had many enemies, particularly when in August 1935 he announced that he would run against Roosevelt in the forthcoming election. Not only were there many attempts to discredit him on a personal level, the police also uncovered a plot to assassinate him. From then on, Long went everywhere accompanied by bodyguards.

At the time, Long was involved in a long-time feud with Benjamin Henry Pavy, state district court judge in St Landry and Evangeline parishes. Unable to unseat him, Long arranged for two of Judge Pavy's daughters, who were teachers, to be sacked from their jobs. He also warned Pavy that he would make it known that the family had what he called 'coffee blood', meaning that a black person had been a member of the family – a damaging accusation in the racist South. Long went further. He got a bill introduced into the Louisiana state legislature changing the borders of Pavy's district, gerrymandering him out of office.

Baton Rouge surgeon Carl Weiss was married to another of Judge Pavy's daughter. The accusation that his wife was mixed race made him furious and he paid a visit to Long in the Capitol Building. At 9.20pm on 8 September, just after the passage of the bill effectively removing his father-in-law from office, Weiss confronted Long as he emerged from the governor's office. He pulled a gun and shot him, hitting him in the stomach. Long's bodyguards then shot Weiss. He was hit over sixty times and died immediately.

During the gunfight, a bullet hit Long in the spine. It is not clear whether this came from Weiss or one of Long's bodyguards. Long was rushed to hospital. At first it was thought he would pull through. He had an emergency operation. However, it seems he had also sustained kidney damage. His condition deteriorated and on 10 September 1935 he died. His sister Lucille said his final words were: 'Don't let me die, I have got so much to do.'

After the death of both Long and his assassin, there was much speculation as to what had actually happened. According to some reports, one of the bodyguard's bullets had ricocheted off a pillar and hit Long. This was the fatal one. There are marks where a bullet nicked the pillar still visible in the hallway to this day. Others said that Weiss was not armed. He had only punched Long as he walked down the corridor. When Long went into hospital for surgery, it was noted that he had a bruised lip which would be consistent with this version. Long's bodyguards had overreacted and opened fire.

There was also speculation about Weiss's motivation. One theory was that Weiss had visited Germany in 1935 and seen parallels between the rise of Huey Long in the US and that of Adolf Hitler in Germany. According to this theory, Weiss saw Long as a demagogue, and was afraid that Long's 'Share the Wealth' campaign was a brand of national socialism. Yet another theory is that the assassination was a plot by powerful elements in the political world to prevent Long from winning the presidential campaign against Roosevelt. Whatever the truth of the matter, the assassination of Huey P. Long brought to an end one of the most colourful, and – many would argue – the most progressive administration in the history of the South.

Tens of thousands saw the funeral in front of the Capitol on 12 September. Presiding was Gerald L. K. Smith, co-founder of Share Our Wealth and subsequently of the America First Party. But with Huey Long dead, Roosevelt romped home in the election to complete the New Deal and guide America through World War II.

Huey Long's wife Rose was named his successor in the Senate, serving in 1936. His brother George served in the US House of Representatives from 1953–58. Another brother, Earl, served three terms as governor of Louisiana but was best known for his affair with stripper Blaze Starr who numbered John F. Kennedy among her lovers. His son Russell was elected to the Senate in 1948 and rose to be chairman of the powerful Finance Committee. Cousin Gillis also served in the US House, as did his nephew Speedy. Both were segregationists and contested the same seat. On the death of Gillis, his widow Catherine took over his seat, serving until 1987.

29

ERNST RÖHM 1934

Ernst Röhm was an early member of the Nazi Party, an ally of Adolf Hitler and a co-founder of the brown-shirted *Sturmabteilung* – *SA*, or 'Storm Battalion' – who provided protection at Nazi rallies and disrupted the meetings of other political parties. Under Röhm's leadership, the brown shirts played a key role in bringing Hitler to power. However, the *Führer* came to see Röhm as a rival and in the 'Night of the Long Knives' in 1934 he was murdered and the *SA* replaced by the ultra-loyal *Schutzstaffel* or *SS*.

Röhm was born in Munich on 28 November 1887, the son of a railway worker who was harsh and domineering. In his memoirs he recalled that 'from my childhood I had only one thought and wish – to be a soldier'. At the age of eighteen, he joined the Royal Bavarian 10th Infantry Regiment Prinz Ludwig at Ingolstadt as a cadet. Within two years, he had reached the rank of lieutenant and by the outbreak of World War I he was an adjutant.

During the war he was injured three times, each time returning to the Front where he was considered a 'fanatical, simple-minded swashbuckler' who frequently displayed contempt for danger. Half his nose was shot away. He had a bullet hole in his cheek and was awarded the Iron Cross First Class after sustaining a serious chest wound at Verdun. More a soldier than an officer, he condemned the cowardice, sensuality and other vices of many comrades, and was considered a traitor to the officer class.

In 1918, he contracted the Spanish flu, but pulled through. By the end of the war he was a captain and was assigned to District Command VII in Munich. Under his influence the army's special intelligence section was formed to maintain a watchful eye over the many political groups that sprang up after the war. As he pointed out in his memoirs, as a soldier 'I was not willing to give up my right to political thought and action within the limits allowed by my military duty, and I made full use of it.'

In 1919, left-wing socialists set up the Bavarian Soviet Republic in Munich. Röhm responded by supplying arms and ammunition to the anti-Communist *Freikorps*. On 7 March 1919, Röhm met Adolf Hitler. They spent the evening discussing ways to combat the revolutionary movement. Both men were possessed of a burning hatred for the new German democratic republic and the 'November criminals' whom they considered responsible for the German capitulation that had ended the war. Both men believed that to build a strong nationalist Germany, a new party had to be built on people from the lower classes, like themselves.

With the weapons Röhm had supplied, the *Freikorps* defeated the Red Guard and overthrew the socialist government. Hitler was arrested and accused of being a socialist, many of whom were beaten and summarily executed. Röhm came to his rescue. Through Röhm, Hitler got to teach courses on history and politics at Munich University. Both Röhm and Hitler joined the small German

Workers' Party, which was then less than fifty strong. With his gift for oratory, Hitler was appointed chief of propaganda, while Röhm was the secret head of a band of murderers – men, it was said, who killed without the slightest qualm. They renamed the German Workers' Party the National Socialist German Workers' Party, or Nazi Party, and it became virulently anti-Semitic.

Like many early Nazis, Röhm was an openly gay man and was accused of using his power in the Party to seduce young recruits. A reactionary homophobe, Joseph Goebbels later brought this to the attention of Hitler, who said: 'Nauseating! The Party should not be an Eldorado for homosexuality. I will fight against that with all my power.'

But still Röhm was the only one among his associates who called Hitler 'Adolf' and used the German familiar '*du*' when addressing him.

By 1921, membership of the Party had swelled to over two thousand and Hitler took over the leadership. That September he went to jail for three months for being part of a mob who beat up a rival politician. When Hitler was released, he formed the *SA* as his own private army. Röhm recruited men from former members of the *Freikorps* who had experience in using violence against their rivals. Röhm quit the *Reichswehr* to commit himself full time to the Party.

In Hitler's Beer Hall Putsch of November 1923, Röhm seized the war ministry. When this failed, Röhm was found guilty of high treason and sentenced to just fifteen months in prison, but the sentence was suspended. Hitler got five years but served only nine months. The *SA* was outlawed, but Röhm merely re-designated them the *Frontbann* and was briefly elected to the Reichstag as member for the National Socialist Freedom Party.

When Hitler was released, he fell out with Röhm, who had used his absence to enhance his power within the movement. In 1928, Röhm accepted a post in Bolivia as adviser to the Bolivian Army. Two years later, Hitler recalled him to become chief of staff to the revived *SA* which then had over a million members. By then, Hitler had set up the *SS*, originally as his personal protection squad.

When Hitler became German Chancellor in 1933, Röhm made a speech where he said: 'A tremendous victory has been won. But not an absolute victory! The *SA* and the *SS* will not tolerate the German revolution going to sleep and being betrayed at the half-way stage by non-combatants. Not for the sake of the *SA* and *SS* but for Germany's sake. For the *SA* is the last armed force of the nation, the last defence against Communism.'

By 1934, Hitler held absolute power in Germany, but there was still no place in his government for Röhm, who complained: 'Adolf is a swine... He only associates with the reactionaries now. His old friends aren't good enough for him. Getting matey with the East Prussian generals. They're his cronies now... Are we revolutionaries or aren't we? The generals are a lot of old fogies. They will never have a new idea... I don't know where he's going to get his revolutionary spirit from. They're the same old clods, and they'll certainly lose the next war.'

While Röhm's homosexuality was ridiculed in the press, his power within the Party grew to the point where Rudolf Diels, head of the Gestapo, reported to Hitler that Röhm was plotting against him. Leading Nazis, including Heinrich Himmler, implored Röhm to 'dissociate himself from his evil companions, whose prodigal life, alcoholic excesses, vandalism and homosexual cliques were bringing the whole movement into disrepute'.

On 4 June 1934, Hitler himself had a five-hour meeting with Röhm, whom he had always suspected of left-wing sympathies, telling him that some people believed that he was 'preparing a Nationalist–Bolshevik revolution, which could lead only to miseries beyond description'.

Hitler then decided to eliminate the socialist wing of the party. Himmler, Heydrich, Hermann Göring and Theodor Eicke, the commandant of Dachau concentration camp, drew up the 'Reich List of Unwanted Persons'. On the top of the list was Ernst Röhm.

On the evening of 28 June, Hitler called Röhm, ordering him to convene a conference of the *SA* leadership at Hanslbauer Hotel in Bad Wiessee on 30 June, assuring him that he would be safe. This had the effect of gathering all the top men together in an out of the way place.

At around 6.30 on the morning of 30 June, Hitler arrived at the hotel in a fleet of cars full of armed *SS* men. Erich Kempka, Hitler's chauffeur, said: 'Hitler entered Röhm's bedroom alone with a whip in his hand. Behind him were two detectives with pistols at the ready. He spat out the words; "Röhm, you are under arrest."'

Other *SA* officers were rounded up. Those caught in compromising situations were dragged out and shot in the road. The rest, around two hundred of them, were taken to Stadelheim Prison. Röhm's boyfriend, Karl Ernst, and the head of the *SA* in Berlin, had just married and was driving to Bremen with his bride to board a ship for a honeymoon in Madeira. His car was overtaken by *SS* gunmen, who shot up the car, wounding his wife and his chauffeur. Ernst was taken back to *SS* headquarters and executed later that day.

Hitler decided to pardon Röhm because of his past services. However, after pressure from Göring and Himmler, Hitler agreed that Röhm should die. Himmler ordered Theodor Eicke to carry out the task. On July 1, Eicke and his adjutant, Michael Lippert, travelled to Stadelheim Prison in Munich where Röhm was being held. Eicke placed a pistol on a table in Röhm's cell and told him that he had ten minutes in which to use the weapon to kill himself. Röhm replied: 'If Adolf wants to kill me, let him do the dirty work.'

Ten minutes later, Eicke and Lippert returned to find Röhm standing defiantly in the middle of the cell stripped to the waist. The two *SS* officers pulled out their revolvers and riddled him with bullets. Eicke later claimed that Röhm fell to the floor moaning: '*Mein Führer.*'

After that, anyone opposing Hitler knew what to expect.

30

VLADIMIR LENIN 1924

Few people know that Russian revolutionary Vladimir Ilyich Lenin, the Bolshevik founder of the Soviet Union, was assassinated. That is because over five years passed between the time he was shot on 30 August 1918 and his death on 21 January 1924. The reason was that in 1918 he had been hit by two bullets. One, in his lung, was removed. The other, in his neck, was left. As a result he died of lead poisoning. In the intervening years, his health and his thought processes gradually deteriorated. This allowed Stalin to manoeuvre himself into a position where he could become Lenin's successor, with disastrous consequences for the rest of the twentieth century and beyond.

Few people also know that Lenin lived in London for nine years. There he mixed with other revolutionary exiles including Trotsky and Stalin. The Second Congress of the Russian Social Democratic Workers' Party, where Lenin's hard-line Bolsheviks broke from the more moderate Mensheviks, was held in Fitzrovia and Islington. Lenin himself lived in Bloomsbury, not far from novelist Virginia Woolf, and his revolutionary newspaper *Iskra* was published in Clerkenwell in the building that is now the Marx Memorial

Library. But while he was in England, no one bothered him. It was only when he travelled back into Russia that the British authorities took an interest.

Lenin was born Vladimir Ilyich Ulyanov on 22 July 1870, on the modern Gregorian calendar, 10 April 1870 on the Julian calendar used in Russia at the time. His father was a school inspector and his mother the daughter of a land-owning physician who had been raised to the rank of state councillor. His mother's inheritance maintained their comfortable lifestyle after her husband died prematurely. Lenin had the money to study to become a lawyer and support himself as a full-time revolutionary after his older brother was hanged for plotting to assassinate the Tsar.

Rusticated for participating in an illegal student assembly, Lenin read Karl Marx's *Das Kapital* and, in 1889, became a Marxist. In 1893, he moved to St Petersburg and joined the Union for the Struggle for the Liberation of the Working Class. For this he was arrested and banished to Siberia. In 1900, he left the country to go into exile, first in Munich, then London.

Opposed to World War I, he found refuge in Switzerland in 1914. For thirty years he had been plotting the overthrow of the Tsar. Then, with the February Revolution of 1917, it happened without him. He thought history was passing him by and was desperate to get back to Russia. With his anti-war stance, he could expect no help from the British or the French. But taking passage through Germany that had been slaughtering Russian soldiers in their hundreds of thousands for nearly three years would look like treachery. The Germans had a solution though.

They were keen for Russia to pull out of the war so they could concentrate their efforts on the Western Front. However, the Provisional Government under Alexander Kerensky in St Petersburg, then called Petrograd, was determined to continue the war and was even planning a new offensive. So the Germans would provide a so-called 'sealed train' to transport Lenin and his party across Germany. Legally the train, or at least the part carrying Lenin and his acolytes, would be an extraterritorial entity. No one and nothing would be allowed on or off it while the train was on German soil. Lenin's party would then take the ferry to neutral Sweden. From there they could cross the border into Finland, then an autonomous region of Russia.

The British and the French knew about the trip and were well aware of its consequences.

'Full allowance must be made for the desperate tasks to which the German war leaders were already committed... Nevertheless it was with a sense of awe that they turned upon Russia the most grisly of weapons. They transported Lenin in a sealed truck like a plague bacillus from Switzerland to Russia,' said Winston Churchill, then minister of munitions.

There was talk of stopping Lenin as he took the train through northern Sweden and killing him, but nobody was willing to take responsibility for this. At Tornio on the Finnish side of the border, Lenin was strip-searched by a British border guard named Harold Gruner. He was questioned for hours and stuck to the story that he was a journalist making his way home. Meanwhile, the British tried to contact the Provisional Government's Foreign Minister Pavel Milyukov to find out what to do. Eventually, Kerensky gave his approval for Lenin's return, saying that a democratic Russia did not deny entry to its citizens, and Lenin arrived at Finland Station in Petrograd on 16 April 1917.

The Bolsheviks' first attempt to seize power in July failed when the Petrograd Soviet refused to endorse it. Lenin fled briefly into Finland, while Trotsky and other Bolshevik leaders were jailed. Kerensky then became prime minister. When Riga fell to the Germans in September, the latest Russian commander-in-chief, General Lavrenti Kornilov, proposed reforms to strengthen the army. Kerensky suspected he was planning a counter-revolution and dismissed him. Kornilov then marched on Petrograd. Kerensky called on the people to defend the capital, arming the leftist Red Guard. In the face of determined opposition, Kornilov's forces melted away. However, this lost Kerensky the support of the right. Needing the backing of the left, he had Trotsky and the Bolsheviks released.

By mid-September the Bolsheviks had majorities on both the Petrograd and Moscow Soviets, or revolutionary councils. Lenin urged his comrades to seize the moment to take power and returned to Petrograd in disguise. On 23 October – 5 November on the Gregorian calendar introduced after the revolution – Kerensky tried to close down two Bolshevik newspapers and re-arrest those who had taken part in the July insurrection. Lenin claimed that this was a counter-revolution. Two days later, troops, sailors and Red Guards took over the key points of the city.

While the Provisional Government was still sitting in the Winter Palace, Lenin issued a proclamation saying that power had passed to the Petrograd Soviet. That night the Bolshevik takeover was endorsed by the All-Russian Congress of Soviets. Early the following morning, troops were sent to the Winter Palace to arrest the Provisional Government, though Kerensky had already fled. All power now lay in the hands of Lenin.

This was disastrous for the British who sent a handful of spies to Russia. These included the novelist William Somerset Maugham and the 'ace of spies' Sidney Reilly. He cooked up a plot with the British consul in Moscow Bruce Lockhart, initially to kidnap Lenin and march him through the streets without his trousers in an attempt to destroy his authority. But this was not good enough for Reilly.

On the evening of 30 August 1918, Lenin addressed a meeting of workers at the newly nationalised Mikhelson plant. As he was leaving the factory, a woman known as Fanny – sometimes Dora – Kaplan approached. She pulled out a Browning revolver and fired three times. Lenin was hit twice and fell to the ground.

'They've killed Lenin! They've killed Lenin!' someone shouted as he fell.

Kaplan dropped the gun and fled. She was later captured and summarily executed.

The Russians knew who was responsible. They called it the Lockhart Plot and arrested Bruce Lockhart. The British embassy in Petrograd was sacked and the military attaché Captain Francis Cromie was shot and killed. Lockhart was later exchanged for a Bolshevik diplomat arrested in London and Sidney Reilly escaped, only to be lured back into Russia in 1925, never to be heard of again.

Against all expectations Lenin pulled through, though the rest of his life was marked by ill health. By 1921, any loud noise upset him and the bells of his telephones were replaced with flashing lights. He frequently withdrew to a dacha in Nizhny Novgorod.

In March 1922 he missed a meeting with Lloyd George at the Genoa Conference, partly through fear of assassination and partly because 'I am ill and stupid', as he said in a letter. He returned to Nizhny Novgorod in April, pleading ill health once more. This allowed Stalin to seize the key position of General Secretary of the Communist Party.

Professor Felix Klemperer, a distinguished German physician, was flown in from Berlin to examine him. It was decided to remove the bullet left lodged in his body in 1918 as Klemperer had diagnosed that Lenin's headaches were caused by lead poisoning from the bullet.

By 26 May, the headaches were accompanied by pains in the stomach and vomiting, more symptoms of lead poisoning. Doctors found partial paralysis in the right leg and right arm, along with a speech disturbance. Lenin had had a minor stroke, which again was thought to have been caused by lead poisoning.

Stalin visited Lenin, who told him: 'I am not permitted to read newspapers. I am not permitted to speak about politics. I carefully make a detour around every piece of paper on the table lest it turn out to be a newspaper and then I would be guilty of a breach of discipline.'

Stalin laughed.

By 4 January 1924, Lenin had reconciled himself with death and wrote a will saying Stalin should be removed from the position of General Secretary. By then he was too weak to implement this himself. Stalin was still in post when Lenin died seventeen days later and, from there, was able to eliminate all opposition.

31

PANCHO VILLA 1923

Years after his death, the Mexican revolutionary Pancho Villa became an emblem of the independent spirit of his country. One of the leaders of the Mexican Revolution, he helped to overthrow the corrupt dictator Porfirio Diaz in 1910, then in 1914 ousted Victoriano Huerta who had seized power in a coup the year before. Villa then fell out with his erstwhile ally Venustiano Carranza, who was elected president in 1917. Their conflict spilt over the border into the US and General John J. Pershing led an expedition to capture Villa, which failed. After Carranza died in 1920, Villa made his peace with the Mexican government and retired, only to be assassinated three years later.

Born José Doroteo Arango Arambula in 1878, Villa grew up in a poor peasant family in Durango. When he was fifteen, his father died and Villa was forced to work as a share-cropper to support his widowed mother and four siblings. One day he returned home to find his twelve-year-old sister being raped by a local rancher. He shot the man and killed him. Fearing for his life, he fled to the mountains and spent the rest of his adolescence as a fugitive, adopting the name Francisco Villa from an earlier outlaw. The diminutive form of Francisco, Pancho, became his *nom de guerre*.

By twenty, Villa had become a fully fledged outlaw himself, and had begun to gravitate towards the city of Chihuahua in the north of Mexico. He occasionally worked as a miner, supplementing his income with cattle rustling. He then took to robbing banks and trains.

By the turn of the twentieth century, Pancho Villa had established a colony of bandits in the Sierra mountains. Unlike other desperados, Villa shared the rewards of his crimes with the local population, making him a Robin Hood figure. His reputation was enhanced as he was working against the background of the unpopular government led by Porfirio Diaz which was hell-bent on exacting oppressive taxes from poverty-stricken rural workers and using the money to line its own pockets. A charismatic leader, Villa was seen to be robbing the rich to give to the poor.

Federal troops caught up with Villa in 1903. He avoided punishment by volunteering to join the 14th Cavalry Regiment. A few months later, he escaped by killing an officer and riding off on his horse. He and his men fled from Durango to the neighbouring state of Chihuahua.

In 1910, there was an uprising against the Diaz government, led by Francisco Madero, a wealthy businessman from Coahuila in northern Mexico. When Villa and his men came down from the hills to join Madero, the revolution immediately gained the support of the peasants. The *bandidos* became revolutionaries, and Villa was able to recruit thousands of peasants into a large people's army. Americans also joined. There was one squadron that was entirely composed of American soldiers.

Villa and Madero's forces managed to overthrow Diaz, who went into exile in 1911. However, though elected, Madero merely took over the existing power structure, including the

Federal Army, even appointing Venustiano Carranza, a one-time supporter of Diaz, as his minister of war and sidelining Pascual Orozco, an ally during the Revolution. At a state banquet in Ciudad Juárez, Villa told Madero: 'You, sir, have destroyed the revolution... It's simple: this bunch of dandies have made a fool of you, and this will eventually cost us our necks, yours included.'

When Madero failed to reward those who had supported him during the Revolution with lands they had captured, Orozco rebelled in March 1912. Although he appealed to Villa to join the rebellion, Villa returned to military service under Madero to fight his former comrade. Villa's irregulars joined forces with the Federal Army under the command of General Victoriano Huerta, who made Villa an honorary brigadier general. The two men did not get on. When Huerta accused Villa of stealing a horse, Villa struck him. As punishment Huerta ordered his death by firing squad. Madero ordered a stay of execution and had Villa imprisoned instead, but he escaped and fled to the US.

Madero was assassinated and Huerta became dictator. Villa returned to fashion his peasant army into the famous *División del Norte* – Division of the North. By then, Villa's fame as a folk hero and leader of a revolutionary army had spread to the US, where his exploits were featured in newspapers and even Hollywood movies.

Villa took over Chihuahua and the northern part of Mexico, forcing the local landowners to give up their extensive lands and hand them over to the widows and orphans of his soldiers who had died in battle. There were celebrations in the army camps, where Villa, though not a drinker, was known to dance all night. He was also a keen swimmer and runner. Keeping himself in good physical shape, he was apparently very attractive to women and was said to have married twenty-six times.

However, his rule was a lawless and violent one. When merchants and shopkeepers refused to do business with him using the army's banknotes, which they issued themselves, they were shot. Villa had others executed on a whim, though the dirty work was usually left to his right-hand man Rodolfo Fierro, who was known as *El Carnicero* – 'The Butcher'.

Villa fell out with fellow revolutionary leaders Venustiano Carranza and Álvaro Obregón, who forced Huerta from office in 1914. Suspecting Carranza also sought to make himself dictator, Villa joined forces with Emiliano Zapata, who was commanding forces in the south.

Carranza and Obregón retreated to Veracruz, leaving Villa and Zapata to occupy Mexico City. However, when Carranza and Obregón combined their armies against Villa's, nothing could prevent his eventual defeat. With just two hundred men left, Villa was forced to retreat into the mountains of Chihuahua.

When Carranza gained the support of the US government, Villa hit back by raiding border towns such as Columbus, New Mexico, where seventeen Americans were killed on 9 March 1916. Although this made him unpopular with the Americans, Villa's popularity with Mexicans, many of whom were deeply anti-American, soared.

In response, President Woodrow Wilson sent five thousand men under General 'Black Jack' Pershing to pursue Villa. But because of Villa's popularity among the peasants and his intimate knowledge of the terrain Pershing was unable to capture him. Each time the US army attacked, he managed to repulse them, leading them on a wild goose chase. When

America joined World War I, Pershing was sent to command US forces in France.

With Villa tied up in the north, Carranza turned his attention to Zapata in the south. Villa fought on until, on 21 May 1920, Carranza was assassinated by supporters of Obregón. On 22 July 1920, Villa sent a telegram to Mexico's interim President Adolfo de la Huerta, which stated that he recognised Huerta's presidency and requested amnesty. They met and successfully negotiated a peace settlement, which granted Villa and his men a 25,000-acre hacienda in Canutillo, just outside Hidalgo del Parral, Chihuahua.

On 20 July 1923, Villa was ambushed and shot while returning in his car from a visit to the bank in Parral. Normally on such trips he would have been accompanied by his large entourage of armed *Dorados*, or bodyguards. That day he had only three. Passing through a village, a pumpkinseed vendor ran into the road, shouting: 'Viva Villa!' This was a signal for a group of seven riflemen to fire. More than forty rounds hit the car. Nine dumdum bullets hit Villa in the head and upper chest, killing him instantly.

Thousands turned out the next day for his funeral. It is not known why Villa was killed. It was suspected that he intended to return to politics in the 1924 election as Obregón could not run again. At the hacienda, Villa's men prepared for a government attack. Six assassins who survived the original shoot-out hid out in the desert and were soon captured, but only two of them served a few months in jail. The rest were commissioned in the army.

Another theory was the Americans were taking their revenge. It was rumoured that the Germans had supported Villa during World War I because they wanted to destabilise America, thus preventing its entry into the war in Europe.

The German interests in the region at the time were revealed by the 'Zimmermann Telegram' – a telegram written in code sent by German foreign secretary, Arthur Zimmermann, to the German ambassador to Mexico, Heinrich von Eckardt, on 19 January 1917. The telegram was intercepted by the British and decoded. In it Zimmermann had asked the ambassador to approach the Mexican government with an offer of alliance, which would mean that the US would have to keep troops on the border, rather than send them to France. As an incentive, the Germans offered Mexico assistance to take back territory ceded to the US – California, Nevada, Utah, most of Arizona, half of New Mexico, some of Colorado and Wyoming, as well as the state of Texas – after the end of the Mexican–American War in 1848.

How much Villa knew about this plan is not known, but throughout his career, Villa had been astute at making alliances with whoever would help his cause. Whatever the truth of the matter, Villa remains a legendary figure in Mexico as a fighter who managed not only to defend his country against Americans, but also to make incursions into American territory.

32

MICHAEL COLLINS 1922

Like many revolutionaries, Michael Collins was consumed by the revolution he fomented. During the Irish War of Independence, he created a special assassination unit called The Squad expressly to kill British agents and informers. He said that this was in line with the universal wartime practice of executing enemy spies who were hunting victims for execution. When the War of Independence was won, he negotiated a treaty that established an Irish Free State as a Dominion within the British Empire. This also allowed Northern Ireland to opt out, resulting in the partitioning of the island of Ireland. A civil war broke out between those who accepted the treaty and those who opposed it. Visiting Cork, Collins was ambushed and shot in the head.

He had always maintained that the Anglo–Irish Treaty he negotiated gave the Irish people 'the freedom to achieve freedom'. Nine years after his death, most of his other demands were ceded by the British government. Only the partition between northern and southern Ireland remained, with its concomitant problems.

Collins was born in County Cork on 16 October 1890. His father had been a member of the Irish Republican

Brotherhood, a secret society dedicated to the establishment of an independent republic in Ireland. Collins was six years old when his father died. At fifteen, he moved to London where he worked, at first, for the Post Office Savings Bank. There he joined the Gaelic Athletic Association, which put him back in contact with the Irish Republican Brotherhood.

Returning to Ireland Collins organised arms and drilled troops in the run-up to the Easter Rising. He served in the Rising and when it was put down he was arrested. The British recognised that he was a particularly dangerous man and he was sent to Frongoch internment camp in Wales, where he organised protests. The execution of the leaders of the Rising meant that Collins became a leading figure in the independence movement. He became a member of the executive of Sinn Féin and director of organisation for the Irish Volunteers.

Elected MP for South Cork in 1918, like other members of Sinn Féin, Collins did not take his seat in the British parliament. Instead, they set up their own parliament, the *Dáil Éireann* in Dublin. Members, including the Sinn Féin leader Éamon de Valera, were arrested. Collins escaped incarceration and engineered de Valera's escape from Lincoln Prison. In de Valera's administration, Collins became minister of finance and issued bonds to fund the new government.

In 1919, *Dáil* declared the IRA – the Irish Republican Army – to be the army of the Irish republic. It ambushed the Royal Irish Constabulary, beginning the War of Independence. Collins became the IRA's director of intelligence, then as adjutant general directed the guerrilla war against the British. The British responded with commissioning special units such as the Black and Tans, who were given a free and brutal hand in dealing with those they considered to be terrorists.

From his secret headquarters in Dublin, Collins organised a special assassination unit called The Squad expressly to kill British agents and informers. The British put a bounty of £10,000 – equivalent to £520,000 in 2020 – on his head. In retaliation for the murder campaign of The Squad, the RIC opened fire on the crowd watching a football match in Croke Park on what became known as Bloody Sunday.

The rebels took control of the countryside, confining the forces of the British Crown to barracks in the larger towns. Collins was planning to execute every British secret service agent in Dublin, along with a major ambush in County Limerick, when a ceasefire was called in July 1921. The *Dáil* declared de Valera President of the Irish Republic and he went to see British prime minister Lloyd George, but he refused to attend the peace conference in London. He sent Collins instead, though Collins had his doubts about participating in the process.

After two months of negotiations, Collins signed the Anglo-Irish Treaty on 6 December 1921, giving Ireland Dominion status similar to Canada. This was a compromise, half-way between being an independent republic and a province of the Empire. While British forces would withdraw from Ireland, there would still be a British governor-general, though the government of the Irish Free State would be formed by the *Dáil Éireann*.

However, under powers granted by the 1920 Government of Ireland Act, Northern Ireland had the right to pull out of the Free State. It remained part of the United Kingdom and a boundary commission was set up to draw a border. Collins argued that the six counties would not be economically viable and would join the Free State when it became a republic. The alternative, he said, was to continue the war which he was not convinced that they would win.

On signing the Treaty, Collins conceded that he may be signing his own death warrant. De Valera condemned the Treaty on the grounds that it had been signed without cabinet consent and that it secured neither the full independence nor Irish unity. Collins retorted that de Valera had refused to lead the negotiations in London in person. Sinn Féin, the *Dáil*, the IRB and the IRA split into pro- and anti-Treaty factions. After a bitter debate the *Dáil* ratified the Treaty and de Valera and his anti-Treaty faction withdrew.

After the anti-Treaty faction of the IRA voted to reject the authority of the *Dáil*, it seized key buildings, including the Four Courts, the seat of the Irish judiciary. Meanwhile Collins and others entered into discussion to heal the rift. He attempted to write a constitution to make the Free State sound enough like a republic for anti-Treaty members to retake their seats in the *Dáil* without swearing an oath to the British Crown.

As chairman of the Provisional Government, Collins said they would not coerce Northern Ireland to join the Free State but would fund county councils and pay the salaries of teachers in Northern Ireland who recognised the Free State. This satisfied no one and fighting broke out between the IRA and the Ulster Special Constabulary along the border, while loyalist paramilitaries in the North drove Catholics out of their jobs. Many civilians were killed.

Collins signed a peace treaty with Sir James Craig, prime minister of Northern Ireland, but violence erupted again. In correspondence with Winston Churchill, the secretary of state for the colonies, Collins warned that breaches of the truce threatened to invalidate the Treaty. Meanwhile he was sending IRA units to the North and supporting the units there, preparing to resume guerrilla warfare. The British sent arms to the government of Northern Ireland and Churchill drew up plans to protect Ulster from invasion by the South. The situation grew confused as Collins tried to cancel an offensive that would involve both pro- and anti-Treaty factions but fighting broke out anyway.

To legitimise Collins as head of government in the Irish Free State, he had to present himself to the Lord Lieutenant of Ireland Viscount FitzAlan, the head of the British administration in Ireland in Dublin Castle. This was spun for the republicans as Collins accepting the surrender of the castle from FitzAlan, who stayed on as viceroy. In a further humiliation, the new constitution had to be submitted to Westminster for approval.

In an attempt to prevent civil war Collins tried to close ranks in the IRA. An equal number of pro- and anti-Treaty officers were to sign 'The Army Document' in May 1922. There would also be fresh elections for the *Dáil* with candidates saying explicitly that they were either pro- or anti-Treaty. Regardless of the outcome the two sides would then join in a government of national unity.

On 22 June 1922, two members of the IRA assassinated Sir Henry Wilson, security adviser to the Northern Ireland government, on the doorstep of his London home. Collins had called him 'a violent Orange partisan'. This caused consternation in London with Lloyd George demanding that Collins' Provisional Government take back control of the Four Courts. The British provided artillery for the purpose. Civil war broke out with Collins setting aside his title as Chairman of the Provisional Government to become Commander-in-Chief of the National Army.

He was largely successful, with the Free State regaining control of most of the country. Nevertheless, Collins still sought a negotiated peace. On 22 August 1922, he went to Cork to propose a truce with the IRA men there. The following day he set out from Cork City. He was spotted on the road in his open-topped car by an anti-Treaty sentry. An ambush was laid and when Collins' convoy returned by the same route, irregulars opened fire with rifles.

Collins jumped from the car. During the action, he was hit in the head. His body was found face down in the road. It was taken back to Cork, then on to Dublin where he was laid in state in City Hall. Tens of thousands of mourners filed past his coffin to pay their respects, including many British soldiers departing Ireland who had fought against him. Some 500,000 people attended his funeral, almost one fifth of the country's population at that time.

There is still some mystery about the death of Michael Collins. The man who is thought to have fired the fatal shot was Denis 'Sonny' O'Neill, a former officer from the Royal Irish Constabulary who served as a sniper in the British Army during World War I, before joining the IRA in 1918. He had met Collins on more than one occasion. In the 1940s the Irish government granted him a military pension.

33

EMILIANO ZAPATA 1919

The Mexican Revolution was characterised by assassination. Revolutionary leaders Francisco Madero, Emiliano Zapata, Venustiano Carranza, Pancho Villa and Álvaro Obregón were all successively assassinated. But although Zapata was killed in an ambush in April 1919, Article 27 of the 1917 Mexican Constitution had been drafted in response to his agrarian demands and in 1920 Zapatistas instituted many of the land reforms he proposed in his home state of Morelos.

Zapata was born on 8 August 1879 in Anenecuilco, a town in the municipality of Ayala, Morelos, in south-central Mexico. It was a pueblo with a history of the local haciendas encroaching on the indigenous people's land. Zapata's family were mestizos of mixed Nahua Indian and Spanish ancestry. They had fought in the various wars that had plagued the country since independence.

When he was sixteen or seventeen, his father died and Emiliano had to support his family. He farmed and bought a team of mules to haul crops and building materials. A skilled horseman, he raced and rode in rodeos, as well as fighting in the bullring as a mounted toreador. He also found work as a horse trainer to the son-in-law of the dictator Porfirio Diaz.

Under Diaz, the owners of the haciendas seized more native land. In response, Zapata and others sought an audience with Diaz. He had them arrested and Zapata was conscripted into the Federal Army. He served for six months, but his equestrian skills were so much in demand he was allowed to return to training horses.

In 1909, Zapata was elected president of the board of defence of Anenecuilco. After pointless negotiations with the local landowners, Zapata and a group of peasants occupied the land that had been appropriated from them and divided it among themselves.

Seeing Francisco Madero as a reformer, Zapata joined his campaign to oust Diaz. First he captured the Hacienda de Chinameca. Then his army of peasants took on the government forces in a six-day siege of the garrisoned and fortified city of Cuautla, emerging victorious on 19 May 1911. He went on to enter Cuernavaca, capital of the state of Morelos with five thousand men.

Diaz resigned and left the country. Zapata went to meet Madero in Mexico City and asked him to put pressure on the provisional president to return the land to the *ejidos* – the former Indian communal system of landownership. Madero refused. Instead he offered Zapata recompense if his men disarmed so that they could buy land. The disarmament began but stopped when the provisional president sent the army under General Victoriano Huerta to Cuernavaca.

After Madero was elected president, Zapata met him again, again fruitlessly. Realising the work of the revolution was incomplete, Zapata withdrew to the mountains of south-west Puebla. There, with former school teacher Otilio Montaño Sánchez, he wrote the *Plan de Ayala*, which called for the lands appropriated under Diaz to be returned immediately.

Further, a third of any large plantation owned by a single family should be given to poor farmers. Any landowner who resisted should forfeit the other two thirds as well.

Adopting the slogan '*Tierra y Libertad*' – 'Land and Liberty' – Zapata began putting his plan into operation by force. A law unto himself, he burnt haciendas and ordered executions. To avoid confrontation with Federal forces, he adopted guerrilla tactics. His men would farm with rifles over their shoulders and, when called for, would assemble in their thousands.

When Huerta deposed and assassinated Madero, he invited Zapata to join him. Zapata refused and he joined Pancho Villa, Venustiano Carranza and Álvaro Obregón. They forced Huerta from office in 1914. Zapata then sided with Villa against Carranza and Obregón. They met at the Convention of Aguascalientes when Zapata managed to get some of his *Plan de Ayala* adopted.

While Zapata let Villa do most of the fighting, he continued putting the *Plan de Ayala* into action in Morelos. However, when Carranza forced Villa onto the back foot in the north, he turned on Morelos. Zapata returned to guerrilla warfare to harry Federal forces. After some initial success, two of Zapata's generals fell out, dividing his forces.

Carranza's forces under General Pablo González Garza took the major cities and Zapata fled to the hills. He regrouped and returned stronger than ever, the brutality of González's forces serving as a recruiting sergeant. Although his advisers urged Zapata to mount a concerted campaign against the Carrancistas across southern Mexico, he concentrated entirely on stabilising Morelos.

Carranza mounted national elections in all state capitals except Cuernavaca and promulgated the 1917 Constitution which incorporated elements of the *Plan de Ayala*. With

Carranza consolidating power, some Zapatistas sought to change sides. Zapata's erstwhile adviser Otilio Montaño moved against the headquarters in Tlaltizapan demanding surrender to the Carrancistas. Zapata had him tried for treason and executed.

The cold winter of 1918 and the onset of Spanish flu cost Morelos a quarter of its population. González went on the offensive again, forcing Zapata to retreat. Nevertheless Zapata wrote an open letter to Carranza urging him to resign. He also tried to rob him of American support by saying Carranza was secretly sympathetic to the Germans. For his part, Carranza wanted to prove himself to the Americans and his Mexican backers by eliminating Zapata.

In March 1919, General González ordered his subordinate Jesús Guajardo to flush the Zapatistas out of the mountains around Huautla. However, Guajardo was caught carousing in a cantina and arrested. Zapata sent a note to Guajardo, inviting him to switch sides. This wound up on González's desk. González told Guajardo that he could escape punishment and redeem himself by feigning defection to Zapata. Guajardo wrote to Zapata telling him that he would bring over his men, along with weapons and ammunition. To prove his sincerity, Guajardo staged a mock battle to take the garrison at Jonacatepec. Those who were killed were former Zapatistas who had defected to the nationalists.

On 10 April 1919, Guajardo and Zapata agreed to meet at the Hacienda de San Juan, in Chinameca, near Zapata's home in Anenecuilco. It was a hot day and, wary, Zapata waited outside. His men scouted the area for more Federal troops in case they were walking into a trap. Guajardo sent a formal invitation for Zapata to join him in the house. Zapata, still suspicious, declined. Then Guajardo sent Zapata a beer.

Though it was hot, Zapata refused it, fearing it might be poisoned.

Eventually a move had to be made. At 2.10pm Zapata and ten of his men rode towards the house, leaving the others in the shade of some trees. As they approached the gates, the sentries saluted him. Guajardo had his men drawn up as if there was going to be a parade. There were nearly a thousand of them. They raised their rifles in the air and fired off a volley into the sky as a salute. Zapata dismounted and a bugle sounded. On its third note, the soldiers lowered their rifles and fired. Zapata died instantly in a hail of bullets.

'Our general Zapata fell, never to rise again,' said one of Zapata's aides.

His horse was wounded and bolted. Guajardo's men loaded Zapata's lifeless body onto a mule and carried it some fifteen miles north to Cuautla. There at the police station, the authorities identified Zapata's remains. They took photographs and the following day, newspapers across the country carried headlines announcing Zapata's death.

In Cuautla, thousands came to view the body before his burial. Many cried, even grown men hardened by war.

'The wings of our hearts fell,' one Zapatista said after seeing the body.

To convince the populous that Zapata was dead, his distinctive clothes were displayed outside a newspaper's office across from the Alameda Park in Mexico City. Along with his large, drooping moustache, Zapata was famous for his *charro* outfit – tight-fitting black cashmere trousers with silver buttons, a fine linen shirt or jacket, a scarf around his neck, boots of a single piece, *Amozoqueña*-style spurs, a pistol at his belt and an oversized sombrero.

However, many refused to believe he was dead. Even some of those who had seen the body refused to believe it was Zapata.

'We all laughed when we saw the cadaver,' one of Zapata's soldiers said. 'We elbowed each other because the *jefe* was smarter than the government.'

They maintained that it was the corpse of Jesús Delgado – a body double who travelled with Zapata. A scar was different, a mole was missing and the body had all ten fingers, when the real Zapata was missing a finger. The *jefe* had been seen on top of a hill, riding away on horseback. Some said he had fled to Arabia, only to return when he was most needed, then only under cover of night.

Several decades later, the daughter of a man appointed by Zapata to look after certain ownership documents, said that she had witnessed Zapata's return. Zapata was an old man by then, too old to continue the struggle.

Partially now a figure of myth, Emiliano Zapata remains a revered national hero. His face has appeared on banknotes. Modern activists seeking social justice for indigenous people often co-opt his name, pointing out his *Plan de Ayala* has not been fully implemented.

34

RASPUTIN 1916

Grigori Yefimovich Rasputin has gone down in history as the mad monk. True, he was a dishevelled lecher – the name Rasputin means in Russian the 'debauched one'. But due to his possibly hypnotic power to staunch the bleeding of the Tsar's haemophiliac son, he achieved influence in the Russian court, particularly with the German-born Tsarina, who was left in charge of the government when the Tsar went to the Front in World War I. In 1916, he was murdered, possibly with the collusion of British intelligence who feared that he was urging Russia to make a separate peace on the Eastern Front.

Rasputin was born in 1869 in a small Siberian village called Pokrovskoye. He had no formal education and was illiterate. After marrying and fathering a number of children, he underwent a religious conversion, undertaking a number of pilgrimages and spending several months in a monastery. He joined the Khlysty, a sect that had broken off from the Russian Orthodox Church. They saw themselves as incarnations of Christ. However, the so-called 'Christy' were nicknamed the Khlysty as *Khlyst* is the Russian for whips or flagellants. They also practised ecstatic dancing and were thought to have held orgies.

With his long-suffering wife Praskovia Feodorovna and his lifelong mistress Dunia Bekyeshova, he was expelled from Pokrovskoye by the local priest. Together they wandered around Russia with Rasputin initiating hordes of other women into the rites of the Khlysty in unrestrained orgies. His wife was not fazed by his numerous mistresses.

'He has enough to go around,' she said.

His doctrine of redemption through sexual release attracted numerous respectable, perhaps guilt-ridden, women, allowing many of his converts to enjoy sex for the first time. His unkempt appearance and peasant manners added to his attraction as a 'holy satyr'. As his biographer Robert Massie said for his followers: 'Making love to the unwashed peasant with his dirty beard and filthy hands was a new and thrilling sensation.' In fact, many of his lovers dowsed themselves in perfume beforehand, his body odour was so powerful.

By the time he reached St Petersburg, he had a powerful reputation as a mystic, a healer and a clairvoyant. In 1905, he was introduced at court. Soon after, he was called on to tend the Tsarevich Alexei. It was found that he could successfully ease the child's haemophilia perhaps due to hypnosis and the Tsarina came to rely on him, believing him to have divine powers.

While Rasputin remained a paragon of chastity and humility in court, outside he continued in his scandalous ways. The ill-kempt 'mad monk' scandalised St Petersburg society by sleeping with scores of women from aristocrats to common whores and drinking to excess. There were even rumours that he was having a sexual relationship with the Tsarina, though there is very little evidence to support this.

Nevertheless, women gathered in his apartment eager for an invitation to visit his bedroom or the 'holy of holies' as he called it. Usually he would be found in the dining room surrounded by female disciples who took turns to sit on his lap while he instructed them on the mysteries of the resurrection. On one occasion, he gave a graphic description of the sex life of horses, then grabbed one of his distinguished guests by the hair and pulled her towards his bedroom, saying: 'Come, my lovely mare.'

He would often sing and they would dance wildly, collapsing in a swoon before being taken into the holy of holies for a personal glimpse of paradise. One disciple, an opera singer, was so devoted to him that she would phone him to sing him his favourite songs. Attendance at his gatherings became so fashionable that cuckolded husbands would boast that their wives had been favoured by Rasputin.

People who tried to convey details of this scandalous behaviour to the Tsar's ears found themselves banished. He was thought to have a strong political influence over the Tsar, as well as the Tsarina, helping to make key government appointments. That began to worry the Russian nobility, as well as the British government. The Romanovs' mysterious friend brought the family into disrepute, and they soon became very unpopular, both at home and abroad.

During World War I, Tsar Nicholas took personal command of his troops, leaving all other government business in the hands of the Tsarina. The granddaughter of Queen Victoria, she was born Princess Alix of Hesse in Darmstadt in the Grand Duchy of Hesse, then part of the German Empire.

In the absence of the Tsar, her personal adviser Rasputin began making disastrous appointments. He also meddled in military affairs to catastrophic effect. To save Russia from his malign influence, a group of young nobles, – Prince Felix Yusopov, Vladimir Purishkevich, and Grand Duke Dmitri

Pavlovich Romanov, a cousin of the Tsar's – plotted to assassinate him.

On the night of 29 December 1916, or 17 December by the old-style Julian calendar still in use in Russia then, Prince Felix invited Rasputin to his palace on the Moika Canal. His incentive was an introduction to Felix's beautiful wife Irina, a niece of the Tsar's. As Yusopov was thought to have been a homosexual who had been rebuffed by Rasputin several times, he may well have had some personal, as well as political, reason to want him dead. At the Moika Palace, Rasputin was ushered into the basement where he was plied with cakes and wine. These had been laced with cyanide. Yusopov waited for Rasputin to drop dead, but the poisoning seemed to have little effect. Rasputin washed down the cakes with Madeira wine. This too had been spiked with cyanide. Again Rasputin showed no signs of dying.

Around 2.30am, Yusopov went upstairs, took a revolver from Dmitri Pavlovich and returned to shoot Rasputin. The conspirators drove to Rasputin's apartment with one of them wearing Rasputin's coat and hat in an attempt to make it look as though Rasputin had returned home that night. When they went back to the palace, they went into the basement to make sure Rasputin was dead. He wasn't. Rasputin suddenly leapt to his feet and attacked Yusopov. Making his way upstairs, he staggered out into the courtyard. To prevent him escaping, Purishkevich shot him again. Rasputin collapsed against the snow bank. They picked him up and took him to the Malaya Nevka river, where they pushed his body through a hole in the ice near the Petrovsky Bridge. He was said to have moved around under the ice for some time, before finally dying.

There are several theories as to why it was so hard to kill Rasputin. It is possible that Rasputin, realising his host's intention, never actually swallowed the poison. It may have been that the sugar in the pastries and wine negated the effect of the cyanide, or that as Rasputin was a heavy drinker, the high level of alcohol in his digestive system protected him from the poison. Some accounts also suggest that one of the nobles may have been double-crossing his co-conspirators by omitting the poison. It also appears that the bullets hit him in the lung and liver which, though fatal, would not have caused instant death.

New evidence has come to light that a British secret service agent may have been involved in the shooting. The British were naturally worried about Rasputin's influence over the German-born Tsarina during World War I. If Russia made a separate peace with Germany, which it eventually did, a huge army of hardened troops from the Eastern Front could be moved on to the Western Front, possibly overwhelming the Allies there.

The head of the British Intelligence Mission to the Russian General Staff Samuel Hoare and British agent Oswald Rayner had been at Oxford with Yusopov. Rayner was thought to have been hidden outside the palace in the bushes observing how the assassination plot was progressing. When he saw Rasputin escaping, he shot him in the head. Hoare sent a report of the murder to the British government written in the racy style of the *Daily Mail*.

Rasputin apparently knew that there were plots afoot to assassinate him. On the night of his murder he is said to have claimed that if the deed was carried out by nobles, Russia would undergo bloody warfare for many years. His prediction came true as following the Bolshevik Revolution his assassination helped precipitate, Russia was plunged into civil war.

Rasputin's assassination redoubled Alexandra's belief in autocracy. She cracked down hard on the Russian people, but within weeks of the death of the mad monk, the Romanovs were swept from power by the Russian Revolution in February 1917 – followed by the Bolshevik Revolution in October. The Romanovs were murdered the following year.

There is a tale that, during the assassination, one of the conspirators pulled out a knife and castrated Rasputin, throwing his severed penis across the room. It was recovered later by a servant who gave it to a maid. In 1968, she was still alive, living in Paris, the owner of a polished wooden box in which she kept what looked like 'a blackened, overripe banana, about a foot long'.

35

ARCHDUKE FRANZ FERDINAND 1914

The assassination of Archduke Franz Ferdinand in Sarajevo on 28 June 1914 sparked off World War I. Many historians argue that the war would have happened anyway because of the network of alliances built up across Europe. Nevertheless, the shot rang out around the world.

During the unification of Germany, which began in 1866, Prussia built the thirty-nine states that made up the German Confederation into a single German Empire with Berlin as its capital. This process ended in 1870 with the six-week Franco–Prussian War, where the Prussian Army crushed the once-mighty French army at the Battle of Sedan and annexed Alsace-Lorraine.

Austria reacted with the *Ausgleich* or Compromise in 1867 which established the Dual Monarchy of Austria–Hungary, giving Hungary internal autonomy while making the empire a single state for the purposes of foreign affairs and war. The two kingdoms under the one emperor, Franz Josef I, also incorporated Czechoslovakia, along with parts of Poland, the Ukraine and the Balkans. From the outset, Austria–Hungary was in conflict with three of its neighbours – Italy, Serbia and Romania – who all had claims on its lands. Consequently, after 1870 Austria–Hungary forged a close alliance with a fourth neighbour, the newly unified Germany. In 1878, with the backing of Germany, the Austrians occupied Bosnia-Herzegovina, then technically still a province of the Ottoman Empire. This outraged Serbia who wanted an outlet to the Adriatic and, as Slavs, had the support of Russia, a fifth neighbour of Austria–Hungary.

As a result of its defeat in the Franco–Prussian War, France signed a secret treaty with Russia in 1894, while Britain had a diplomatic agreement with France called the *Entente Cordiale*. But it was Britain's guarantee of Belgian neutrality when Belgium was established as an independent country by the Treaty of London of 1839 that eventually brought Britain into World War I.

Kaiser Wilhelm II, the grandson of Queen Victoria, had come to the throne in 1888. Born with a withered arm, he turned against his English mother and became virulently anti-British. He adopted an aggressive policy of colonial expansion in Africa and the Pacific and began an arms race with Britain. In 1897, Germany began a crash course of shipbuilding with the aim of rivalling Britain's Royal Navy, then the biggest in the world.

Archduke Franz Ferdinand was the nephew of Emperor Franz Josef I of Austria and heir presumptive to the Austro–Hungarian throne. His politics were relatively liberal, considering he was a member of one of the oldest and wealthiest dynastic houses of Europe. Ferdinand was in favour of keeping the peace between the warring nations of the Balkans and supported liberal causes such as giving the vote to all citizens of all classes (as long as they were male, that is). These views, of course, did not endear him to the higher echelons of the aristocracy in Austria who were terrified that his plans would end their privileged way of life. It was even suspected, after the event, that the assassination was a plot by the Austro–Hungarian establishment to rid themselves of the archduke, who was seen as a threat to their privilege and power. However, as no evidence has ever been uncovered to support this theory, it remains in the realms of conjecture.

On 28 June 1914, Archduke Franz Ferdinand and his wife, Countess Sophie, paid a formal visit to General Oskar Potiorek, the governor of the Austrian province of Bosnia-Herzegovina, who had invited them to the opening of a hospital in the capital Sarajevo. Although Ferdinand knew that the visit would be dangerous, and there was a threat of terrorist attack from Bosnian Serb nationalists who wanted freedom and independence from the Austrian empire, he accepted the invitation.

Precautions were taken. The Archduke and Countess Sophie arrived unannounced by train. However, they then made the mistake of riding through the streets in an open-topped car with their host, Oskar Potiorek, who wanted to show off his honoured guests. Crowds turned out to greet them. They waved back, clearly relying on their security forces to deal with any potential troublemakers.

Just after ten o'clock, the motorcade passed the city's police station, where a young man named Nedeljko Cabrinovic was waiting, one of six would-be assassins lining the route. They were members of a terrorist organisation known as the Black Hand. Their leader Dragutin Dimitrijevic had managed to persuade them to assassinate the archduke and die in the course of their duty if necessary. To this end, Dimitrijevic had handed out vials of cyanide to the men, in case they were arrested.

Cabrinovic stepped forward and threw a grenade at the archduke's car. Seeing it coming, the driver accelerated and the grenade ended up hitting the car behind. Two of its passengers were injured and members of the crowd were hit by shrapnel.

Swallowing the cyanide, Cabrinovic ran down to the River Milijacka to drown himself. But the river turned out to be just four inches deep. The cyanide was out of date and he was arrested by the police. Brought to trial, he was convicted and given a fifteen-year prison sentence. Already suffering from tuberculosis, he died in jail in 1916.

The Archduke and Countess Sophie arrived at the town hall, telling the mayor: 'Mr. Mayor, I came here on a visit and I am greeted with bombs. It is outrageous.' After making a speech to the civic dignitaries, Archduke Ferdinand thanked the people of Sarajevo for 'their joy at the failure of the attempt at assassination'.

It was then suggested that the imperial couple stay at the town hall until troops could be brought in to guard the streets. Potiorek vetoed the suggestion on the grounds that, coming straight from manoeuvres, the soldiers would not be in dress uniforms befitting the occasion.

'Do you think that Sarajevo is full of assassins?' he asked.

Archduke Ferdinand then decided that he would pay a visit to some of the injured citizens at the local hospital. For safety's sake they decided to take a different route. Unfortunately, not familiar with the city, the driver lost his way and ended up driving down Franz Josef Street.

Purely by chance, one of the other terrorists from the Black Hand group, a nineteen-year-old man named Gavrilo Princip, was eating a sandwich in the Moritz Schiller café on Franz Josef Street. Earlier, like several of his comrades, he had not been able to get close enough to the archduke's car because of the crowds. He thought the opportunity to assassinate the archduke had passed. Now he saw the car passing by the window of the café.

He leapt to his feet and ran out into the street, though the archduke's car had already passed him. However, by this time, the driver of the car had realised he was lost and was backing slowly up the street. There were no crowds. Princip pulled out his revolver and opened fire on the passengers who were now only a few feet away from him.

The first to be hit was Countess Sophie. The bullet hit her in the stomach. Sadly, she was pregnant at the time. She collapsed in front of her husband and died within minutes. The archduke was in shock. Apparently thinking his wife had just fainted, he tried to rouse her, but was then shot in the neck himself. A few minutes later, he also died.

Like his comrade Cabrinovic, Gavrilo Princip took a vial of cyanide before the police came to arrest him. Again, the cyanide failed to kill him. After his arrest, he was brought to trial, convicted and given a twenty-year prison sentence. Had he been older, he would have been sentenced to death. It was immaterial. He too died of tuberculosis a few years later, while still in prison.

Austria blamed Serbia for the assassination and issued an ultimatum. Russia backed Serbia, while Germany backed Austria who hoped they could defeat Serbia quickly before Russia could intervene. News of the ultimatum reached Tsar Nicholas II on the 24th and he ordered his army to prepare for mobilisation. Austria–Hungary mobilised too. Kaiser Wilhelm returned early from his annual cruise to read the Serbian response to the Austrian ultimatum, which conceded Austria's demands, and he decided there was no justification for war. Despite attempts at mediation by Britain, Austria declared war on Serbia on 28 July. Germany stayed its hand. If there was to be a war, it was vital that Russia ordered a general mobilisation first. Then the war would appear to be Russia's fault. That way, there was a possibility that Britain might stay out of it.

When Britain made it clear that it would not remain neutral in any war between Germany and France, the Kaiser sent a telegram to his cousin by marriage Tsar Nicholas asking him to halt any general mobilisation. The Tsar also sought to avoid war, writing to the Kaiser in English, he said: 'To try and avoid such a calamity as a European war, I beg you in the name of our old friendship to do what you can to stop your allies going too far.' He signed the message 'Nicky'.

It was too late. On 29 July, Austrian riverboats bombarded the Serbian capital Belgrade. The Russian generals prevailed on the Tsar to resume the mobilisation. German generals did the same with the Kaiser.

The French also held back. They wanted any German attack to be seen as unprovoked. That way, they would have more of a chance of involving the British. When the Germans heard of the Russian mobilisation, they ordered troops up to the French and Belgian borders. The German chancellor then sought to provoke the French, asking them to promise to remain neutral if Germany went to war with Russia, knowing France would not abandon its ally.

The British were also asked to stay out of any European war. The government asked in reply if Germany would respect Belgian neutrality. They got no answer.

At 3.55pm on 1 August 1914, the French ordered a general mobilisation. The Germans followed suit five minutes later. On the Continent, the mobilisation of troops was done by railroad for the first time, making any planned offensive almost impossible to call off. At 7pm, Germany declared war on Russia. The following day, Germany sent troops into neutral Luxembourg and sent an ultimatum to Belgium demanding free passage of German troops across its territory.

Two days later, Belgium rejected Germany's ultimatum. Germany invaded. Britain mobilised and World War I was underway.

36

WILLIAM MCKINLEY 1901

William McKinley was the last Civil War veteran to enter the White House. The seventh of nine children, he was born on 29 January 1843 in Niles, Ohio, where his father managed a blast furnace and foundry. The family moved to the town of Poland in 1852, where the young McKinley attended the Union Seminary. He went on the Allegheny College in Meadville, Pennsylvania, in 1859. After a year, he became ill and returned to Poland. By the time he had recovered, there was no money to resume his education and he went to work in the Post Office.

When the Civil War broke out, McKinley enlisted as a private in the 23rd Ohio Volunteer Infantry. He was commissioned as a second lieutenant for conspicuous valour at the Battle of Antietam in 1862. He also saw action at the battles of Winchester, Opequon, Cedar Creek and Fisher Hill, reaching the rank of major before leaving the army in July 1865. His commanding officer, Rutherford Hayes, himself later US president, described him as 'one of the bravest and finest officers in the army'.

Back in civilian life, McKinley studied law in Youngstown, Ohio, then enrolled at the Albany Law School. Admitted to the Ohio bar in 1867, he practised in Canton, Ohio, before being elected prosecuting attorney in Stark County in 1869.

McKinley was elected to Congress in 1896 and re-elected for seven consecutive terms. By 1889, he was chairman of the powerful Ways and Means Committee and introduced the McKinley Tariff Bill, which raised tariffs to the highest level they had been up to that time.

Defeated in the 1890 Congressional race due to gerrymandering of his constituency, his staunch protectionist views had already caught the eye of Cleveland industrialist Marcus Hanna. With Hanna's support, McKinley was elected Governor of Ohio, serving two terms while he laid his presidential plans. In 1896, he won the nomination at the Republican National Convention in St Louis. His opponent, the candidate of both the Democratic and Popularist parties, was William Jennings Bryan, a silver-tongued orator who laid the country's problems at Wall Street's door. 'The Boy Orator of the Platte' – as Bryan was known – toured the country four times, covering over 18,000 miles in his whistle-stop campaign. McKinley, a quiet man, knew he could not compete with this, so he stayed at home and ran a 'front porch' campaign. Hanna negotiated discount rail fares and paid for 750,000 people to travel to Canton to hear McKinley. Each trainload was canvassed on the way, so McKinley could tailor his speech to individual grievances.

The major issue of the day was 'hard money' versus 'free silver'. McKinley promised prosperity and a 'full dinner pail' by keeping the dollar on the gold standard. Bryan wooed the farmers of the West and South with the bimetallic standard, increasing the money supply with silver coinage. McKinley won by 271 to 176 electoral votes.

Once in office, McKinley immediately restored the high tariffs abandoned by Grover Cleveland in 1894. The Dingley Tariff was set at a higher rate than ever before. But soon domestic concerns were obscured by the nationwide outcry over Cuba. In 1895, the Cuban sugar market collapsed and plantation workers rebelled against their Spanish overlords, destroying millions of dollars of American-owned property in the process. However, the Spaniards' brutal suppression of the revolt turned American public opinion against Spain.

McKinley did not want war and tried negotiation, but the press was against him, On 9 February 1898, the *New York Journal* leaked a letter from the Spanish ambassador in Washington which described McKinley as 'weak and a bidder for the admiration of the crowd... a would-be politician who tries to keep the door open behind him while keeping on good terms with the jingoes of the party'. If that was not bad enough, six days later, the US battleship *Maine* mysteriously blew up in Havana harbour, killing 260 officers and men. The American yellow press blamed the Spanish and adopted the slogan: 'Remember the *Maine*, to hell with Spain.'

America went to war on 24 April. On 1 May, Commodore George Dewey on board the flag ship *Olympia* steamed into Manila harbour with four cruisers and two gunboats. Within a few hours, Dewey had silenced the shore batteries and destroyed the Spanish fleet. Ten Spanish ships were sunk, 167 men were killed and 214 wounded. The Americans lost not a single ship, no men and only eight Americans were lightly wounded.

The war ended with the capture of Santiago, Cuba, and on 26 July the Spanish sued for peace. The peace treaty was signed in the White House on 12 August. The war was the shortest America ever fought. The US suffered not a single defeat. Not a soldier, colour, gun or an inch of territory was lost. Spain gave up Cuba, ceded Guam, Puerto Rico and the Philippines to America. The problem was that the US did not know quite what to do with them.

America was loath to become a colonial power, but McKinley declared that Guam, Puerto Rico and the Philippines must not be allowed to fall into unfriendly hands. They were made US dependencies, which meant that America inherited the guerrilla war the Spanish had been fighting against Filipino insurgents.

With the end of the war, attention focused again on the question of currency. The Gold Standard Act was signed in 1900, making gold the only metal that the dollar could be redeemed in. However, the increased availability of gold made the silver question a dead issue.

In 1900, McKinley faced Bryan again in the presidential race. This time the thrust of Bryan's campaign was that America's new colonial acquisitions would lead to national decay. McKinley's Vice President Garret A. Hobart had died during his term of office, so McKinley replaced him with hero of the Spanish–American War Theodore Roosevelt. Again Hanna organised the campaign, shipping voters into Canton. McKinley defeated Bryan by an even greater margin – 292 to 155.

On 6 September 1901, President McKinley visited the Pan-American Exposition in Buffalo. He was shaking hands with visitors in the Temple of Music. A young anarchist named Leon Czolgosz took his place in the reception line with a .32-calibre revolver hidden in a handkerchief, wrapped around his hand like a bandage. When McKinley reached him, Czolgosz fired two shots. One hit McKinley's breastbone, the other ripped through his abdomen. McKinley died eight days later with the words: 'Goodbye,

goodbye, it's God's way.' He was laid in state in the Capitol Rotunda, before being buried in Canton.

'I thought it would be a good thing for the country to kill the President,' Czolgosz said from his cell. He went to the electric chair four to five days after McKinley's death, leaving Americans to wonder how they had lost three Presidents to the assassin's bullet since Abraham Lincoln just thirty years earlier.

After the assassination of President McKinley, Theodore Roosevelt took office, promising that there would be no change in policy. But instead of backing big business, Roosevelt soon became known as a 'trust-buster' and pushed for a 'Square Deal' between capital and labour. He also supervised America's rise to become an international power.

America and Columbia were deadlocked over the building of the Panama Canal. The situation was resolved when Roosevelt's administration engineered a bloodless coup d'état. This resulted in the establishment of the breakaway Republic of Panama, which quickly reached agreement with the United States over the canal.

'I took the Canal Zone, and let Congress debate,' said Roosevelt with an arrogance that alienated most of Latin America. Roosevelt was not fazed by other countries' reaction. He said his foreign policy was summed up by an old African saying: 'Speak softly and carry a big stick.'

Roosevelt became the first overtly imperialist President. He believed that strong nations thrived, while weak ones went to the wall. He built the US Navy into a major sea power. In 1909, he also paid $25,000 to the Wright brothers for a plane, beginning the US Army Air Force. When Britain, Germany and Italy blockaded Venezuela, he added the 'Roosevelt Corollary' to the Monroe Doctrine – the United States alone would police the Western hemisphere.

37

ALEXANDER II OF RUSSIA 1881

Tsar of Russia from 1855 until his assassination in 1881, Alexander II was known as Alexander the Liberator for freeing the serfs in 1861. However, poverty was still rife and revolutionary fervour grew through the country. There were assassination attempts on him in 1866, 1879 and 1880. Security forces were on high alert. Even so, Alexander was eventually killed in a bomb attack that not only blew him apart, but also killed his assassin and twenty others, injuring many more. The snow was turned red as the wounded bled to death and strips of human flesh were left hanging from the trees and lamp posts in the street.

Ironically, the assassination of Alexander did not immediately forward the revolutionaries' cause. His successor Alexander III was profoundly reactionary. The target of assassination plots himself, by the end of his reign he had become so unpopular that he was virtually a prisoner in his own palace. When his son Nicholas II came to the throne, he had little alternative but to continue the repression. In 1917, this led to the Russian Revolution, after which Nicholas was brutally murdered, along with his entire family. So the assassination of Alexander II was the beginning of the end for the Romanovs and tsarist rule and ushered in the Bolsheviks.

Alexander II Nikolaevitch was born in 1818, the eldest son of Tsar Nicholas I of Russia and Princess Charlotte of Prussia. As a boy, he was educated by romantic poet Vasily Zhukovsky. To the disappointment of his father, he showed little interest in the military or politics. He toured Russia and was the first Romanov heir to visit Siberia. He also toured Europe and met the twenty-year-old Queen Victoria.

In 1841, Alexander married Princess Marie of Hesse who gave him six children. After his wife died, he married his mistress, Princess Catherine Dolgoruki, who gave him four more. When Nicholas died, Alexander became Tsar, overseeing the final year of the Crimean War. Then he devoted himself to reforms in the hope that Russia could catch up other European powers. Without relinquishing his powers as an autocrat, he began to pass laws to help modernise industry and commerce, extending the railways across the country. It became clear to him that Russia could not advance any further under the system of serfdom, where peasants were tied to the land with very few rights of their own. But once they had been emancipated the serfs were subject to taxation, leaving them materially little better off.

Following the 1863 uprising in Poland, where Alexander was also king, he stripped the country of its constitution and incorporated it into the Russian Empire. Minority languages were banned, leading to resentment and unrest.

In 1866, Dmitry Karakozov, a student, arrived in St Petersburg with the intention of assassinating the Tsar. On 4 April, he went to the gates of the Summer Garden, drew his gun, and was about to shoot Alexander when a peasant named Osip Komissarov jogged his elbow. It is not clear whether this was an accident. Karakozov tried to make a run for it but was arrested and hanged in public. Komissarov was rewarded with a title and money but was exiled from St Petersburg for his uncouth behaviour. Meanwhile, Alexander commissioned a new gate for the city to celebrate his escape from death – 'The Great Gate of Kiev' commemorated by Mussorgsky in *Pictures at an Exhibition*, though it was never built.

On the morning of 20 April 1879, thirty-three-year-old Alexander Soloviev fired five times at the Tsar, missing Alexander as he fled, dodging the bullets. Soloviev was arrested and hanged the following month.

In December 1879, a group of radicals called *Narodnaya Volya* – 'Will of the People' – attempted to blow up a train the Tsar was in. The Tsar usually travelled with two trains – the first to test the safety of the track and a second carrying him following. However, on this occasion Alexander was travelling in the first train; the plotters blew up the second.

Narodnaya Volya tried again on 5 February 1880. This time they set off explosives in a box with a clockwork timer in the guards' rest room in the Winter Palace, directly under the Tsar's dining room. But Alexander and his family had been delayed by the late arrival of the Tsar's nephew, the Prince of Bulgaria, and were saved.

Security was tightened. The Tsar no longer travelled by train, taking boats wherever possible, and cutting down on public appearances. However, Alexander knew that to continue in power he had to show the people that he was not afraid. After all, he had already survived several assassination attempts and had lived longer than most of his ancestors. His confidence was misplaced, as it turned out.

On 13 March 1881, Alexander went to review his troops as he did every Sunday. He travelled in his bulletproof carriage accompanied by six Cossacks. His carriage was followed by two sleighs carrying, among others, the chief of police and the chief of the emperor's guards.

Two members of *Narodnaya Volya*, Andrei Zhelyabov and his lover Sophia Perovskaya, had rented a shop along the route where they sold cheese. From there, their group tunnelled out under the street, packing the culvert with dynamite. They also positioned four men in the street, armed with bombs.

Before the attack the police arrested Zhelyabov. Perovskaya was left in charge of the attack, but the Tsar took an unscheduled route down the next street. Alerted, the bomb attackers leapt into action. Nineteen-year-old student Nikolai Rysakov threw the bomb at the Tsar's carriage, damaging the door and rocking it from side to side, but the coach continued on its way. A butcher's boy who was standing in the street was killed, along with two of the Tsar's Cossack escorts and several horses. Others were also hurt. Rysakov was arrested. In an attempt to save his own skin he co-operated with the authorities, betraying his comrades, but was later executed anyway.

Against the advice of his coachman, the Tsar had stopped his carriage and got out to see what was going on. Emerging shaken but unhurt, he walked around to offer encouragement to those who were wounded.

Police Chief Dvorzhitsky heard Rysakov shout out to someone else in the gathering crowd. Fearing there may be an armed accomplice nearby, he offered to drive the Tsar back to the palace in his sleigh. They were ready to drive away when a second assassin named Ignacy Hryniewiecki ran up and threw a nitroglycerine bomb at the Tsar's feet. The bomb blew Alexander's legs off below the knee, tore open his torso and took out one of his eyes. Hryniewiecki was also fatally wounded. He was taken to a military hospital where he refused even to give his name, dying after a few hours. Some twenty onlookers were also killed and many more were injured.

The mortally wounded Alexander knew he was dying and ordered his aides to get him to the palace to say farewell to his loved ones. An hour later, he died, attended by his family.

This did not spark a revolution as the assassins had hoped. Instead liberal and left-wing opposition to the regime collapsed. The surviving conspirators were tried, found guilty and executed.

As a result of Alexander II's bloody end, his son and successor, Alexander III, clamped down on any form of political activism. Radicals all over the country disbanded their organisations and went into hiding. An extremely repressive monarch, deeply opposed to any kind of reform, Alexander determined to turn the clock back. For over a decade, any kind of opposition to the government was banned, and Russia's social system returned to the backwardness that had characterised it before the reign of Alexander II.

On the sixth anniversary of the assassination of Alexander II, there was a planned attempt on the life of Alexander III. Police suspected that when Alexander III visited church on the anniversary of his father's assassination, members of *Narodnaya Volya* would throw bombs into the emperor's carriage. Three would-be assassins were arrested in Nevsky Prospect. One of them was Aleksandr Ulyanov, the elder brother of Vladimir Ulyanov, later known as Vladimir Lenin. In court Ulyanov gave a political speech. The conspirators were sentenced to death; all but five were pardoned by Alexander III. Ulyanov was not among them. His death turned Lenin into a revolutionary.

When Alexander III died prematurely in 1894, Nicholas II took over, becoming the last Tsar to rule Russia. He and his entire family were eventually shot by ruthless revolutionaries on the orders of Lenin. There followed a bloody civil war, then seventy years of a repressive Soviet state. While this proved vital in the defeat of Nazi Germany, it brought the world to the brink of extinction in the Cold War that followed. It extended its brutal repression across eastern and central Europe and, in competition with the West, spread terrorism, revolution and theatre wars around the world, including the wars in Korea and Vietnam. With Vladimir Putin in power in Russia, one could argue that the effects of the assassination of Alexander II are still being felt today.

38

JAMES A. GARFIELD 1881

James A. Garfield was in office for less than four months before he was assassinated. He had never wanted to be president in the first place. His assassin was a would-be politician who thought that he was responsible for Garfield's victory in the 1880 election and should, at least, have been rewarded with a consulship to Vienna or Paris. When no position was forthcoming, he decided the remedy was to remove Garfield from office with a gun.

The last of the 'log cabin' presidents, Garfield was born on 19 November 1831 in a shack at Orange, Cuyahoga County, Ohio. His father died when Garfield was two years old. He helped his mother work their small farm, taking what schooling he could during the winter months. When he was seventeen, he worked driving the horses and mules that pulled flatboats along the Ohio canal – and in typical Horatio Alger-style beat up the tow-path bully.

With the money he earned he enrolled in a local school run by the Disciples of Christ and became a preacher. Working as a carpenter during the summer, he put himself through Geauga Seminary in Chester, Ohio, then paid his way through Hiram Eclectic Institute (now Hiram College) by teaching English and ancient languages. He was a passable poet and an accomplished classical scholar. His party trick was simultaneously writing Greek with one hand and Latin with the other.

By 1854, he had saved enough money to travel east to the prestigious Williams College in Williamstown, Massachusetts, where he worked his way through college by teaching. He graduated with a BA in 1856 top of his class. Then he returned home to Ohio, where he was soon made president of Hiram and married his childhood sweetheart Lucretia Rudolph.

A 'free-soiler', an anti-slavery faction, he joined the newly formed Republican Party and was elected to the state senate, where he quickly made a reputation for himself as an orator. He also found time to study law and was admitted to the Ohio bar in 1860.

As Republican Party leader in the Ohio state senate, he called for an end to slavery and for the use of force to put down any rebellion in the South. When the Civil War came, he raised a regiment of volunteers, the 42nd, partly from his old students. He joined up as their lieutenant colonel and was soon made full colonel in command of the 18th Brigade.

At the Battle of Middle Creek he was promoted brigadier general. Just thirty, he was the youngest brigadier general in the army. He went on to fight at Shiloh and, as chief of staff to General W. S. Rosecrans, managed to turn the tide at Chickamauga.

Garfield was elected to Congress while still in uniform, but at Abraham Lincoln's request, he resigned his commission when he went to Washington in 1862. He served on the Committee on Military Affairs and repeatedly called for the complete conquest of the South. Then, as a leading Radical, he helped lead the movement to impeach President Andrew Johnson, Lincoln's successor.

Garfield managed to avoid most of the scandals of the notoriously corrupt administration of Ulysses S. Grant. Like other Congressmen, he had been offered stock in Credit Mobilier, a fraudulent company set up by Union Pacific Railroad to inflate construction cost. While he did not take it up, he was paid a dividend of $329, which he innocently accepted.

In the contentious politics of the Reconstruction era, he also sat on the electoral commission which looked into the disputed returns in the 1876 presidential election, where the Democrat Samuel Tilden won the popular vote. A staunch Republican, Garfield brokered the deal with southern Democrats that gave disputed electoral college votes to Rutherford Hayes, making him president, in exchange for withdrawing Union troops from the South.

Garfield had served eighteen years in the House when, in 1880, the Ohio state legislature elected him to the US Senate. He never took his seat. The Republican National Convention in Chicago that year was sharply divided between the 'Stalwarts' – backers of Grant who was running for a controversial third term – and the more moderate 'Half Breeds' who backed James G. Blaine. As head of the Ohio delegation, Garfield was chosen to put forward the name of Treasury Secretary John Sherman and did so eloquently. This led to a three-way deadlock, with Grant leading the vote on the first thirty-five ballots.

In an attempt to break the impasse, Garfield assembled an anti-Grant coalition which overturned the 'unit rule' where a state's entire vote was cast by the majority of delegation. Then, on the second day of the convention, Sherman withdrew and asked his supporters to vote for Garfield instead. Garfield protested: 'No man has a right, without the consent of the person voted for, to announce that person's name and vote for him in this convention. Such consent I have not given.'

It made no difference. On the thirty-sixth ballot there was one candidate the entire party could rally behind – Garfield. The Stalwart Chester Arthur was nominated as vice president to balance the ticket.

There were few issues in the 1880 election and Garfield ran his campaign largely from the front porch of Lawnfield, the house he had bought in Mentor, Ohio, in 1876. He beat the Democratic candidate Winfield Scott Hancock by only ten thousand popular votes out of a total of some nine million. But this gave him 214 of the 369 votes in the electoral college.

Garfield's election marked the end of the old bitterness between North and South. Reconstruction was over and the old white aristocracy had re-asserted itself in the secessionist states. At Garfield's inauguration parade a group of Confederate veterans broke through the crowd, waving the Union flag and cheering Garfield and Hayes. And on 4 March 1881, the six-foot tall, portly, blue-eyed, blond, bearded Ohioan was sworn in as the 20th President of the United States.

Garfield immediately took on the Stalwarts, appointing Blaine secretary of state. The leader of the Stalwarts, US Senator Conkling and his fellow New York Senator Thomas Platt resigned, hoping that the New York state legislature would back them and return them to the Senate with a fresh mandate. The gamble failed and New York's legislature refused to re-elect them.

The new administration's Postmaster General Thomas L. James and Attorney General Wayne MacVeagh uncovered the Star Route Frauds. Huge sums of money had gone missing over the granting of mail delivery contracts in the West – much of it going into the pockets of Republican officials in previous administrations. Garfield let the investigation continue, despite the damage it was doing to his party.

On 2 July 1881, President Garfield was waiting with Secretary of State Blaine in the Baltimore and Potomac Railroad depot for a train to Massachusetts, where he planned to visit his alma mater, Williams College. They were approached by Charles J. Guiteau, a lawyer who had failed to secure the position of minister to France in Garfield's administration. Guiteau drew an English bulldog pistol, yelled: 'I am a Stalwart and now Arthur is President.' He fired.

The first bullet grazed Garfield's arm; the second lodged in his back. He need not have died. Alexander Graham Bell was called to the White House to find the exact location of the bullet using an induction-balance device he had invented. The bullet was safely lodged in a muscle and could have remained there. But the surgeon probed for it with his bare fingers and unsterilised instruments, fatally contaminating the wound.

Garfield lingered on through the long hot summer, unable to perform any executive acts except for signing one extradition order. The Constitution was unclear about what should happen in such circumstances. Should the vice president take over the presidency or merely govern in the president's name? Congress was not in session to debate the matter. The cabinet met but decided they could take no action without consulting Garfield. This was impossible the doctors said.

On 6 September 1881, Garfield was taken on special train to Francklyn Cottage, Elberon, New Jersey, where it was hoped the sea air would revive him. With the constant attention of his wife, Garfield seemed to rally. But on the morning of 19 September 1881, he woke with a chill and grew progressively weaker. He died at 10.30 that night.

His body was taken to Cleveland, Ohio, for burial. As the train passed through Princeton, New Jersey, the students covered the railroad tracks with flowers as a mark of respect.

A month later, Guiteau was brought before the Supreme Court of the District of Columbia. Although he ranted incoherently throughout the ten-week trial, he was found guilty and sane. On 30 June 1882, he was hanged in a Washington jail in front of a crowd of over two hundred people, many of whom had paid exorbitant prices for tickets. On the gallows, he read a poem he had written for the occasion and continued babbling even after the black hood had been pulled over his face.

39

ABRAHAM LINCOLN 1865

The assassination of Abraham Lincoln on 15th April 1865 is seen as the first modern political assassination. It raised Lincoln to be a figure of almost mythological proportions. Certainly he confronted and resolved the issue that had threatened to tear the republic apart, preserved the Union – at the cost of the bloody and divisive Civil War – and freed the slaves, albeit reluctantly. Few remember that this great champion of freedom defied the Constitution, spent large amounts of money without Congressional approval, suspended habeas corpus and ordered suspected traitors to be tried by military tribunals. However, these things are forgotten – or forgiven – because, at the moment of victory, Lincoln died a martyr's death. What remains is Lincoln's eloquent defence of democracy. He believed that the Union was worth preserving, not just for its own sake, but because it embodied an ideal – that people were capable of governing themselves.

Born in rural Kentucky, Lincoln was raised in a series of backwoods cabins. His schooling never amounted to more than a year. The young Lincoln helped his father clear the fields and tend the crops, but he took an early dislike to fishing and hunting. After moving to Indiana, his mother died and his stepmother encouraged him to read.

While working as a clerk in a general store in New Salem, Illinois, he ran for the state legislature as a Whig and won on his second attempt in 1834. He taught himself law and was admitted to the bar two years later. It was in the state legislature that Lincoln first outlined his views on slavery, which he had witnessed first-hand on river trips to New Orleans. He said that slavery was 'founded on injustice and bad policy'. But he was no abolitionist. 'The promulgation of abolition doctrines tends to increase rather than abate its evils,' he maintained.

Elected to the US House of Representatives in 1846, he introduced a bill that gradually emancipated slaves in the District of Columbia and compensated their owners. But this should only happen with the consent of the 'free white citizens' of the district, he argued. Consequently, he managed to alienate the abolitionists as well as the slave-owners.

In 1856 he joined the newly formed Republican Party and ran against Democratic incumbent Stephen Douglas for the US Senate in 1858. During the campaign, Lincoln challenged Douglas to a state-wide series of debates on slavery which were widely followed. In them, Lincoln asserted: 'A house divided against itself cannot stand. I believe the government cannot endure half slave and half free… It will become all one thing or all the other.'

Lincoln lost the election, but the debates had brought him to nationwide prominence. At the Republican National Convention in Chicago in 1860, he was nominated on the third ballot. In a four-cornered race, 'Honest Abe' won no votes in the Deep South and carried no more than 40 per cent of the country as a whole, but the Democrats were so divided that Lincoln won 180 of the 303 votes in the electoral college.

South Carolina seceded immediately. When an attempt at compromise between the slave states and free states failed in Congress, six more states followed, forming the Confederacy. A scheduled stop at Baltimore on his way to the inauguration had to be cancelled after a plot to assassinate him was uncovered.

The bone of contention between the Union and the Confederacy were the Federal forts in the South. In his inauguration address, Lincoln maintained that it was his duty to hold onto government property. The war broke out when Confederate artillery fired on the Union garrison at Fort Sumter in Charleston, South Carolina, in April 1861.

The Civil War dragged on for four years with possibly as many as a million dead. By the time of Lincoln's death the Union had prevailed. During the course of the war he had signed the Emancipation Proclamation, freeing the slaves.

As a result, there were many who wanted Lincoln dead, both aggrieved supporters of the Confederacy and those who believed in slavery. One such man was the actor John Wilkes Booth, who had been a leading actor before the war. A southern sympathiser and confirmed racist, Booth loathed Abraham Lincoln.

By the late summer of 1864 it had become clear that the Union was winning the war. Booth's original plan was to kidnap Lincoln and take him to Richmond, the Confederate capital. By January 1865, Booth had gathered a group of like-minded conspirators who met in a boarding house belonging to Mary Surratt.

The kidnap was planned for 17 March 1865 when the president was due to attend a play at a hospital near

Washington. However, Lincoln cancelled at the last moment. Before a new plot could be put in place, General Robert E. Lee, leader of the Confederate forces, surrendered to Union commander General Ulysses S. Grant at Appomattox on 9 April 1865, ending the Civil War. Two days later, Booth was present when Lincoln made a speech in Washington suggesting that voting rights should be extended to African Americans.

The conspirators came up with an ambitious plot to assassinate not just Lincoln but also the vice president Andrew Johnson and the secretary of state William Seward. The aim was to cause chaos in Washington, so that the Confederates, who had not yet disbanded, could rally and seize one last chance to strike back. Craving the limelight, Booth wanted to be the one who actually shot Lincoln.

On the morning of Friday 14 April, Booth visited Ford's Theatre and discovered that the president was planning to watch the play *Our American Cousin* there that night. It was decided that Booth would shoot Lincoln at the theatre, while co-conspirators George Atzerodt and Lewis Powell were to shoot Andrew Johnson and William Seward respectively. All three attacks were planned for 10.15 that night.

President Lincoln arrived at the theatre at about 8.30pm with his wife Mary, Major Henry Rathbone and Clara Harris. Booth turned up an hour later, carrying a single shot derringer and a hunting knife. Booth left his horse with a boy holding it in the back alley, while he went to the saloon next door for a drink. Around 10.07pm he entered the theatre and gradually made his way towards the box where the Lincolns were sitting. The policeman who was supposed to have been guarding the box door had sloped off to slake his thirst.

At about 10.15pm, Booth slipped into the box and shot Lincoln in the back of the head at near point-blank range.

Rathbone grabbed Booth, who stabbed him in the arm. Booth then leapt over the balustrade to the stage some eleven feet below. The spur on his right foot caught on the Union flag draping the box and he fell with such force that he broke his leg. Brandishing the bloody dagger, he shouted what those who heard it said sounded something like '*sic temper tyrannis*' (ever thus to tyrants) and limped from the stage.

There was a piercing scream from the box and the scene in the theatre became pandemonium. An army doctor in the audience rushed to the box and quickly saw that the wound was fatal. The doctor ordered the dying President to be carried from the theatre to a small lodging house across the street. At 7.22 the next morning, Lincoln died.

The other conspirators had been less successful. Atzerodt lost his nerve and never even tried to kill Johnson, while Powell stabbed Seward, but failed to kill him.

In the uproar, Booth had escaped from the theatre. At around midnight he reached Mary Surratt's boarding house where he met accomplice David Herold, before heading to a sympathetic doctor who set and splinted Booth's broken leg. Booth and Herold then fled the city on horseback over the Navy Yard Bridge.

A few days later, they rowed across the Potomac into Virginia. They stopped at the farm belonging to Richard Garrett near Park Royal and Garrett, thinking they were returning Federal soldiers, let them sleep in the barn.

It was there on 26 April 1865 that Union cavalrymen caught up with them. Herold gave himself up. But Booth, who had avoided action by spending most of the war in the North, said that he would never be taken alive. The soldiers set fire to the barn, a shot was heard and the dying Booth was dragged out. He had probably shot himself, although a Sergeant Boston Corbett was to claim that he disobeyed orders and fired the fatal shot.

Within days, the rest of the gang had been rounded up and given a military trial before uniformed judges appointed by the War Department. Three were sentenced to life imprisonment. David Herold, Lewis Powell, George Atzerodt and Mary Surratt were sentenced to be hanged. The execution took place on 7 July 1865 in front of a detachment of Union troops.

A black-draped funeral car bore Lincoln's body on its last journey. It travelled across the country, stopping at cities on the way, where the body was taken from the car to lie in state. The train took twelve days to travel from Washington to Springfield, Illinois. There the body was interred in the Oak Ridge Cemetery.

40

SHAKA 1828

Shaka was the father of the Zulu nation, who subsequently nearly destroyed it. Born the illegitimate son of the Zulu chief Senzangakhona around 1787, he was driven out with his mother Nandi, a Langeni, which the Zulu considered an inferior clan. Even his name was an insult – 'iShaka' was an intestinal parasite thought to be responsible for menstrual irregularities and said, by Zulu elders, to be the true cause of Nandi's pregnancy.

At sixteen, he was taken under the protection of Dingiswayo, king of the Mtetwa, and was trained in his army, excelling in single combat. When Senzangakhona died, Shaka returned to the Zulu – then numbering just 1,500 – as their chief. He quickly reorganised his army. Any opposition resulted in instant death and the people who had made his childhood a misery were impaled on the sharpened stakes of their own *kraal* fences.

Before Shaka, the Zulu were armed with oxhide shields and light throwing spears, and battles were desultory affairs which were broken off before there were many casualties. Shaka rearmed his men with short-bladed assegais for stabbing at close quarters. He also developed a heavier shield that was used to force his opponent to expose his side to the thrust of his assegai. Some were also armed with knobkerries or cudgels.

Shaka instituted a regimental system, with each regiment or *impi* composed of men roughly the same age and housed in their own separate *kraal*. They were distinguished by different headdresses and coloured markings on their shields. Officers directed battles by hand signals, while Shaka sent instructions by runner. He also developed the famous 'buffalo' formation, with the men forming the 'chest' pinning the enemy down while the 'horns' encircled them. The 'loins' were the reserve, who sat looking away from the action to prevent them from becoming unduly excited.

Zulu males were raised as warriors from the age of six. They dispensed with their traditional oxhide sandals and were trained to outrun a horse, covering as much as fifty miles a day barefoot. They swore loyalty to the Zulu king and were not allowed to marry before they had proved their courage in some way. In wartime, warriors painted their upper bodies and faces with chalk and red ochre. They were also famous for their customary 'washing of spears' in their enemy's blood. They cut open the belly of their victims – sometimes, allegedly, while they were still living. This was supposed to allow the release of the enemy's spirit so it could not haunt the killer.

Using such terror tactics, Shaka set about destroying all the tribes around him, integrating any survivors into the Zulu nation which, within a year, had quadrupled in number. Soon he was fielding *impis* a thousand strong, accompanied by young boys who carried cooking pots and sleeping mats.

Then when Dingiswayo died, Shaka took over the Mtetwa Empire. Fighting against the Ndwandwe, he introduced a tactic new to Africa, the scorched earth policy. The Ndwandwe were finally defeated in a two-day battle at the Mhlatuzi fords. In 1820, Shaka began the Mfecane – 'the Crushing' – arbitrarily wiping out clans across the plateau of Natal. The devastation was so complete that the Boer's Great Trek of the 1830s passed through uninhabited land. The Zulu nation grew to 250,000 with an army of 40,000 and occupied territory that stretched from the Cape nearly two thousand miles to the north. To create this empire, it is estimated that Shaka killed over two million people, often in mass executions.

When Shaka was wounded in 1824, he was treated by a visiting Englishman. In recompense, he allowed English traders to operate out of Port Natal and a *kraal* a hundred miles to the north at Bulawayo. He even tried to exchange ambassadors with George IV. In 1827, his mother Nandi died. In grief, Shaka killed seven thousand Zulus. No crops were planted for a year and milk – a Zulu staple – was banned. Milch cows were slain so that calves could know what it felt like to lose a mother and pregnant women were slain with their husbands. Enforced chastity had already dispirited Shaka's army. When they were sent further and further from home to find more lands to conquer, they rebelled.

Two of Shaka's half-brothers Dingane and Mhlangana made at least two attempts to assassinate him. Then, sometime in 1828, with the aid of a general named Mbopa they succeeded. Shaka died without dignity, begging for mercy. His body was dumped in a grain pit that was then filled in. The location is unknown but is believed to be somewhere under the Natal village of Stanger.

However, there are various versions of his last words. According to Zulu myth, he told Dingane and Mhlangana that they would not rule the Zulu nation. Instead it would be taken over by the 'white people who will come up from the sea'. In another version he said it would be ruled by swallows, a reference to white people because they build houses of mud as swallows do.

A more plausible version comes from Mkebeni kaDabulamanzi, King Cetshwayo's nephew and grandson of King Mpande, another half-brother to Shaka. He said Shaka had told Dingane and Mhlangana: 'Are you stabbing me, kings of the earth? You will come to an end through killing one another.'

This, too, was prescient. After Dingane assumed the throne, he purged loyalists to Shaka. He allowed the troops to marry and set up a homestead, which built loyalty within the military. However, his half-brother Mpande came to prominence when Dingane was defeated by the Boers at the Battle of Blood River in December 1838. With the help of the Boers, Mpande defeated Dingane at the Battle of Maqongqo. After executing his own general Ndlela kaSompisi, Dingane escaped, but was soon murdered in Hlatikhulu Forest and Mpande became king.

In 1843 Mpande ordered the death of his brother Gqugqu, who was said to be plotting to kill the king. Gqugqu's wives and children were also killed. The throne was taken by the last great king of the Zulus, Mpande's eldest son and Shaka's nephew Cetshwayo.

Born in 1826, Cetshwayo began taking part in raids on European settlers at the age of twelve, distinguishing himself in the war against the Swazis of 1853–54. He became heir by defeating Mpande's favourite, Cetshwayo's younger brother Mbuyazi, at the Battle of Ndondakusuka in 1856. The survivors were massacred, including five of Cetshwayo's brothers.

Cetshwayo then became de facto king, with Mpande only performing a ceremonial role. He became so fat he was unable to walk. Nevertheless, Cetshwayo also kept an eye on his father's new wives and children for potential rivals, ordering the death of his favourite wife Nomantshali and her children in 1861. She and her daughters were hacked to death. Though two sons escaped, the youngest was murdered in front of the king. Cetshwayo was proclaimed king on Mpande's death in 1872.

The infighting among the Zulus after the death of Shaka weakened them. In 1877, the British decided to annex the Transvaal and the Boers began to encroach on Zulu land. In response, Cetshwayo increased the size of his army. The British High Commissioner, Sir Bartle Frere, decided to eradicate the menace. In December 1878, he sent an ultimatum, insisting that Cetshwayo disband his army. When he refused, the British invaded. But on 22 January 1879, the Zulus, armed only with spears, wiped out an entire British regiment at Isandhlwana. The famous action at Rorke's Drift occurred that same day.

The British recovered and defeated the Zulus at Kambula on 29 March 1879 and took the Zulu capital Ulundi on 4 July 1879. During the battle the only son of Napoleon III, then exiled in England, was killed. Cetshwayo was captured. However, he was allowed to visit Queen Victoria in England and was restored as ruler of Zululand, by then a dependency, in 1883. But those who had ruled in the meantime refused to accept him. Defeated by a rival, he sought refuge with the British resident in Eshowe, where he died of a heart attack in 1884.

The line of Cetshwayo continued to be nominal rulers of Zululand, which was made a British Crown colony in 1887 under the Native Law of Natal. Rebellions in 1888 and 1906 were put down. Cetshwayo's son Dinuzulu led an army against the British in 1890 and was exiled to the island of St Helena for seven years. He was tried for treason following the rebellion in 1906 and jailed, but was released when an old friend of his, General Louis Botha, became prime minister of the Union of South Africa.

The Natal Native Code of 1894 had confiscated two thirds of the Zulu's land and they were confined to native reserves. In 1897, Zululand was incorporated into Natal. The Bantu Homeland – later called a Black state – KwaZulu, composed of some areas of the historical Zululand, was established in the 1970s.

Although Shaka's rule and his assassination ultimately led to the downfall of the Zulu nation, his legend lives on. But while some see him as an heroic king and nation builder, others see him as a depraved monster.

41

SPENCER PERCEVAL 1812

Spencer Perceval was the only British prime minister to be assassinated. He was in office from 4 October 1809 until 11 May 1812, leading a weak administration following the falling out of George Canning and Lord Castlereagh, the leading Tory statesmen of the day. He faced a number of crises during his term in office, including the failure of the Walcheren expedition to the Netherlands during the Napoleonic Wars, the madness of King George III which brought the Prince Regent to power, the economic depression brought on by the war against France, and the Luddite riots where aggrieved workers smashed textile machinery. He was resolute in the face of these difficulties and successfully pursued the Peninsular War, where the British and Portuguese overcame the French forces in Spain. However, his murder had little to do with the major political issues of the day, rather it was over a personal claim for compensation from the government.

The son of the Earl of Egmont, Perceval was educated at Harrow and Trinity College Cambridge. While his eldest brother took his seat in the House of Lords, Perceval studied law and was called to the bar. He came to the attention of the Tory administration of William Pitt the Younger as junior counsel in the prosecution of the radical Thomas Paine, a leading figure in both the American and French Revolutions.

Perceval was elected to parliament in a by-election in May 1796, inheriting the seat from his cousin Lord Compton, and won acclaim in January 1798 with a speech defending Pitt's government against attacks by the radicals Charles James Fox and Francis Burdett. He was generally seen as a rising star in his party. His short stature and slight build earned him the nickname 'Little P'.

He was appointed solicitor general in 1801 and attorney general in 1802. Following Pitt's death, he joined the new Tory administration of the Duke of Portland as chancellor of the exchequer and leader of the House of Commons. In August 1809, Portland had a stroke. Perceval hoped to become home secretary in the new administration, but when contenders for the premiership fell out he was appointed First Lord of the Treasury – the formal title by which prime ministers were then known. Forming a cabinet was made more difficult as Castlereagh and Canning had ruled themselves out of consideration by fighting a duel.

While British forces were withdrawn from the Netherlands, the army of Sir Arthur Wellesley, the future Duke of Wellington, was pinned down in Portugal. George III lapsed into insanity and the Prince of Wales became Prince Regent, who was less sympathetic than his father to Perceval. A bill passed making Luddism a capital offence and, due to the embargo imposed by Napoleon, Orders in Council permitted the Royal Navy to detain any ship carrying goods to France. This affected trade with the United States, damaging British industry. After riots in Manchester in April, the House of Commons set up an enquiry into the operations of the Orders in Council. Perceval was expected to attend the session on 11 May 1812 which was due to start at 5.30pm. Waiting in the crowded lobby was a Liverpool merchant, John Bellingham.

Bellingham's father died in a mental asylum. John then signed on as an officer cadet on a ship bound for India. It was shipwrecked off the Cape Verde Islands. He survived and returned to London, where he set up in business, but went bankrupt in 1794. Escaping debtors' prison, he became a book-keeper and was sent to Archangel in Russia as a commercial agent.

Returning to England, he moved to Liverpool where he set up his own trading company and returned to Archangel. In the autumn of 1803, a Russian ship was lost in the White Sea. It had been insured at Lloyd's of London. The owner Soloman van Brienen filed a claim, but an anonymous letter to Lloyd's said the ship had been sabotaged. Van Brienen believed that Bellingham had written the letter and retaliated by accusing him of a debt of 4,890 roubles in a bankruptcy where he was a guarantor.

Bellingham was about to return to England when his travel documents were cancelled and he was imprisoned for debt. He accused the local authorities of improper detention and made repeated appeals for help to the British consul and ambassador. They did not act, saying the case was one for the Russian authorities alone. After appealing to the Tsar, he was eventually released in October 1809 and returned to England, determined to gain redress.

He petitioned the British government for compensation but was refused as the UK had broken off relations with Russia. Successively he petitioned the Foreign Office, the Treasury, the Privy Council and Perceval himself. Each time he was rebuffed. His wife Mary-Anne begged him to drop the matter. He returned to her in Liverpool where he remained for eighteen months.

Returning to London in December 1811, he resumed his campaign for redress. This time he petitioned the Prince Regent before contacting the Privy Council, the Home Office and the Treasury once more. Copies of his petition were sent to every member of parliament, again getting nowhere.

He took the matter through legal channels, writing to Bow Street Magistrates' Court on 23 March 1812. They refused to consider the case. Bellingham turned to his own MP, Isaac Gascoyne, Tory member for Liverpool. He too was no help.

Just a month before the assassination, Bellingham was once again at the Foreign Office where he met a civil servant named Hill and told him that if he could get no satisfaction he would take justice into his own hands. Hill, apparently not perceiving these words as a threat, told Bellingham he should take whatever action he deemed proper.

Two days later, he bought two .50-calibre pistols and had a tailor sew an inside pocket on his coat to conceal the weapons. On 11 May 1812, he went to the lobby of the House of Commons, where he was seen frequently so his presence warranted no undue attention.

At around 5.15pm Perceval arrived, having walked from Downing Street. As Perceval entered the lobby, Bellingham confronted him. Drawing a pistol, he shot Perceval in the chest. Perceval staggered forward a few steps and exclaimed: 'I am murdered!' In other accounts, he said 'Murder' or 'Oh my God.'

Then he fell face down at the feet of William Smith, the MP for Norwich. Smith only realised that the victim was the prime minister when the body was turned face upwards. Perceval was carried into another room. He was unconscious, but a faint pulse was detected. By the time a doctor arrived, it had stopped and Spencer Perceval was declared dead.

Despite the pandemonium, Bellingham sat quietly on a bench. In the confusion, he then got up to walk about but was seized by an official who had witnessed the murder. He was taken to the Serjeant-at-Arms' quarters where MPs who were also magistrates set up a makeshift court.

Volunteering to explain himself, Bellingham said calmly: 'I have been ill-treated... I have sought redress in vain. I am a most unfortunate man and feel here' – indicating his heart – 'sufficient justification for what I have done.'

Having exhausted all proper avenues, he said he had informed the authorities that he intended to take independent action. Told to do his worst, he said: 'I have obeyed them. I have done my worst, and I rejoice in the deed.'

Formally charged with murder, he was taken to Newgate Prison. At his trial at the Old Bailey on 15 May, Bellingham said: 'Recollect, Gentlemen, what was my situation. Recollect that my family was ruined and myself destroyed, merely because it was Mr Perceval's pleasure that justice should not be granted; sheltering himself behind the imagined security of his station, and trampling upon law and right in the belief that no retribution could reach him. I demand only my right, and not a favour; I demand what is the birthright and privilege of every Englishman.

'Gentlemen, when a minister sets himself above the laws, as Mr Perceval did, he does it as his own personal risk. If this were not so, the mere will of the minister would become the law, and what would then become of your liberties?

'I trust that this serious lesson will operate as a warning to all future ministers, and that they will henceforth do the thing that is right, for if the upper ranks of society are permitted to act wrong with impunity, the inferior ramifications will soon become wholly corrupted. Gentlemen, my life is in your hands, I rely confidently in your justice.'

Evidence was presented that Bellingham was insane, but this was discounted by the trial judge, Sir James Mansfield. After considering the matter for just fifteen minutes, the jury returned a verdict of guilty. Bellingham appeared surprised.

There had been rejoicing around the country at news of the death of Perceval and, when Bellingham was hanged in public outside Newgate Prison on 18 May, troops were on hand to prevent any attempt to rescue him.

On 15 May, the House of Commons voted for the erection of a monument to the assassinated prime minister in Westminster Abbey. Later, memorials were placed in Lincoln's Inn, and within Perceval's Northampton constituency. Parliament also made generous provision to Bellingham's widow and children. She remarried the following year.

42

PAUL I OF RUSSIA 1801

Paul I of Russia was the son and successor of Catherine the Great, who ruled as empress of Russia from 1762 to 1796. Her feeble-minded husband, Tsar Peter III, had only been on the throne for seven months when Catherine conspired with her lover Alexei Grigoryevich Orlov and other members of the guard to depose him when she suspected that he intended to divorce her. After Paul had formally abdicated, he was killed, an event which ever afterwards preyed on the mind of their son, then a boy of eight.

However, it was suspected that Paul was not even Peter's son, but that of another of Catherine's lovers, Sergei Saltykov. There is no reliable evidence to support this, but Paul was born after ten years of married life during which the royal couple had remained childless. Upon his birth, the Empress Elizabeth, Peter's mother, whisked the newborn away from his parents and raised him on her own. Elizabeth also died in 1762, further leaving Paul rudderless.

On Catherine II's accession to the throne, the army swore an oath to her and to the young heir, Paul. However, Catherine did not fancy being regent and wanted to rule as an autocratic monarch in her own right. As a result, mother and son became estranged, and Catherine did everything in her power to keep Paul far from both the court and from government affairs.

She married him off to a German princess, Princess Wilhelmina of Hesse-Darmstadt, and settled them on an estate at Gatchina, away from the centre of affairs at St Petersburg, where Paul could play at soldiers and hold the meaningless military parades in which he delighted. He admired the Prussian army and was obsessed with exacting drill movements and the precise tailoring of uniform.

When Wilhelmina died in childbirth, there was talk of Paul becoming co-ruler of Russia with his mother. She found him another bride, the beautiful Sophia Dorothea of Württemberg, who bore him a son, Alexander, in 1777. Catherine had him brought up at her court, and as the empress neared her death, it seemed that she might name Alexander, not Paul, as her successor. However, when Catherine died in November 1796, Paul succeeded at the age of forty-two. His first act was to try and find Catherine's testament, if she had left one, and destroy it in case it excluded him from the succession. At his coronation, Paul decreed a law of hereditary succession to the crown down the male line, rather than leaving it to the whim of the reigning sovereign.

The remains of Peter III were removed from the sepulchre in which they had been deposited in the church of St Alexander Nevsky. Then after lying in state for three weeks, they were interred in the sepulchre of Catherine II in the Cathedral of St Peter and St Paul. The aged Count Aleksei Grigoryevich Orlov, who had been involved in Peter III's murder thirty-five years earlier, was forced to carry the imperial crown behind the coffin on the way to its new resting place. Paul responded to the rumours of his illegitimacy by parading his descent from Peter the Great. The inscription on the monument to the first emperor of Russia near St Michael's Castle reads in Russian 'To the Great-Grandfather from the Great-Grandson'.

Before she died, Catherine had planned to invade Prussia. Paul immediately recalled the troops. He put his men into Prussian-style uniforms and took much satisfaction in reviewing them as they paraded outside his Mikhailovsky Palace in St Petersburg at 11am every day, regardless of the weather. The elite guards officers, forced to take part in these charades, did not enjoy them. They had little time for the Prussians.

Paul was a martinet. He would personally sentence soldiers to be flogged if they made a mistake. On one occasion he ordered a guards regiment to march to Siberia after they became disordered during manoeuvres, although he changed his mind after they had walked about ten miles. He attempted to reform the organisation of the army in 1796 by introducing *The Infantry Codes*, a series of guidelines for the army based largely upon show and glamour. Those who did not share his views were dismissed or excluded from court – 7 field marshals and 333 generals fell into this category.

Paul then set about reversing many of his mother's policies and weakening the influence of the aristocracy. The only *grands seigneurs* in Russia, he once remarked, were those men who were speaking to the Tsar, and then only for as long as the conversation continued. He tried to lighten the burden on the serfs, at the expense of the landowners, and appointed bureaucrats to run central and local government. Emperor Paul also ordered the bones of Grigory Potemkin, one of his mother's lovers and for seventeen years her most powerful minister, dug up and scattered.

In an attempt to curb inflation, five million paper roubles were burnt outside the Winter Palace. The minting of silver roubles was also ordered. Paul himself sacrificed part of the palace silver for this cause, saying that he would eat his meals with tin plates and cutlery 'until the rouble reaches its proper conversion rate'.

The belief in his own Divine Right, which made some monarchs more humane, had the opposite effect on him. He was perceived to be an aloof, haughty, lonely figure, yet he had loaves sold from special crown storehouses in an attempt to reduce the cost of bread.

Fearing a French-style revolution, Paul forbade his subjects travelling abroad and banned the import of foreign books and periodicals. His foreign policy was a disaster. Without diplomatic relations with Austria, he got Russia into a coalition against Napoleon in 1798, while pursuing an anti-British policy. So in 1800 he was officially at war with France, while unofficially at war with Britain. He expelled the British ambassador, closed British trading posts in St Petersburg, impounded British ships and cargos, and was on the verge of sending a Cossack army through unmapped regions of Central Asia to invade British India. Britain responded by signing treaties with Persia, which threatened Russia's southern flank.

On a cold Monday night in St Petersburg which was to be the last of his life, Paul hosted a dinner party at the palace. Those present included his son, the Grand Duke Alexander, who ate little and seemed ill at ease. After dinner the Tsar retired to his private apartments. There are conflicting accounts of what happened later, but a group of conspirators led by General Leo Bennigsen and Count von Pahlen, the military commander of the city, were quietly admitted to the palace. Von Pahlen went to Alexander's rooms, while Bennigsen led a party of guards officers to the Tsar's suite. The conspirators had had a good deal to drink. They broke down the door and went into the bedroom, which seemed empty. One of them said the bird had flown, but Bennigsen felt the bedclothes and found that they were still warm. Paul was soon found cowering in terror behind a screen.

The conspirators pulled him out and forced him to the table, where they tried to compel him to sign a document of abdication. When Paul offered some resistance, General Nikolay Zubov struck him with a sword. After that, the assassins strangled him with a scarf and trampled his body. It was shortly before one o'clock in the morning.

As the conspirators had an abdication document for Paul to sign, they may not originally have intended to kill him. On the other hand, von Pahlen, asked beforehand what would happen to the emperor, had replied that making an omelette required the eggs.

Twenty-three-year-old Alexander, who succeeded Paul as Tsar Alexander I, was certainly party to his father's deposition, if not to the murder. He had a guilty conscience for the rest of his life. Zubov swept his misgivings aside, saying: 'Time to grow up. Go and rule!' Alexander I did not punish the assassins, while Russia's court physician, the Scot James Wylie, declared apoplexy the official cause of death.

Alexander I's first act was to open peace negotiations with Britain as Nelson was sailing towards St Petersburg and had reached Reval, now Tallinn, the capital of Estonia. Alexander led Russia to victory over Napoleon when his 600,000-strong Grand Army invaded in 1812. When Napoleon entered Moscow after the Battle of Borodino, Alexander said:

'Napoleon or I: from now on we cannot reign together.' And the burning of Moscow, he said, 'illuminated my soul'.

Russia, Austria, Prussia, Great Britain, Sweden, Spain and other nations then formed a sixth coalition with Alexander as its supreme commander. Coalition forces entered France in January 1814 and Paris surrendered on 31 March. It was the first time in four hundred years that a foreign army had entered the city. On 4 April, Napoleon abdicated and went into exile on Elba.

As the most powerful ruler in Europe, Alexander inspired the Congress of Vienna which attempted to restore peace in the Continent. The settlement agreed there formed the framework for European international politics until the outbreak of World War I in 1914.

43

JEAN-PAUL MARAT 1793

The assassination of French revolutionary leader Jean-Paul Marat on 13 July 1793 was immortalised by the painter Jacques-Louis David. It shows Marat in his bath where he spent most of his time to ease an unpleasant skin condition. A board placed across it served as a writing desk. On this Marat was said to have written lists of the names of those he considered to be counter-revolutionaries who were to be guillotined. His young assassin, Charlotte Corday, believed that Marat was a bloodthirsty monster whose excesses were a threat to the newborn Republic. However, her action did not halt the Reign of Terror, rather it intensified it, and David's *The Death of Marat* turned him into a martyr.

Born on 24 May 1743, Marat was a doctor and scientist who became a journalist and politician at the time of the French Revolution. On the eve of the Revolution he began writing political pamphlets. Then in September 1789, he began his own newspaper *L'Ami du Peuple* – 'The People's Friend', where he called for radical action and attacked the aristocracy. He also condemned revolutionaries less radical than him, saying: 'Five or six hundred heads cut off would have assured your repose, freedom and happiness. A false humanity has held your arms and suspended your blows; because of this, millions of your brothers will lose their lives.'

Between 1790 and 1792, Marat was often forced into hiding, sometimes in the Paris sewers, which almost certainly aggravated his debilitating skin disease, thought to be *dermatitis herpetiformis*. Marat emerged publicly on the 10 August insurrection, when the Tuileries Palace was invaded and the royal family forced to shelter within the Legislative Assembly.

Corday thought that Marat was responsible for the September Massacres of 2 to 6 September 1792, where over a thousand prisoners – men, women and children – were sent to the guillotine. Largely they were non-political, mainly common criminals and Catholic priests. Marat knew that many of them were innocent of any crime but felt that a steady supply of victims was necessary to keep the crowds baying for blood sympathetic to the Revolution. The violence spread to the countryside. Marat was a member of the vigilance committee of the Commune that published a circular calling on provincial patriots to defend Paris by eliminating counter-revolutionaries.

Marat was elected to the National Convention which declared France a republic on 22 September 1792. He was one of the radical Montagnards, or 'Mountain Men', who sat on the highest benches of the assembly. They were opposed by the more moderate Girondins or Girondists who the Montagnards claimed were 'a counter-revolutionary faction [which] had coalesced around deputies of the department of the Gironde'.

After Louis XVI had gone to the guillotine on 21 January 1793, Marat called for violent tactics to be used against the Girondins, who he saw as enemies of the

Republic. He signed a circular that called for the recall of those who had voted for the decision to execute the king to be referred back to the people. The Girondins fought back. On 24 April 1793, Marat was brought before the Revolutionary Tribunal on charges that he had printed in his paper statements calling for widespread murder as well as the suspension of the Convention. Marat defended his actions, presenting himself as 'the apostle and martyr of liberty'. The case against him collapsed. Two days later, members of the Paris Commune responded by bringing a case to the Tribunal against twenty-two leading Girondins. Others fled to the provinces. With Marat acquitted on all charges, Charlotte Corday decided to take matters into her own hands.

Born in 1768 in Normandy, she was educated at a Roman Catholic convent in Caen, and as a young woman became a supporter of the moderate Girondins, who wanted to retain the monarchy but make reforms in France. However, she was in favour of the Revolution when it began in 1789, but as it progressed she was appalled by the violence the radical Jacobins, such as George Danton, Maximilien Robespierre and Jean-Paul Marat, had unleashed.

By the summer of 1793, the Girondins were a spent force in the Convention and they met at Caen to discuss how to orchestrate their opposition. Corday, a devoted party follower, was there. She heard a speech denouncing Marat as 'unfeeling, violent and cruel' and proclaiming that liberty could not be established again until he was dead. Corday set off to Paris, determined to kill Marat herself.

Arriving on 9 July, she took a room at the Hôtel de Providence and bought a butcher's knife with a six-inch (15cm) blade. Over the next few days, she wrote her *Adresse aux Français amis des lois et de la paix* – 'Address to the French people friends of Law and Peace' – explaining her reasons for assassinating Marat.

She planned to kill him in front of the National Convention to make an example of him. Then she learned that, because of his skin disorder, he no longer attended the Convention, though tried to make his influence felt with letters which were largely ignored.

On 13 July 1793 she called at Marat's apartment and asked to see him, saying that she wished to 'put him in a condition to render a great service to France'. However, she was turned away by Catherine Evrard, the sister of Marat's fiancée Simonne.

That evening she returned. This time Simonne barred her from entering Marat's room, but Marat heard the commotion and told Simmone to let Corday in. Once she was alone with Marat, she began giving him the names of the Girondists in Caen who had spoken out against the Montagnards. Marat wrote down their names and told her that they would be rounded up and sent to the guillotine. In fact, Marat's influence had already waned and he had no power to send anyone to the guillotine.

Corday then pulled out the butcher's knife she had hidden in her dress, and plunged it into Marat's chest, severing an artery. He called out: *'Aidez-moi, ma chère amie!'* – 'Help me, my dear friend!' As the bathwater turned red, Simonne Evrard rushed into the room. She was joined by a distributor of Marat's newspaper, who seized Corday and restrained her. Two neighbours, a military surgeon and a dentist, attempted to revive Marat, but he was already dead. Republican officials arrived to interrogate Corday and to calm a hysterical crowd who were ready to lynch her.

During her interrogation, Corday insisted that she had acted alone and was not part of a wider Girondist conspiracy. She also said that she was a Republican, citing ancient Rome as the ideal model. Marat, she said, had no respect beyond the *sans-culottes* of Paris. At her trial, she justified her actions, saying: 'I knew that he [Marat] was perverting France. I have killed one man to save a hundred thousand.'

A letter written to her father that had been intercepted was read out during her trial to show that her actions had been premeditated. It read:

Forgive me, my dear papa, for having disposed of my existence without your permission. I have avenged many innocent victims; I have prevented many other disasters. The people, one day disillusioned, will rejoice in being delivered from a tyrant. If I tried to persuade you that I was passing through England, it was because I hoped to keep it incognito, but I recognised the impossibility. I hope you will not be tormented. In any case, I believe that you would have defenders in Caen. I took Gustave Doulcet as a defender: such an attack allows no defence, it's for the form. Goodbye, my dear papa, please forget me, or rather rejoice in my fate, the cause is good. I kiss my sister whom I love with all my heart, as well as all my parents. Do not forget this verse by Corneille: Crime is shame, not the scaffold!

It is tomorrow at eight o'clock that I am judged. This July 16.

When she was sentenced to death for her crime, she said that she had nothing to say 'except that I have succeeded'. She reiterated that she had intentionally assassinated Marat, adding, 'that is the only defence worthy of me'.

Before she died, Corday's portrait was painted by Jean-Jacques Hauer, a National Guard officer who had already begun sketching her from the gallery of the courtroom. It was completed shortly before Corday was summoned to the tumbril. To thank him, she gave him a lock of her hair, as a souvenir 'of a poor dying woman'.

On 17 July 1793, four days after Marat was killed, Corday was guillotined in the Place de Grève wearing the red overblouse denoting a condemned traitor who had assassinated a representative of the people. A witness to her execution, Pierre Notelet, was impressed by her courage and described her as 'calm and beautiful at the end'. She was twenty-four years old.

Despite Corday's protestations that she had acted alone, the Montagnards insisted that she was part of a conspiracy and the Girondins charged before the Revolutionary Tribunal were executed and the Reign of Terror against those suspected of being counter-revolutionaries took off.

David, Marat's colleague in the Convention, was called in to arrange the funeral and to paint a portrait of his friend. He had visited Marat the day before his death. Ignoring Marat's skin condition, David painted a highly idealised portrait. Later, when Robespierre was guillotined and the Jacobins fell from grace, the painting was returned to David. It became famous as a depiction of one of the most dramatic events of the French Revolution.

44

HENRY IV OF FRANCE 1610

Between 1562 and 1598, France was plagued by the Wars of Religion which consumed the lives of three million people. One of the casualties was Henry III of France, whose authority was undermined by violent political parties funded by foreign powers – the Catholic League, supported by Spain and the Pope, and the Protestant Huguenots, supported by England and the Dutch. Before he ascended to the throne, Henry was leader of the royal army that won significant victories over the Huguenots and was one of the figures behind the St Bartholomew's Day Massacre, the targeted assassinations of key Huguenot leaders in 1572.

On 1 August 1589, Henry III was with his army at Saint-Cloud, preparing to retake Paris, when a young fanatical Dominican friar named Jacques Clément, carrying false papers, arrived saying he had important documents for the king. After handing over the documents, he said that he also had a secret message. As Clément bent forward to whisper in Henry's ear, he plunged a knife into the king's abdomen. Clément was killed on the spot by the guards.

Henry had no children and, fatally wounded, he enjoined the officers around him to be loyal to Henry of Navarre as their new king. The following morning Henry III died and Henry of Navarre succeeded him as Henry IV.

Good King Henry or Henry the Great, as he became known, was born in Pau in 1553. While baptised a Catholic, he was brought up as a Protestant by his mother Queen Joan III of Navarre, who declared Calvinism to be the state religion. During the Wars of Religion, he joined the Huguenot cause.

When his mother died in June 1572, he became king of Navarre. It was arranged that he should marry Margaret of Valois, daughter of Henry II and Catherine de' Medici. Margaret was a Catholic and the wedding, which took place on 18 August outside Notre Dame Cathedral in Paris, was supposed to symbolise the reconciliation between Catholics and Protestants. However, on 24 August the St Bartholomew's Day massacres began in Paris, where several thousand prominent Protestants who had come to Henry's wedding were killed. With the help of his Catholic wife, Henry escaped the slaughter. But he was forced to convert to Catholicism and live in the French court.

In 1576, he escaped and renounced Catholicism at Tours, then rejoined the Huguenot forces. Despite this, Henry became heir presumptive to the French throne in 1584 upon the death of Francis, Duke of Anjou, brother and heir to the Catholic Henry III. As Salic law prevented inheritance through the female line, Henry III had no choice but to recognise him as his successor. However, Henry I, Duke of Guise, head of the Catholic League, maintained that no Protestant could wear the crown of France. This precipitated the War of the Three Henries, forcing Henry III to ally himself with Henry of Navarre. The matter was resolved after Guise took Paris and seemed to have the upper hand.

Henry III summoned him to an audience at the Château de Blois. He was then assassinated by forty-five of the king's bodyguards while Henry III looked on. The following year Henry himself was assassinated when he and Henry IV tried to retake Paris.

The pope excommunicated Henry IV and said, as a Protestant, he had no right to inherit the crown. The Catholic nobles who had supported Henry III then abandoned Henry IV, who renewed the onslaught on Paris with German troops and English money. The Catholic League proclaimed Henry's Catholic uncle Charles, Cardinal de Bourbon, king. But having been captured by Henry III, he was then Henry IV's prisoner and, whether voluntarily or not, renounced the crown. When he died the following year, the Catholic League could not agree on a new candidate. If they abandoned Salic law forbidding succession down the female line, the English would again have title to the French throne.

Henry sought to solve the problem by converting to Catholicism once more, saying: '*Paris vaut bien une messe*' – 'Paris is well worth a mass.'

With the Catholic League occupying Rheims where French kings were traditionally crowned, the coronation took place at Chartres Cathedral on 27 February 1594. The pope lifted his excommunication the following year. Then in 1598, Henry issued the Edict of Nantes, extending religious tolerance to Protestants.

His marriage to Margaret of Valois was childless and they had separated even before he had taken the throne. He wanted to annul it and take his mistress Gabrielle d'Estrées as his wife. She had already borne him three children but died in 1599 giving birth to a fourth. The annulment went ahead anyway and, the following year, Henry married Marie de' Medici, who gave him a male heir who became Louis XIII of France and a daughter Henrietta Maria who became Queen of England after marrying Charles I.

During his reign there were a number of attempts on his life. In 1593, Pierre Barrière, a soldier in the Catholic League, planned to assassinate Henry, but he sought absolution from Dominican priest Father Banchi who denounced him. Arrested at Melun on 27 August in commission of his attack, he was executed four days later by breaking on the wheel and quartering. Until his death, he maintained that he had been encouraged by Aubry, parish priest of Saint-André-des-Arcs in Lyon and by Father Varade, rector of the Jesuits in Paris.

The following year, Jean Châtel, the nineteen-year-old son of a cloth merchant, gained entrance to the king's chamber. When Henry stooped to help two officials who had knelt before him rise, Châtel attacked him with a knife, striking his lip. He was arrested.

When questioned Châtel revealed that he had been educated by the Jesuits of the Collège de Clermont. With the Wars of Religion still underway, it was inevitable that the Jesuits would be accused of inspiring Châtel's attack, though he denied it. His former teachers, Fathers Hay and Guéret, were lucky to be exiled. A third teacher, Father Guignard, was hanged and burnt at the stake for his presumed part in the affair. The Collège de Clermont was closed, and the building forfeited, while the Jesuit Order was banished from France, although this ban was lifted in 1605.

Châtel was convicted of the crime of *lèse majesté*. As the law prescribed, first Châtel's hand, which he had attacked the king with, was burnt with molten sulphur, lead and wax. He was then executed by dismemberment.

Then on 14 May 1610, Henry IV was killed by François Ravaillac, who stabbed him in the Rue de la Ferronnerie. Henry's coach had stopped in traffic congestion caused by the queen's coronation ceremony.

Ravaillac was a Catholic fanatic. His mother Françoise Dubreuil was known for her Catholic piety and her two brothers were canons of the Cathedral of Angoulême. Obsessed by religion, he sought admission to the ascetic Feuillants, an order of Cistercian monks. But after a short probation, he was dismissed as being 'prey to visions.' An application in 1606 for admission to the Society of Jesus was again unsuccessful.

In 1609, Ravaillac claimed to have had a vision telling him to persuade Henry IV to convert the Huguenots to Catholicism. Between Pentecost 1609 and May 1610, Ravaillac made three separate trips to Paris to tell the king of his vision, lodging with Charlotte du Tillet, mistress of Jean Louis de Nogaret de La Valette, duc d'Épernon. Unable to secure an audience with the king, Ravaillac interpreted Henry's decision to invade the Spanish Netherlands as the start of a war against the pope. To prevent this, Ravaillac decided to kill the king.

On 14 May, Ravaillac lay in wait in the Rue de la Ferronnerie in Paris. When the king passed, his carriage was halted and Ravaillac seized the opportunity to stab Henry to death. Pierre de l'Estoile, the chronicler, stated of the king:

His coach, entering from St Honoré to Ferronnerie Street, was blocked on one side by a cart filled with wine and on the other by a cart filled with hay… Ravaillac climbed on the wheel of the above-named coach and with a knife trenchant on both sides stabbed him between the second and third ribs.

During interrogation, Ravaillac was frequently tortured for the names of his accomplices, but he insisted that he had acted alone. His knowledge of the king's route and the blockage of traffic that put the king within reach excited speculation. The king had been on his way to the Arsenal to make final preparations for imminent military intervention in the disputed succession to the united Duchies of Jülich-Cleves-Berg after the death of Duke John William. This involvement on behalf of a Calvinist candidate would have brought France into conflict with the Catholic Habsburg dynasty. Ravaillac seems to have learned of the plan. In his tortured mind this was part of the king's preparations to make war on the pope and transfer the Holy See to Paris.

Ravaillac had no regrets. During his interrogation, he said of the king: 'I know very well he is dead; I saw the blood on my knife and the place where I hit him. But I have no regrets at all about dying, because I've done what I came to do.'

On 27 May 1610, he was taken to the Place de Grève and was tortured one last time before being pulled apart by four horses, a method of execution reserved for regicides. Historian Alistair Horne described Ravaillac's suffering: 'Before being drawn and quartered... he was scalded with burning sulphur, molten lead and boiling oil and resin, his flesh then being torn by pincers.'

Following his execution, Ravaillac's parents were forced into exile, and the rest of his family was ordered never to use the name 'Ravaillac' again.

Henry IV's widow, Marie de' Medici, served as regent for their nine-year-old son, Louis XIII, until 1617. When she continued her husband's policy of religious tolerance, the princes of the blood and the great nobles revolted. An accomplished intriguer, she bought them off. Louis went on to destroy the castles of any who defied him and abolished private armies, centralising power. He also established the Académie française.

45

LORD DARNLEY 1567

Henry Stewart, Duke of Albany, also known as Lord Darnley, was the second husband of Mary Queen of Scots. He fancied himself king of Scotland, but he fell out with the queen and was murdered, perhaps at her behest. This led to her downfall, her exile in England and, ultimately, her beheading. Their son, James VI of Scotland, went on to become James I of England, uniting the two kingdoms. James was the first to style himself king of Great Britain.

Born in 1545 or 1546 in Yorkshire, Darnley's father was Earl of Lennox and Henry's title came from the barony of Darnley in Renfrewshire, an early possession of the Lennox Stewart family. Through his parents he had claims to both the Scottish and English thrones, being descended from both James II of Scotland and Henry VII of England. Educated at home, he spoke Scots, English, French and Latin.

Darnley's father had been declared guilty of treason and his Scottish estates forfeited in 1545 for his part in the 'rough wooing' – that is, an invasion by the English to destroy Scotland's alliance with France. Keen to recover his estates, Lennox sent his teenage son to congratulate Mary on becoming queen of France as wife to François II in 1559.

He crossed the Channel again after the death of François in December 1560 to offer condolences. As a result, the family were arrested by the English for consorting with the French, though Darnley escaped.

When the family were pardoned in 1563, Darnley and his mother were invited to stay at the court of Elizabeth I who wrote to Mary about the restoration of the Lennox estates. Mary agreed to return them and the family went back to Scotland.

There was already talk of a marriage between Mary and Darnley, and when he arrived in Edinburgh, courtier Sir James Melville reported: 'Her Majesty took well with him, and said that he was the lustiest and best proportioned long man that she had seen.'

They danced a galliard together. Darnley then fell ill and she nursed him. After swearing allegiance to Mary on 15 May 1565, he was created knight of Tarbolton, Lord Ardmannoch, and Earl of Ross. This was tantamount to announcing their engagement. Elizabeth was furious. She sent Darnley's mother to the Tower and confiscated Lennox's English estates.

It made no difference. On 22 July Darnley was created Duke of Albany in the abbey of Holyroodhouse and the banns of marriage were called in the parish of Canongate. A week later the proclamation was issued saying that they would govern jointly and a silver coin was struck with both their heads on.

The wedding on 29 July 1565 took place in Mary's private chapel at Holyrood by Catholic rites. Afterwards Darnley left Mary to hear the nuptial mass alone. He was flexible when it came to religion – sometimes a professed Catholic, sometimes a follower of John Knox. When Darnley was proclaimed king Henry the following day, only his father shouted: 'God save His Grace.' He was Darnley's only real supporter in Scotland.

Within weeks the marriage began to break down. It became clear to Mary that Darnley was arrogant, vain, and unreliable, preferring pleasure to the affairs of state. Darnley insisted that he be granted the crown matrimonial – under Scots law, this meant that he would rule in his own right in the event of her death and any children of a second marriage would inherit the crown. Mary told him that he must wait until he came of age and that the crown matrimonial could only be granted with the consent of the Scottish parliament.

The coin with their two heads on it was withdrawn from circulation and another struck naming Darnley only as 'the queen's husband'. In February 1566, Darnley was invested by the French ambassador with the order of St Michel, France's highest chivalric order. At the celebrations afterwards, it was reported that: 'All people say that Darnley is too much addicted to drinking… and gave her such words that she left the place in tears.'

Darnley grew jealous of Mary's private secretary, Italian Catholic David Riccio, who was suspected of being a papal agent. Suspecting adultery, Darnley conspired with disaffected nobles, promising them indemnity and his conversion to the Protestant religion in return for their support in his quest for the crown matrimonial.

On 9 March 1566, while Mary and Riccio were having supper together, the conspirators burst in and brutally murdered him. Darnley wanted this done in front of the queen, perhaps in the hope that she might miscarry. The conspirators fled to England, sending Mary a copy of the indemnity that Darnley had promised, thus implicating him in the murder.

There were rumours that Mary sent emissaries to Rome to ask for a divorce. Fearing for his own position, Darnley tried to curry Mary's favour, joining her at the Easter celebrations and hearing mass every day. Meanwhile he sought support from abroad.

On 19 June, Mary gave birth to the future king James. He was baptised with full Catholic rites. Darnley refused to attend. Towards the end of 1566 Mary met with her lords of council to discuss the 'Darnley problem', asking those present to seek 'the means that your majesty shall be quit of him without prejudice to your son'. They agreed to murder him.

Meanwhile Darnley fell ill with what seems to have been syphilis. Mary nursed him in the Old Provost's Lodge at Kirk o' Field. On 9 February 1567, the night before Darnley was due to return to Holyrood, there was a huge explosion that completely destroyed the house. The bodies of Darnley and his servant were found under a tree in the garden, with a chair, a dagger, a coat, and a cloak beside them. There was no sign of damage by the explosion on the bodies, nor had they been stabbed, shot, strangled or beaten. It was concluded they had probably been suffocated. Neighbours later stated that Darnley had cried out: 'O my brothers, have pity on me for the love of him who had mercy on all the world.'

Other witnesses said that they saw eleven men riding away after the explosion. One shouted after them that they were traitors. Another grabbed one of the men and asked about the explosion but got no reply.

It was clear that Mary was complicit in the murder. Elizabeth I wrote to her, saying: 'I should ill fulfil the office of a faithful cousin or an affectionate friend if I did not… tell you what all the world is thinking. Men say that, instead of seizing the murderers, you are looking through your fingers while they escape.'

Chief among the suspects was James Hepburn, Earl of Bothwell. He was charged, tried and acquitted on 12 April. On 24 April, Bothwell and his eight hundred men took Mary to his castle at Dunbar. There, it is alleged, he raped her. On 12 May she created him Duke of Orkney and Marquess of Fife, and on 15 May they were married in the Great Hall at Holyrood, according to Protestant rites. Catholics denied the validity of the marriage, refusing to recognise Bothwell's divorce from his first wife just twelve days earlier. Both Protestants and Catholics were shocked that Mary should marry the man accused of murdering her husband.

Twenty-six Scottish peers, known as the confederate lords, turned against Mary and Bothwell and raised an army against them. Mary and Bothwell confronted them at Carberry Hill on 15 June. There was no battle as Mary's supporters had deserted her.

After one final embrace Bothwell was given safe passage from the field. He was stripped of his titles and estates, and fled to Denmark, where he was arrested and died in jail. Some of his followers who remained in Scotland were executed.

Mary was taken to Edinburgh, where crowds denounced her as an adulteress and murderer. She was then imprisoned in Loch Leven Castle, on an island in the middle of Loch Leven. Mary was forced to abdicate on 24 July and her one-year-old son James was crowned five days later.

The following May, Mary escaped and headed for Dumbarton Castle where her supporters had rallied. In a battle at Langside near Glasgow, they were scattered and she fled to England. However, Elizabeth saw Mary as a threat. As a granddaughter of Henry VII, she had a claim to the throne of England. Many Catholics viewed Elizabeth as illegitimate, making Mary the rightful queen of England. She was imprisoned.

Although she pledged loyalty to her cousin Elizabeth, she became the centre of Catholic plots. In 1586, she was implicated in the Babington Plot. Tried for treason at Fotheringhay Castle, she was convicted and sentenced to death. On 1 February 1587, Elizabeth signed the death warrant. A week later, Mary was beheaded. Her body was embalmed and she was given a Protestant burial at Peterborough Cathedral.

Mary's son James VI of Scotland became James I of England in 1603. Her body was exhumed in 1612, when her son, king James VI and I, ordered that she be reinterred in Westminster Abbey in a chapel opposite the tomb of Elizabeth.

46

THOMAS BECKET 1170

The son of a merchant, Thomas Becket, often known as Thomas à Becket, rose to be royal chancellor then Archbishop of Canterbury. He fell out of favour with Henry II, who was trying to rein in the powers of the Church which was both a law unto itself and loyal to the pope rather than the crown. It is not entirely clear whether Henry ordered his murder, or whether the assassins misunderstood him. However, his murder before the altar in Canterbury Cathedral made him a martyr and a saint, revered down the centuries.

Born in London's Cheapside in 1120, he was the only surviving son of Gilbert Beket and his wife Matilda. They were Normans and Becket's mother tongue was French. This may have been the origin of his misattributed name à Becket, stressing his French origins.

The Bekets became wealthy property owners and had a fine house in the City. This gave Becket a privileged childhood, learning to ride, hunt and joust. At the age of ten he was sent to board at the Augustinian priory at Merton in Surrey, which had a good scholastic reputation. Later he went to one of the London grammar schools. When he was twenty, he was sent to Paris for a year to continue his studies.

However, the Bekets lost their money and Thomas went to work as a clerk at the banking house of a rich relative, then entered the household of the Archbishop of Canterbury Theobald of Bec.

Better educated than the other clerks, Becket found favour with the archbishop who sent him to study law at Bologna and Auxerre and even on missions to the papal curia. On his return, Theobald made him an archdeacon.

After the death of king Stephen in 1154, Theobald was involved in the negotiations that put Henry II on the throne. Becket then became chancellor, perhaps forced on the twenty-two-year-old Henry as the church's agent to restrain a youthful ruler who they thought was headstrong and anti-clerical. However, Becket became Henry's close friend and was generously rewarded.

The high points in his career as royal favourite were leading a legation to the French king in 1158, and his participation the following year in Henry's campaign to 'recover' Toulouse where he had seven-hundred knights under his command and took an active part in the fighting. However, the campaign was paid for by a tax on the church, which lost him friends there.

When Becket fell ill, he was visited by both Henry and the French king Louis VII who had made a truce. When Theobald died in 1161, he wanted Becket, his protégé, to succeed him. Henry wanted that too, to have a friend and ally as the head of the English church. However, since the Norman conquest all archbishops of Canterbury had been monks, and the monks of the cathedral see, Christ Church, claimed sole right of election. Monastic bishops were available for the post, primarily Gilbert Foliot, bishop of Hereford, a pious theologian who later became bishop of

London. Becket himself did not want the post. He enjoyed to the full his life at the royal court. But Henry had his way. Becket's election was confirmed on 23 May 1162 by a royal council of bishops and noblemen.

Becket first had to be ordained a priest on 2 June 1162. The following day he was made archbishop. Henry now hoped that, by making his friend Becket the most important religious leader in the land, he would ensure that the church would take the side of the monarchy. However, once Becket became archbishop, Henry began to realise he had made a mistake. Having lived an ostentatious life at court and been a worldly companion to the king, Becket now became serious and ascetic, adopting coarse robes and solemnly attending to his religious duties. Rather than being at the king's beck and call, he was now loyal to the church.

Becket worked to ensure that the church had its own sphere of influence, separate from that of the crown. A bone of contention was that the king wanted priests who had committed criminal offences to be tried in the crown courts. Becket argued that they should be tried by religious authorities under canonical law in the church's own courts where clerics often received lighter sentences or were acquitted. Unscrupulous criminals took advantage of this by taking minor orders and claiming the right to be tried by ecclesiastical courts 'by benefit of clergy'.

There was a case where the archbishop had prevented a clerk, convicted in a lay court of a felony, from suffering the proscribed lay penalty of mutilation or death. Henry II called a church council at Westminster on 13 October 1163 and asked them to overturn this ruling. Becket and the bishops refused. The following morning the king sought to disgrace Becket by removing his son Henry from the archbishop's tutelage and depriving him of all the custodies and honours he had granted him as chancellor.

Both Henry and Becket appealed to the pope. Henry also sought to increase the powers and privileges of the Archbishop of York which would allow his use as an alternative primate in England. When Pope Alexander III prevaricated, Henry called a great council at Woodstock where he browbeat Becket into declaring that he would observe the laws and customs of the kingdom over those of the church. In doing so, Becket accepted that he had sinned. He suspended himself from priestly duties and imposed penance on himself.

Henry then accused Becket of embezzlement. He was also found to be in breach of the Constitutions of Clarendon Henry had passed in 1164, to curb the power of church courts. But before the judgment was given, Becket walked out of the court. In disguise, he made his way to Sandwich, crossed the Channel and sought asylum in France. He stayed there for six years.

When he returned, relations between Henry and Becket had not improved. Henry wanted Becket to pardon the bishops of London whom he had excommunicated for siding with the king. Becket refused. Infuriated, Henry was said to have shouted: 'What cowards have I brought to my court, who care nothing for allegiance to their lord? Will no one rid me of this meddlesome priest?' In other accounts this is rendered as: 'What miserable drones and traitors have I nurtured and promoted in my household who let their lord be treated with such shameful contempt by a low-born clerk!'

Seeking to curry favour with the king, four knights – William de Tracy, Hugh de Morville, Reginald Fitzurse and Richard Brito – set off for Canterbury. They arrived on 29 December

1170 and accosted Becket. Realising he was in danger, his household bundled him into Canterbury Cathedral where they left him though Becket had not ordered the doors to be barred. He could have hidden, but he decided to face his assailants.

The knights followed him up to the altar and demanded that he withdraw the excommunications. He refused. When Fitzurse tried to arrest him and hoist him onto William de Tracy's shoulders, he fought back fiercely. Insults were traded. Finally, they pulled their swords. While Hugh de Morville kept onlookers at bay, Fitzurse and the others struck in turn. The first blow was partially deflected by the arm of Edward Grimm, a monk who was standing near the altar. But still it took off the top of Becket's head. He fell face down, commending his soul to God, the Blessed Mary, St Denis and the patron saints of his church. The four knights then hacked Becket to pieces, with Richard Brito delivering the *coup de grâce*. Becket's brains were spilled on the floor in full view of the congregation. The knights then fled from the cathedral.

Besides being a horrifyingly brutal murder, this was also a sacrilegious act when performed in a church. This appalled Christians throughout Europe. Becket was quickly canonised, Henry vilified for the cold-blooded murder of the most important religious leader in England.

For his part, Henry claimed that he had merely spoken in anger; he had not meant his outburst to be taken seriously. Such was the public outcry at the murder that, four years later, the king was forced to do penance for the crime. He walked barefoot through the streets of Canterbury, wearing the simple robe of a pilgrim with a hair shirt underneath. At Becket's tomb in the cathedral, he knelt down, confessed and asked for the dead man's pardon. He then bared his back and was lashed with branches by eighty monks, until his skin was covered in welts.

He negotiated a settlement with the papacy, effectively overturning the Constitutions of Clarendon, and swore to go on a crusade, though he did not do so. Louis VII used the murder as an excuse to make renewed inroads into Henry's possessions in France. Meanwhile the cult of Becket went from strength to strength.

47

CALIGULA 41

The third Roman emperor Caligula, or Gaius Caesar Germanicus as he was more properly known, was viewed as a mad tyrant who drained the treasury faster than he could replenish it through taxes and extortion. In AD41 Caligula was stabbed to death, by officers of the Praetorian Guard led by Cassius Chaerea. Roman historian Cassius Dio remarked that Caligula 'learned by actual experience that he was not a god'.

The Senate wanted to use the removal of Caligula as a pretext to re-establish the Roman Republic, but the Praetorian Guard put Claudius on the throne. He extended the Roman Empire in North Africa and made Britain a province and Roman emperors continued to rule for another four hundred years in the West and fourteen hundred years in the East.

Born in AD12, he was brought up in the military camps of his father, Roman general Germanicus Caesar, and got his nickname Caligula – which means 'Little Boots' – from the scaled-down army footwear he wore as a youth.

His father died in AD19, and his mother and two older brothers were executed by the Emperor Tiberius during his paranoid purges. But after being summoned to Capri,

Caligula managed to ingratiate himself with Tiberius, being constantly at the emperor's beck and call. It was said of Caligula that no one ever made a better slave or a worse master. Not only did he have to tolerate the whims of the man who had killed half his family, he also had to witness the old man's sexual depravity and his delight in torture and mass executions. As Tiberius's favourite, he got to indulge sadistic whims of his own.

'Even at that time he could not control his natural cruelty and viciousness,' wrote first-century historian Suetonius. 'He was a most eager witness of the tortures and executions of those who suffered punishment, revelling at night in gluttony and adultery, disguised in a wig and a long robe, passionately devoted besides to the theatrical arts of dancing and singing, in which Tiberius very willingly indulged him, in the hope that through these his savage nature might be softened. This last was so clearly evident to the shrewd old man, that he used to say now and then that to allow Gaius to live would prove the ruin of himself and of all men...'

It was said that Caligula then poisoned Tiberius. According to Suetonius he did this little by little so that Tiberius, fearing he was dying, would take the ring from his finger and hand it over, thus transferring power. Tiberius did take the ring off but did not hand it over. He held on to it, so Caligula put a pillow over his face to smother him – or, in other versions, he strangled him.

The Romans were delighted that Tiberius was dead, making Caligula a popular figure. His father was remembered with affection and Caligula was widely pitied because of the destruction of his family by Tiberius. When he accompanied the dead emperor's funeral cortege on its journey to Rome, the crowds along the way turned out to cheer him.

When the procession reached the capital, Tiberius's will, which named his grandson Tiberius Gemellus as his successor, was voided and absolute power was put in Caligula's hands by the unanimous consent of the Senate and the acclamation of the mob outside. According to Suetonius: 'So great was the public rejoicing that within the next three months, or less than that, more than a hundred and sixty thousand victims are said to have been slain in sacrifice.'

Initially Caligula was popular, largely because Tiberius was so hated. He restored the honour of his family, having his mother and brothers' ashes moved into the Emperor Augustus's mausoleum. He renamed the month September Germanicus after his father, declared a general amnesty for all Romans imprisoned or exiled by Tiberius and stopped the old emperor's treason trials. To further boost his popularity, the vast coffers that the miserly Tiberius had amassed were squandered on magnificent games.

For the first months of his reign Caligula openly flaunted his incest with his favourite sister Drusilla. They lived openly together as lovers, even though she was married. They planned to have a child who would succeed as emperor and, when he fell ill, he named Drusilla as his successor.

One sycophantic senator said that he would be willing to sacrifice his own life if Caligula's was spared. Caligula rallied and took him at his word. He was put to death on the spot. Caligula then ordered the execution of all those who had anticipated his death and had their severed heads piled on his sick bed, believing that he would draw strength from them.

As soon as he recuperated, he instigated a series of treason trials of his own. Tiberius's chosen heir Gemellus was disposed extrajudicially of by Caligula and Naevius Sutorius Macro, the prefect of the Praetorian Guard. Increasingly paranoid,

Caligula began to fear the growing power of Macro and had him arrested for being his wife's pimp after Caligula himself had seduced her. Macro was forced to commit suicide.

While Drusilla remained in favour, Caligula's other two sisters, Agrippina the Younger and Livilla, came under suspicion. He spared their lives but ordered that they be handed over to the mob as sex slaves.

Although when Caligula came to power he promised that philosophers would have their freedom to say or write anything they liked, those who did not extol Caligula's policies found their mouths sewn up and their hands chopped off. And prisoners released in the first flush of the new regime who were too debilitated by incarceration to celebrate their new-found freedom or heap praise on their liberator were sent to the arena.

When Drusilla died suddenly at the age of twenty-three, temples were consecrated to her throughout Rome and the empire, and coins were minted in her honour. Those who questioned her deification found themselves being crucified upside down and burnt alive. A season of public mourning was announced, during which it was a capital offence to laugh, bathe or dine with members of your own family.

Caligula built vast galleys, villas and country houses regardless of expense. Guests at banquets would find gold moulded in the shape of food on plates in front of them. He would dissolve valuable pearls in vinegar and drink down the mixture. Soon he had squandered the vast fortune Tiberius had left.

To raise money, he started a fresh round of treason trials. Those condemned would forfeit their property. He would name the amount he sought to raise and keep signing death warrants until he had amassed that sum. In one afternoon he condemned as many as forty men to raise the desired figure, complaining afterwards what a tiring day he had had. Others were murdered for no reason.

He ate and drank to excess and had sex with any man or woman who took his fancy. None dared refuse him. Among his gay lovers he counted a beautiful young pantomime actor Marcus Lepidus Mnester, who he kissed in public, even – scandalously – in the theatre. He also had an affair with his own brother-in-law.

Gradually Caligula's behaviour became increasingly sadistic. He would close the granaries so that the people would go hungry, or scatter free tickets to the arena among crowds, causing stampedes where many people died. He put on contests between mangy beasts and people who were crippled or infirm. When one contestant complained, he had his tongue cut out before being returned to the arena.

Caligula came to believe that he was a living god and had temples and statues built. The deification of Julius Caesar and Augustus were revoked. Meanwhile he continued to humiliate those of rank around him. He would insist on sleeping with their wives and, afterwards, tell the woman's husband publicly that his wife was no good in bed or hire her out as a whore to any low life who wanted her. The prefect of the Praetorian Guard Cornelius Sabinus was humiliated in this way. The other prefect Cassius Chaerea – there were always two – had distinguished himself as a soldier in the Rhine mutiny of AD14, but he had a high squeaky voice and Caligula teased him unmercifully. As a result Sabinus and Chaerea organised a plot to rid themselves of their unruly emperor.

On 24 January AD41, Caligula attended the Palatine Games, where Chaerea and the Praetorian Guard advanced on him. The first blow hit him on the shoulder, slicing six inches into his upper body. Chaerea then stuck his sword into Caligula's stomach until it came out of his back, then twisted it.

Chaerea pulled out the blade, raised it and with one stroke neatly decapitated Caligula. As his body crumpled, the rest of the Praetorian Guard cut him to pieces, paying special attention to the mutilation of his genitals. Caligula was just twenty-nine and had ruled for less than four years when he died.

48

JULIUS CAESAR 44BC

The murder of Julius Caesar in the Senate in Rome on 15 March 44BC was a turning point in history. It marked the end of the Roman Republic, which had endured for nearly 500 years, and the beginning of the Roman Empire, which would dominate in one form or another for another 1,500 years.

Gaius Julius Caesar was born on 12 or 13 July probably in the year 100 or, perhaps, 102BC – sources differ. Or rather he was born on 12 or 13 Quintilis in 638 or 640 as Quintilis – the fifth month in the Roman calendar whose year began in March – was later renamed July in his honour and, until the Christian era, the Romans numbered their years from the mythical foundation of Rome in 738BC.

Gaius was Julius Caesar's given name, Julius was his clan name, and Caesar his family name. The Julii were patricians – that is they were members of Rome's original aristocracy – and the Caesars traced their lineage back to the goddess Venus. However, by the time Gaius was born, they were neither rich nor particularly influential.

The great hope for the family was Caesar's uncle, the general and statesman Gaius Marius. He opposed Lucius Cornelius Sulla in a brutal civil war. When Sulla took Rome in 82BC after Marius's death, Caesar sought military service in the east to stay out of Sulla's way. He won his laurels for taking Mytilene, the capital of Lesbos.

When Sulla died in 78BC, Caesar returned to Rome, where he started a career as a criminal lawyer and quickly gained a reputation for being on the side of the people by prosecuting several prominent Romans for corruption.

In 75BC, Caesar left Rome to study rhetoric in Rhodes. On the way he was captured by pirates. The ransom paid, he was freed, then returned with a fleet to have the pirates crucified. After more military action in the east, Caesar returned to Rome to begin his political career in earnest. He held a number of elected offices, including military tribune in 72BC.

When his first wife died, he seized the opportunity to marry Pompeia, Sulla's granddaughter, a relative of the great general Gnaeus Pompeius Magnus – Pompey the Great – who had recently reconquered Spain. This increased Caesar's political influence. By 63BC, he was *pontifex maximus* – highest of all priests – a position held for life.

But bribery and extravagance had left him bankrupt. He borrowed money from Marcus Licinius Crassus, the richest man in Rome, got himself elected governor of Further Spain, where he plundered the silver mines of Galicia, and returned in triumph, a rich man. Elected consul he avoided prosecution. With Pompey and Crassus, he formed the First Triumvirate which ran Rome from behind the scenes. Caesar took control of the army and began the conquest of Gaul. During the campaign, he invaded Britain. He went on to pacify Gaul, earning him another twenty-day thanksgiving.

While Caesar was away things had changed in Rome. Crassus had been killed out east and Pompey was made sole consul in 52BC with near dictatorial powers. The Senate then feared a war between Caesar and Pompey and sought to prosecute Caesar for bribery. To secure immunity, he needed to be consul again. To run for office, he would have to renounce the command of the army in Gaul and return to Rome.

Instead, at the head of his army, he marched on Rome, crossing a small stream called the Rubicon on the way, which was considered an act of war. Pompey and his supporters in the Senate fled across the Adriatic. Caesar took Rome unopposed. After defeating Pompey's legions in Spain, Caesar returned to Rome to be made dictator. But he laid down the dictatorship to pursue Pompey who was then in Greece.

After defeat in the Battle of Pharsalus, Pompey fled to Egypt, where he was assassinated. Caesar followed, taking the country and marrying Cleopatra. When he returned to Rome, Caesar publicly refused to wear a crown. But he wore a purple robe as Alexander the Great had swathed himself in the Emperor Darius's purple robes after conquering the Persian Empire. He also wore the red boots of Etruscan kings and sat on a gold throne in the Senate. This hardly allayed fears that he wanted to be king, a thing that was anathema to republican Romans.

Plainly Caesar had to be stopped and the only way to do that was to kill him. The man best fitted for the task was Marcus Junius Brutus as he was one of the family of Lucius Junius Brutus, the man who rid Rome of its last king five hundred years earlier. It is likely that Brutus was Caesar's son as his mother Servilia was one of Caesar's many mistresses. During the Civil War Brutus had backed Pompey but had been pardoned by Caesar.

According to the Greco-Roman historian Plutarch, Gaius Cassius Longinus urged Brutus on. They gathered some sixty conspirators around them. Most had been pardoned by Caesar or raised to high office by him. Cassius convinced Brutus that Caesar intended to have himself proclaimed king of those parts of the empire outside Italy. That way, the Senators would either have to vote for his kingship or reveal that they opposed him.

But Caesar, frustrated by the politics of Rome, was planning a new campaign in the east. A meeting of the Senate was announced for the Ides of March – that is, the fifteenth day of the month – to discuss the campaign. The conspirators decided to kill Caesar at the Senate because they could gather there without inviting suspicion. They also thought it propitious as, with the new Senate house under construction, the Senate was meeting in the Theatre of Pompey, where a statue of the famous general had been erected.

Caesar was aware that he was in danger. At dinner on the night of 14 March, the topic of death came up in conversation. The question was asked 'which death is the best?' Before anyone could answer, Caesar said: 'An unexpected one.'

He had been warned by a seer named Spurinna some time earlier to 'beware the Ides of March'. His own wife Calpurnia feared that he would be killed if he attended the Senate that day. Despite these warnings Caesar left home without a bodyguard.

On the steps of Pompey's Theatre, he was met by the seer Spurinna.

'The Ides of March have come,' said Caesar.

'Aye, they have come,' replied Spurinna, 'but they have not yet gone.'

As planned, Trebonius, a former military commander, and now consul, took Caesar's co-consul Mark Antony aside for a chat outside the Senate to keep him out of the way. When Caesar took his seat inside, the other conspirators crowded around him. One of them, Tillius Cimber, pretended to submit a petition on behalf of his exiled brother. Suddenly Cimber grabbed Caesar's purple robe and wrenched it away from his neck.

'This is violence,' said Caesar. Violence of any sort was not allowed in the Senate.

It was the signal for attack. Immediately Publius Servilius Casca struck the first blow, just below the throat. But the wound was not deep or life threatening.

'Accursed Casca, what have you done?' cried Caesar, stabbing Casca in the arm with the only weapon he had to hand – the stylus he used for writing on wax tablets.

Caesar tried to get to his feet but was stopped by a second blow. The other conspirators surrounding him drew their daggers. Seeing a knife glint in Brutus's hand, Caesar said – not '*Et tu, Brute?*' ('And you, Brutus?') in Latin as Shakespeare would have us believe – but '*Kai su, Technon?*' ('You too, my child?') in Greek.

'When he saw that he was beset on every side by drawn daggers, he muffled his head in his robe, and at the same time drew down its lap to his feet with his left hand, in order to fall more decently, with the lower part of his body also covered,' said Suetonius.

Such a storm of blows followed – directed particularly at his face, eyes and groin – that 'many of the conspirators were wounded by one another, as they struggled to plant all those blows in one body'.

Apart from a groan on the first blow, Caesar said nothing more. Unable to defend himself Caesar pulled his toga down over his head and sank down against the pedestal of Pompey's statue. 'And the pedestal was drenched with his blood, so that one might have thought that Pompey himself was presiding over this vengeance upon his enemy, who now lay prostrate at his feet, quivering from a multitude of wounds,' said Plutarch.

With Caesar dead, Brutus and his followers marched up to the Capitol, displaying their knives openly.

For hours, nobody dared to come close to Caesar, until three common slaves put his corpse on a litter and carried him home, 'with one arm hanging down'. A physician named Antistius was then called to conduct what must have been one of the world's first autopsies. He found that Caesar's body had twenty-three stab wounds. But in his opinion none of them were mortal – 'except the second one in the breast'.

Several days later, Caesar's funeral was held in the Forum. When the Roman mob saw Caesar's blood-stained cloak and heard of the money that was to be distributed among them, they burst into a frenzy of posthumous adulation. Then, Mark Antony delivered the funeral oration, in which he further inflamed their emotions.

While Mark Antony was in charge in Rome, Gaius Julius Caesar Octavianus, Caesar's nephew and adopted son, was his chosen successor. They joined forces and, in 42BC, defeated Brutus and Cassius at Philippi in Macedonia. The assassins committed suicide – Cassius, Plutarch said, killed himself with the same dagger he had used to stab Caesar.

Octavian and Mark Antony then fell out. Mark Antony committed suicide after his defeat at the Battle of Actium in 31BC. In 27BC Octavian became Rome's first emperor under the name Augustus.